The What, Where, When, How & Why
Of Gardening In Virginia

Virginia

GARDENER'S GUIDE

JACQUELINE HÉRITEAU

COOL
SPRINGS
PRESS

First printing 1997
Printed in the United States of America
02 01 00 99 98 97 96   10 9 8 7 6 5 4 3 2 1

Hériteau, Jacqueline.
    Virginia gardener's guide / by Jacqueline Hériteau.
        p.   cm.
    Includes bibliographical references and index.
    ISBN 1-888608-11-0 (trade paper)
    1. Landscape gardening--Virginia. 2. Plants, Ornamental--Virginia.   I. Title.
    SB470.54.V8H47   1997
    635.9`09755--dc21   97-19411
                                                                CIP

Published by
Cool Springs Press, Inc.
118 Fourth Avenue South
Franklin, Tennessee 37064

Map provided by Agricultural Research Service, USDA.
Horticultural Edit by Andrew Bunting.
On the cover (clockwise from top left): Plumbago, Camellia, Carolina Jessamine, Dogwood.

DEDICATION

FOR CINDI FESTA LITTLEDALE, Virginia's most passionate gardener—with love.

ACKNOWLEDGEMENTS

*S*O MANY HORTICULTURISTS, FRIENDS AND GARDEN-
ERS have contributed to the information it's impossible to
acknowledge all. I owe much to Virginia nurseryman André Viette,
former President of the Perennial Plant Association; Dr. H. Marc
Cathey, whose Garden Show based on our ten-year collaboration on
the question/answer column, Dr. Cathey Says; Holly Shimizu, former Curator of the U.S. National Herb Garden, who taught me so
much about herbs and flowers in this region; Brent Heath, third-
generation commercial grower and owner of the Daffodil Mart in
Gloucester; of Charles Thomas, President of Lilypons Water
Gardens, whose knowledge is the basis of our book, *Water Gardens*;
Erick Neumann, Head, now retired head of Education and Public
Services at the U.S. National Arboretum, my generous and indefati-
gable liaison with the National Arboretum staff when I was
working on the *National Arboretum Book of Outstanding Garden
Plants*; the late Charles A. H. Thomson, who headed the new edition
of *Successful Gardening in the Greater Washington Area*, published by
the Men's Garden Club of Montgomery County. I am indebted to
gardeners Cindi and Kris Littledale, June Stewart, Myra Johnson,
Rue Judd, the church that allowed me to plan its garden, and many
other friends and associates.

I also wish to thank the man whose knowledge of word proces-
sors has made it possible to produce this work in such a short time,
Tom Robertson, and Cool Springs Press Publisher Roger Waynick
and Editor Hank McBride, who invited me to write about gardening in Virginia.

My deepest appreciation is given to my husband, Earl Hubbard,
for bearing with my working weekends and midnight oil.

CONTENTS

INTRODUCTION

Virginia Gardening

*V*IRGINIA IS A STATE WHERE WONDERFUL GARDENS HAVE FLOURISHED FOR 400 YEARS, and a wonderful state for gardening in general, with almost four seasons. In most of the state, winter is mild enough to allow pansies and early narcissus to flower. Spring lasts many weeks and is graced from February on by the lavish bloom of flowering bulbs, trees, and shrubs. Summer is hot and stormy, but from mid-September on, Virginia creeper, maples, oaks, euonymus and dozens of other trees color brilliantly. A scattering of bulbs bloom in fall, and hollies, cotoneasters, winter-berries, and barberries redden their berries with the changing autumn colors.

The chapters that follow discuss garden ornamentals I've seen thriving in Virginia gardens. These plants are exceptionally beautiful, have modest maintenance requirements, and are pest and disease resistant, according to consultants recommended by the National Arboretum in Washington, D.C. I could have added dozens more to each chapter—but this is a beginning. Master what's here, then explore your many options.

A very pleasant way to learn about other plants that will thrive in your own garden is to visit Virginia's many magnificent public gardens. The Appendix includes the locations of 35 historic garden restorations recommended by The Garden Club of Virginia. In Tidewater, Virginia, there's beauty as well as wisdom in the Colonial Williamsburg Restoration, where flower beds brighten the orchards and kitchen gardens that fed the early households. Central Virginia is home to a personal favorite, Jefferson's Monticello, where a sumptuous vegetable and herb terrace over-looks vineyards, orchards, and the valley below.

Northern Virginia has access to many historic gardens. In the District of Columbia there's much to learn by visiting Dumbarton Oaks and its 28 garden rooms, the open air gardens surrounding the U.S. Botanic Garden, and the U.S. National Arboretum. The Arboretum includes the U.S. National Water Garden, the U.S. National Herb Garden, and much more. In Alexandria, the American

Introduction

Horticultural Society offers membership to interested gardeners, and can also put you in touch with local garden groups, which are matchless sources of information about plants and gardening where you live. They're able to explain, for example, which of Virginia's five climate zones apply to you.

Our Climate

Winter cold dictates, and summer heat limits, the plants that will thrive year in and year out in your garden. A climate zone map prepared by the USDA shows each region's average lowest winter temperature. Literature about garden ornamentals—except for annuals, plants that live only one season—usually includes the zones where plants survive the particular extremes of temperature—for example, "sweet box, Zones 5 - 8." I haven't added zone hardiness designations to the plants in this book, because those I've recommended do well in Virginia. But when you buy plants not discussed here, be sure they are recommended for your zone.

If you live in the level area 10 to 20 miles inland from the southern tip of the state—the Tidewater area between Norfolk, Virginia City, and the border of North Carolina—you're in Zone 8A. Minimum cold in winter ranges between 10 and 20 degrees Fahrenheit. Subtropical plants like camellias and live oaks survive your winters, along with many of the plants that do well in the cooler parts of the state. The weather comes from the sea and is humid, and winters are brief. The soil is sandy and drains well, but most ornamental plants will do better if you add humus to the planting holes.

If you live inland on the Coastal Plain—where the land rises west of the Dismal Swamp—you are in Zone 7 B. In winter, temperatures there fall to minimums around 10 degrees Fahrenheit. Soil on the Coastal Plain still tends to be sandy, but elsewhere it usually includes clay. West of Greenville and Lunenburg, Zone 7A begins, and winter temperatures can fall even farther, to 0 degrees Fahrenheit. Zones 7 A and B extend northward to Northern Virginia, Washington D.C., and the Maryland border. Winter cold usually lasts about four months. The high heat of summer can come in mid-June and stay until mid-September, punctuated by afternoon thunderstorms, which can be destructively heavy, with an extended period of drought in August. A 3-in. mulch helps to keep the ground cool around plant roots. In high heat we don't try to force plant growth by feeding, and we avoid pruning, which stimulates growth. The plants will shut down as protection against weather extremes.

If you live westward, up in the foothills of the Blue Ridge Mountains, you're in the cooler Zone 6, where the skiing is wide open, but the range of plants that survive the winter is slightly more restricted. Here in the Piedmont (French for "foot of the mountain"), winter temperatures can go down to 0 and -10 degrees Fahrenheit. Zone 6 follows the mountains northward to D.C. and Maryland, where winters are short, summers moderate, and there's plenty of rain most years.

Your Microclimates

This is a simple description of the climate in Virginia. But gardening is never very simple—just very rewarding. Actually, the plants you can grow are not entirely governed by the zone where you live. Cold falls, so valleys are cooler than the prevailing area. High hills are also colder than their respective zones.

And within every garden there are microclimates—places warmer or cooler than the prevailing temperatures, which will allow you to grow plants that normally don't succeed in your zone. For example, a south-facing wall can warm a corner, and shade can cool it. White and reflective surfaces increase light and heat, whereas a windbreak, a vine-covered pergola, a large tree or a high hedge can lower temperatures. Also, proximity to moving water tempers temperature extremes, and cities are 5 to 10 degrees warmer than the suburbs and the country. Mulch protects roots from extremes of heat and cold.

Perennials must survive winter, so climate, microclimate, and weather are important considerations in choosing species and vari-

Introduction

⚜

eties. Plants describes as "annual" live one season. It is a group comprised primarily of flowers and of vegetables, although I haven't dealt with vegetables here, because they need a book of their own. Climate and hardiness affect only how early annuals can be planted in spring, or can be expected to survive in fall. A "hardy" annual can be set out earlier than one not said to be hardy, and will stand up for some time to cold at the end of the season. Select only perennials, and especially flowering trees and big shrubs that are within their cold hardiness range in your garden. Late frosts can devastate the flower buds on a camellia that isn't hardy in your zone, even though the leaves and the plant will do well there.

Many plants are offered in varieties described as early, midseason, or late, and you can use this to your advantage. Where the growing season is shortened by unusually cool weather in spring or fall, plant early varieties. If you wish to enjoy a very long season of bloom of any particular plant, look for varieties of all three types: early, midseason, and late.

Another way to outwit your season's limitations is to extend it by starting seeds early indoors, in winter for spring planting, and in summer for early fall planting. The subject is more fully discussed in the chapter on annuals. You also can start seeds early in a cold frame, or a hot bed—projects that require more space than we can give them here. You can also protect seeds and seedlings from early and late cold by covering them with "hot caps," or plastic tenting. The first frost dates of the year in and around D.C. and Northern Virginia are October 19; October 16 in Culpepper; November 13 in Richmond; and October 28 in Williamsburg.

Two weeks after the date of the last annual frost, it is generally safe to transplant out into the open those garden seedlings started indoors or purchased at your garden center. The last frost of the year in Williamsburg is about April 14; in Culpepper, April 17; in Richmond, May 4; and in D.C. it is March 25. These are generally true—but as mentioned above, there are microclimates, and the suburbs and country are 5 to 10 degrees cooler than the cities.

Introduction

The outside temperature should have reached at least 55 degrees Fahrenheit during the day. Transplanting too early just leaves seedlings sulking and yellowing. Before planting seedlings—your own, or seedlings from the garden center—it's a good idea to let them acclimate a bit in a sheltered location protected from direct sun and wind.

When a flowering species fails to flower, check the hours of direct sun it receives: unless noted as flowering in shade, plants require 6 hours of direct sun to bloom well. They will flop forward when they lack sun, and in the hottest parts of the country, some noon shelter may be beneficial—a light trellis, for instance, or the dappled shade of tall trees. Plants receiving full sunlight are often the most cold hardy.

PREPARATION OF YOUR SOIL

The best garden is one you can maintain without more effort than you have time to give. It begins with well prepared, good garden loam and sound gardening practices.

When the soil is right, plants thrive. Almost all of my planting instructions begin with recommendations to add sand or chicken grit to the soil to improve drainage. Take the sand out of the mixture if the soil already contains a good amount. I also suggest adding humus to improve moisture retention. A more thorough approach is to start a new garden by planting green cover crops in the fall and winter, and then to turn them under. But so few gardeners today have the time or the will to go through it that I won't go into great detail here. Cover crops are fast-growing legumes or grasses, dug back into the soil before they go to seed. They improve soil structure, add nutrients, increase microbial activity, and help break up compacted areas. Some of the many plants used as cover crops are: alfalfa, fava beans, clover, cowpeas, soybeans, vetch, ryegrass, mustard, and barley.

The attributes of soil are structure or composition, fertility (see Fertilizers, below), and pH. Structure governs the soil's ability to

Introduction

absorb and maintain moisture. Soil containing gritty particles is loose enough to allow tender rootlets to seek moisture and the nutrients it contains, and it also allows water to drain through before it becomes stagnant. When soil contains a balanced proportion of humus, it also retains enough moisture to keep the rootlets from drying out. Good garden soil feels silky, and you can dig in it with your fingers.

Fertility refers to the nutrients in soil. But their accessibility depends on moisture, and on the soil's pH, or potential of hydrogen. The pH reaction refers to the relative acidity or alkalinity of soil. A pH of 7.0 is neutral, below is acidic, and above is alkaline. Most garden ornamentals do best toward the middle range, between 5.0 and 7.0. Trees and shrubs are more apt to be finicky about pH than are herbaceous plants.

Relatively inexpensive testing kits available at garden centers can help you to determine the pH of your soil, and how to adjust it. To correct excessive alkalinity, you just add aluminum sulfate at the rate recommended on the package. Adding 60 percent sphagnum peat moss to the soil will also lower the pH as it breaks down by about two points. Sphagnum is a beneficial soil amender and decomposes rather rapidly, so you must add sphagnum peat moss annually to keep the pH down. To correct acidity, dig in a dusting of lime at the rate recommended on the package.

I also recommend maintaining a 2- to 3-in. layer of organic mulch on all plantings. This is only in part to buffer soil temperatures and maintain soil moisture: an organic mulch decomposes slowly on the underside, and that replenishes the soil's supply of humus, which is dissipated during the growing season.

Creating a Raised Bed
Most Virginia gardens need the amendments recommended in the planting instructions because of the prevalence of clay. Not only does clay soil drain poorly, but it is also hard for the plants to grow into. A highly respected Virginia nurseryman of national acclaim, André Viette of Fishersville, goes so far as to recommend creating

Introduction

raised beds for all gardens. Here are some of André's thoughts about creating a raised bed:

- Fall is the ideal time to start a new bed, but spring is fine, too.

- Use string or a hose to outline the area in lazy curves.

- Apply weed killer. (At this writing, RoundUp is recommended.)

- Bring in enough topsoil to raise the level 12 to 15 in.—buy soil advertised as weed free.

- Determine the pH of the soil, and adjust it to something in the range of 5.5 to 6.5. That suits most flowers and nearly all plants that are acid-loving. Unless limestone is prevalent in your area, chances are that your soil falls in this range.

- Add 2 to 4 in. of coarse sand or chicken grit, of leaf mold, or sphagnum peat moss. Decomposed bark, compost, leaf mold (partially decomposed leaves), sphagnum peat moss (dried, compressed sphagnum), black peat humus (composted peat), decomposed animal manures, composted sewage sludge, and seaweed, are some of the sources of humus. There are many others.

- Spread on superphosphate at the rate of 50 pounds per 1000 square feet. Bonemeal is a source of phosphorous, which is important for good root development, but it adds calcium, which injures Japanese iris and acid-loving plants.

- Spread on fertilizer at the rate recommended on the package. For a bed being prepared in fall for spring planting, apply Osmocote in 8- or 12-month slow-release formulations—12 will take you through summer.

- Spread on gypsum at the rate of 50 pounds per 1000 square feet in clay soil, and double the rate if the soil is very heavy clay.

- Mix all this into the soil with a rear-tine rototiller, which you can rent from your hardware store or garden center.

- Rake out the rocks and clumps of earth when you are ready to plant.

Introduction

WATERING

After planting, water gently and slowly with a sprinkler that lays down 1 to 2 in. in 5 to 12 hours. Use an empty coffee tin to measure.

During the growing season, flower beds and new plants thrive with two to three hours of gentle rain every 10 days to 2 weeks. Water, if you can, before the sun reaches the garden in the early morning. I find soaker hoses are the best method for watering where mildew is a problem, and where the weather is muggy. But overhead watering is fine as long as you water deeply, and the foliage has a chance to dry between sessions.

In summer's high heat, if your plants are wilting (especially new plantings), don't wait 10 days—WATER! Daytime watering lowers leaf temperatures and reduces stress, but evening watering is fine. Again, let me warn you against forcing plants to flower by watering and fertilizing when the heat is beyond their comfort zone. With summer-flowering roses, it is a temptation!

FERTILIZING

With fertilization, less is usually better than more. The numbers on fertilizer labels describe the balance of the elements in the language of NPK ratios: (N) for nitrogen; (P) for phosphates; (K) for Potash. Nitrogen greens the leaves. Phosphates help develop good root systems and flowering. Potash promote bloom, strengthens stems, and increases resistance to diseases. Fertilizer that contains all three are known as "complete" or "balanced." The fertilizer many nurserymen use is a high-nitrogen mix such as 18-6-12, which greens plants and encourages leaf growth. High-phosphorous 5-10-5 helps young plants grow roots. A high-potash composition such as 7-6-19 helps established plants to stay healthy.

A fertilizer described for "acid-loving" plants, or for azaleas and gardenias which are acid lovers, is the best choice for plants that need acidic soil—rhododendrons, for example. But keep track of the pH. If you find the soil growing too acidic, a dusting of lime will correct the pH.

Introduction

Light Requirements

For best growing results, plants need to be placed where they will receive the proper amount of sunlight. I have indicated the amount of sunlight suitable for each plant's growing requirements. The following symbols indicate full sun, partial sun, and shade.

Full Sun   Partial   Shade
                Sun

Healthy Garden Practices

To avoid dealing with solutions, avoid problems by following healthy garden practices. There's a huge bonus: lower maintenance. Here are some of the approaches that will help your garden to avoid difficulties:

Introduce diversity into your plantings and into your neighborhood. Give cultivars of native plants a place in your design, and buy only healthy plants that are pest and disease resistant. Limit your choices to plants that thrive in your climate and your soil. These will best withstand insects attacks and diseases to which the species may be susceptible, and they survive the normal droughts.

When planting trees and shrubs described as hard-to-transplant, set out young, container-grown plants. They adapt better to the new environment and grow faster. Plant in early spring when growth is most vigorous.

When you can, buy from the nearest reliable nursery and ask for field-grown stock, since it has proven successful in your particular area.

Pests

Dealing with deer is a distressing garden problem. There's no spray that keeps them away. Barriers work, and there is dark, unobtrusive—if not inexpensive—fencing. Deer can't stand Milorganite,

Introduction

Milwaukee's composted municipal sludge, which has been sold as an organic fertilizer since 1926. It is certified by the U.S.D.A. as suitable for all crops, including food. A study commissioned in 1991 by the Cornell Cooperative Extension Service in Millbrook, N.Y., confirmed that it does keep deer away as long as it is not stale. Deer especially dislike Milorganite in spring, summer, and fall, when the air is warm enough to hold its odor. Thus, it does not appear to be as effective in the winter. The odor is lost with rain, and snow and ice will smother it, so it must be reapplied after a storm.

Deer have less liking for prickly things; and, I have heard, for ginkgoes, crape myrtle, junipers, spruces, pines, sumacs, yarrow, asters, English daisies, baby's breath, poppies, phlox, tuberous begonias, crocus, scilla, daffodils, forget-me-nots, portulaca, dusty miller, and hollyhocks, to name a few. Tulips are not, however, on their hate list.

Tolerate a natural complement of insects. If you work with disease-resistant plants, there will be more friendly insects in your garden than bad guys. New growth will eventually cover their depredations, even that of the gypsy moth. Let the seeds and berries of summer's flowers stand through fall and winter to feed birds. Birds eat insects and bring great charm to the garden setting. If you can obtain decomposed horse manure, fertilize with it in late winter: manure and compost keep earthworms active in the soil, and birds love worms.

GIVING BACK TO THE EARTH

Many municipalities in Virginia now mandate that all yard and kitchen wastes be kept out of landfills, and others will surely follow suit. Some counties give away free wood chip mulches, and some are marketing composted waste. In Northern Virginia, we can buy ComPRO and LeafGRO, which I find effective and modestly priced.

Compost is black, soillike stuff that is the end product when nature has put organic material through a process of decomposition. It is produced commercially from animal manures—rotted horse or cow or sheep manure, often mixed with soil.

Introduction

There are many ways to compost: in a garbage bag, in a plastic bin (my method), or in a state-of-the-art, solar-powered compost tumbler. The ingredients that we compost are brown dead leaves, fresh weeds, grass clippings, and vegetable or fruit peels. Don't compost garden debris that appears diseased. The basic method is to build a pile of leaves, preferably shredded to speed decomposition, about 4 ft. deep and 3 or 4 ft. square. Top it with a layer several inches deep of green garden or kitchen waste, then top that with a similar layer of soil. Sprinkle a cupful of fertilizer over the pile, make a depression in the center, and soak the pile. Every six weeks until it has disintegrated, turn the pile with a pitchfork. In summer, our bin composts these materials in a couple of months if I remember to keep it moistened and poked up. In winter, it decomposes slowly until spring warmth arrives. This is a very simple approach. If you are interested in more scientific approaches, *The Rodale Book of Composting* is a sound reference.

Compost amends the soil. It can be used as is as a mulch, or spread over the soil to a depth of 2 or 3 in. and dug or rototilled in. A handful of compost scratched into the soil around plants during the growing season is beneficial.

Nourish the earth, and Virginia will fulfill your most cherished garden dreams.

USDA HARDINESS ZONE MAP

Virginia

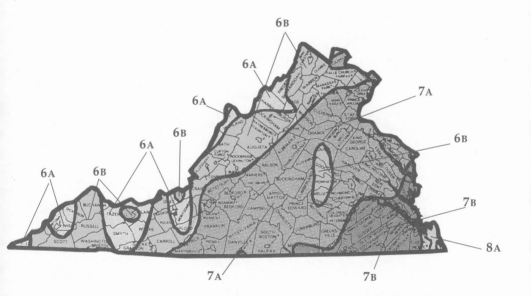

AVERAGE ANNUAL MINIMUM TEMPERATURE

Zone	Temperature
6A	-5° F TO -10°F
6B	0° F TO -5° F
7A	5° F TO 0° F
7B	10° F TO 5° F
8A	15° F TO 10° F

CHAPTER ONE

Annuals

*A*NNUALS AND TENDER PERENNIALS ARE ONE-TIME, "FILLER-INNER" FLOWERS that are colorful over a long period and provide quick, vivid color for garden spaces left empty by the fading of bulbs and perennials. Several self-sow and may spare you the trouble of replanting the next year. Some are planted for their foliage color—the brilliant shade-loving coleuses and ornamental cabbages and kales that brighten in fall, for example. But most are planted simply for the beauty of their bright flowers.

Annuals have two seasons in Virginia: summer and fall. In early to mid-May, I plant marigolds, zinnias, ageratum, snapdragons, geraniums, and the other summertime favorites in the sun; and impatiens, nicotiana, and coleus in shaded places. I keep my baskets and the flower beds lush by planting seedlings of annuals every week or two throughout the season. In fall, I plant pansies and ornamental cabbages and kales, and any other seedlings the garden center is offering for fall color. The pansies are still there in spring, so I fertilize them, firm them into their planting holes, and fill gaps with fresh seedlings. The show lasts until the summer heat does them in. In hill country, pansies will last through July 4 if given a little shade.

Most annuals will grow rapidly in rich, well-drained soil. For basket and container plants, I recommend a commercial potting mix. Many annuals are shallow rooted and can't stand drought. Sustained moisture from overhead watering is the best way to get seedlings off to a good start. After that, an occasional soaking from a soaker hose will take care of their needs. I hide our soaker hoses under mulch.

Provided the soil has been well prepared, and provided they have sustained moisture as they knit into their environments, annuals rarely fail. To keep the flowers coming, remove blossoms as they fade. When deadheading or cutting annuals for bouquets, make the cut beyond the next set of leaves to encourage the plant to branch out and deflower. Pinching out annuals that have leaders also encourages branching. In midseason, shear back long-branched plants such as petunias to encourage a new round of flowers.

PLANTING ANNUALS

You'll find seedlings of the most popular annuals at garden centers in April and May. I always buy seedlings of annuals that are slow to germinate and grow, petunias for example. Already in their first flush of bloom, seedlings satisfy the spring hunger for instant gardens. But to provide your garden with the diversity which catalogs display, you must sow seeds.

Fast-growing annuals start easily from seed sown in the garden as long as the soil and the air have warmed somewhat, usually in early to mid-April. Flowers that tolerate the first frosts, like the little wax begonias, you can sow sooner than those that prefer warmth, like cosmos. Annuals with a showtime in late summer and fall can be sown in June—cosmos, for example. Some early-blooming annuals can be planted in fall, such as foxglove. But even cold-tolerant annuals won't germinate and start to grow until the soil grows warm in the spring or fall. Most will come into flower soonest if sown where they are to flower.

Seeds are sown "broadcast," that is, sprinkled thinly over the planting area; in "hills," that is, in groups of four to six, or three to five, equidistant from each other; vegetables often are sown in "drills," that is, dribbled at spaced intervals along a shallow furrow drilled in the soil by dragging the edge of a rake along the planting line.

For planting depth, follow the instructions on the seed packet. If the seed packet has no specific instruction regarding depth, sow the seeds at a depth that is about three times the seed's diameter, not its length.

In windy locations, tall plants may need support. Set a stake close to the plant stem while it is still young. Then, as it leafs out, it will hide the stake. Use green wool, raffia, cotton string or twist ties to hold the plant to the stake.

Starting Seeds Indoors

You might enjoy trying your hand at starting seeds early indoors. Seed packets suggest planting 1 to 12 weeks for slow growers like petunias, and 4 to 6 weeks for fast growers like zinnias. Most seeds germinate well at temperatures of 65 to 70 degrees Fahrenheit. If they don't sprout in 20 days, start over again with a fresh batch of seed. Once germinated, they grow best in a cool sunroom or basement under fluorescent lights.

Sow seeds of plants identified as difficult to transplant directly into peat pots so the seedlings can be transplanted without being unpotted. Soak the pot and break the bottom third open when you transplant.

To plant in flats, fill the containers to within 1/4 in. of the top with moistened and sterilized commercial potting mix. Press the seeds into the mixture to a depth equal to their diameter. Sprinkle very small seeds over the surface and cover thinly with growing medium. Mist the surface after sowing and label the flats. Then, tent them with plastic (cleaner's bag) and set them in strong, indirect light at temperatures between 60 and 75 degrees Fahrenheit. Water from the bottom until you can see moisture rising to the top.

When the seeds germinate, make small holes in the plastic for ventilation. After the second set of leaves appears, remove the plastic, reduce moisture, and place the flats in full sun. Turn the flats often to keep the stems growing straight. When the seedlings become crowded, transplant them to jiffy pots to allow room for the development of individual plants. Before transplanting seedlings to the garden, harden them off for a week in a sheltered position in bright shade.

It is generally safe to transplant the seedlings outdoors two weeks after the date of the last annual frost in your area. Many annuals won't start growing until the ground warms up in spring, and transplanting too early just leaves them sulking.

Chapter One

Seeds grow very well indoors under grow lights, but this is a fairly complex task best undertaken with a good book on the subject as a guide.

Annual flowers that sow their own seeds will naturalize under good conditions. Self-sown seedlings are called "volunteers." Petunia, snapdragon, and some zinnia volunteers turn up every year in my garden; but they're slow to flower, so I count on them for late summer and fall bloom. Other self sowers are so productive in some places that they become weeds—morning glory is one which springs to mind.

To encourage self sowers, spread a 1- or 2-in. layer of soil around the crowns of the parent plants, dampen the soil, gather the seeds as they ripen and scatter them over the soil. Or, wait until the seeds are dry and loose in their casings, then shake the flower heads vigorously over the soil.

Ageratum

*S*et out in mid-spring, ageratum will keep your garden supplied with touches of blue until frost. The flowers are tiny puffs of color—in addition to blues there are pinks and whites—that bloom in round-topped clusters. The plant is a pretty little mound 6 to 12 in. high with bright-green, pointed leaves arranged as neatly as a nosegay. I plant seedlings in sets of 3 just behind mats of white sweet alyssum and pink, large-flowered wax begonias. My favorite varieties are the compact, lavishly blooming lavender-blue 'Blue Danube' (Blue Puff), the extra-early bright blue 'Adriatic' and 'Blue Surf', which grows to 9 in. tall. But you can find this indispensable blue flower in sizes 18 in. tall and suitable for planting farther back in the garden. They are lovely with pink-and-white snapdragons and silver artemisia. If you plant ageratum seedlings rather than seeds, you can have blue in the garden from May on. High heat can cause ageratum to brown, but it comes back in my garden with the September rains.

WHEN TO PLANT

Sow seeds or plant seedlings after the soil has warmed—April in Zone 8, mid-May in Zones 6 and 7. Ageratum can take quite a lot of cold, but not frost and excessive heat. Or start ageratum seeds indoors in flats 3 to 4 months before planting time.

WHERE TO PLANT

In warm parts of Zone 7 plant ageratum in dappled light; in cool, hilly regions, it can take 4 to 6 hours of direct sun, especially morning sun. Ageratum needs lots of direct sun to keep blooming all summer, but it can't take a full day of direct sun once summer has warmed up. If you are starting seeds in the garden, sow them where the plants are to bloom.

HOW TO PLANT

Prepare the bed by digging in 1 in. of coarse sand or chicken grit, 2 in. of humus, and a slow release 5-10-5 fertilizer. In clay soil, add a small handful of gypsum and superphosphate for each plant. Work the soil 8 to 12 in. deep. Ageratum does well in soil whose pH is 5.5

to 7.0. Sow seeds following package instructions, or mark planting holes for seedlings 6 to 8 in. apart around a system of soaker hoses. Divide plants in flats with a sharp, clean knife, giving each a good root system. Half fill each hole with diluted fertilizer, plant the seedling high, and press the soil down around the stem firmly enough so the plant resists a tug. Water with a diluted fertilizer solution. Apply a 3-in. mulch starting 3 in. from the stems.

How to Provide Care and Maintenance

To promote rapid, unchecked growth, for the next 2 or 3 weeks water often enough to sustain the soil moisture. After that, water deeply every week unless you have a soaking rain. Once the plants show signs of new growth, to encourage branching, pinch out the top 3 to 4 in. of the lead stem. After the first flush of bloom, fertilize again, and repeat every 3 to 5 weeks through August. Deadhead to promote flowering. If the flower tips brown out in July and August, cut them off and make sure the plants don't go dry. They will freshen when fall comes.

Additional Advice

The seedlings will sulk if the ground is icy cold when they are set out. Wait to plant until 2 weeks after that last frost date: in the Williamsburg area that is April 14; Culpepper, April 17; Richmond, May 4; Washington, D.C., March 25.

Other Cultivars and Species

I like to pair ageratum with the look-alike perennial called hardy ageratum, *Eupatorium coelestinum.* Together, these will keep the garden in blue from mid-spring to late fall.

Centaurea cyanus

Bachelor's-button

OTHER COMMON NAME: Cornflower

*B*achelor's-button is an upright, branching summer flower 1½ in. across with a thistle-like center surrounded by a ring of ray petals. The plant grows quickly to 2 or 3 ft. tall, producing handsome, gray-green leaves and masses of flowers if you deadhead it. These are good cutting flowers, and they dry well. The color associated with bachelor's-buttons is true deep-blue, but there are purples, pinks, whites, luscious maroons, all intensified by a colorful brown eye. Improved plants have large double flowers; for instance 'Blue Diadem', 2½ in. across on stems to 24 in. tall. The taller cultivars fall forward as they mature, but the little 12- to 18-in. 'Polka Dot' series of mixed colors, and the deep corn-flower blue cultivar 'Jubilee Gem', stay upright. Bachelor's-button often self-sows. I recommend that you let the plants grow up and become fillers for your perennials.

WHEN TO PLANT

Start seeds indoors in flats 10 to 12 weeks before planting time—April in Zone 8, mid-May in Zones 6 and 7. Or sow seeds in the garden in early fall or in mid-spring. You can keep bachelor's-buttons blooming in your garden all summer and early fall by making successive sowings.

WHERE TO PLANT

Sow seed, or plant seedlings, in full sun. If you are starting seeds in the garden, sow them where the plants are to bloom.

HOW TO PLANT

Prepare the bed by digging in 2 in. of coarse sand or chicken grit, 2 in. of humus, and a slow-release 5-10-5 fertilizer. In clay soil, add a small handful of gypsum and of superphosphate for each plant. Bachelor's-buttons succeed even in poor soil. Sow seeds following package instructions, or mark planting holes for seedlings 6 to 8 in. apart around a system of soaker hoses. Divide plants in flats with a sharp, clean knife, giving each a good root system. Half fill each hole with diluted fertilizer, plant the seedling high, and press the soil down around the stem firmly enough so the plant resists a tug. Water with a diluted fertilizer solution. Apply a 3-in. mulch starting 3 in. from the stems.

HOW TO PROVIDE CARE AND MAINTENANCE

To promote rapid, unchecked growth, for the next 2 or 3 weeks water often enough to sustain the soil moisture. After that, water deeply every week unless you have a soaking rain. Thin the seedlings if they become crowded. After the first flush of bloom, fertilize lightly.

ADDITIONAL ADVICE

To encourage the plants to self sow, spread a 1- or 2-in. layer of well-prepared soil around the feet of the parent plants, dampen the soil, gather the seeds as they ripen, and scatter them over the prepared soil—or monitor the seeds as they ripen and when they are dry and loose in their casings, shake the flowerheads vigorously over prepared soil.

Bedding Begonia

OTHER COMMON NAME: Wax Begonia

*B*egonias are small, mounded non-stop bloomers whose crisp, shiny leaves make a real contribution to the front rows of the garden from mid-spring to late fall. The leaves are fresh green or rosy bronze or both and the blossoms range from white to pale pink, rose, coral, deep pink and red. I love them because they fill out so beautifully, and because they flower all summer long. I love them especially when summer ends and September rains cool the air because then they are fullest and the flowers are bigger and prettier than ever. The prettiest wax begonias are the green-leaved Wing F1 hybrids which are 10 to 12 in. tall and have 3-in. flowers. 'Picotee Wings' is a treasure, a soft white edged in rose. For edging, choose dwarf Semperflorens. For hanging baskets, choose Semperflorens hybrids with cascading branches. These wonderfully carefree little plants need no deadheading to keep blooming. They are tender perennials that can take a lot of cold but no frost. Potted up and brought indoors to a sunny window in October, they bloom all winter.

WHEN TO PLANT

Plant seedlings after the soil has warmed—April in Zone 8, early May in Zones 6 and 7. Begonias can take quite a lot of cold, but not frost. I do not recommend starting your own plants from seed unless you have a greenhouse—they need 4 to 5 months to come into bloom.

WHERE TO PLANT

Plant wax begonias in direct sun or dappled light—either way they seem able to bloom profusely. If you live in a very hot area, choose dappled light or part shade. If your region is cool, they'll do better with 4 to 6 hours of direct sun. In real shade begonias keep their leaves but do not fill out.

HOW TO PLANT

Prepare the bed by digging in 2 in. of coarse sand or chicken grit, 2 in. of humus, and a slow-release 5-10-5 fertilizer. In clay soil, add a small handful of gypsum and of superphosphate for each plant. Work the soil 8 to 12 in. deep. Wax begonias do well in soil whose pH is 5.5 to 7.0. Sow seeds following package instructions, or mark planting holes for seedlings 6 to 8 in. apart around a system of soaker hoses. Divide plants in flats with a sharp, clean knife, giving each a good root system. Half fill each hole with diluted fertilizer, plant the seedling high, and press the soil down around the stem firmly enough so the plant resists a tug. Water with a diluted fertilizer solution. Apply a 3-in. mulch starting 3 in. from the stems.

HOW TO PROVIDE CARE AND MAINTENANCE

To promote rapid, unchecked growth, for the next 2 or 3 weeks water often enough to sustain the soil moisture. After that, water deeply when other flowers show signs of wilting. Wax begonias are able to remain crisp even in the first stages of water deprivation. Fertilize every 3 to 5 weeks through August.

ADDITIONAL ADVICE

These seedlings seem to grow the best root systems while the weather is stillcool. Set them out right after the last frost date: in the Williamsburg area that's April 14; Culpepper, April 17; Richmond, May 4; Washington, D.C., March 25.

OTHER CULTIVARS AND SPECIES

There is an attractive 24-in. perennial begonia, *Begonia grandis,* known as the hardy begonia. It is also known as 'Evans Begonia' (formerly *B. evansiana*). The hardy begonia survives winters in all but the coldest areas of Virginia and thrives in lightly shaded gardens and under tall shrubs like laurel and rhododendrons. There are white and pink-flowered varieties.

Burning Bush

OTHER COMMON NAME: Summer Cypress

*T*his is a foliage plant with many uses. Started from seed, or set out as a seedling in mid- to late spring, by August, kochia grows into a leafy 2- to 4-ft., pale-green bush that looks quite like an evergreen. Then with the coming of frost-touched nights, the 2-in. leaves burn purplish to bright red, justifying the common name of burning bush. The form when it is full grown is more or less oval. The flowers are tiny and unremarkable. Kochia makes a great low, temporary hedge. Planted as backdrop and filler for a flowering border, it guarantees vivid fall color for the garden. For a wild display of late color, plant kochia in sets of 3 to 5 with ferny cosmos in mixed colors and big, bold Joseph's-coat, *Amaranthus tricolor* 'Molten Fire'. Kochia is a tough annual that succeeds even in hot, polluted areas.

WHEN TO PLANT
Sow seeds outdoors or plant seedlings after the soil has thoroughly warmed—mid-April to early May in Zone 8, mid-May in Zones 6 and 7. Seeds can also be started indoors 4 to 6 weeks earlier.

WHERE TO PLANT
Plant kochia in full sun. If you are starting seeds in the garden, sow them where the plants are to bloom.

HOW TO PLANT
Prepare the bed by digging in 2 in. of coarse sand or chicken grit, 2 in. of humus, and a slow-release 10-10-5 fertilizer. In clay soil, add a small handful of gypsum and of superphosphate for each plant. Work the soil 8 to 12 in. deep. Sow seeds following package instructions or mark planting holes for seedlings 6 to 8 in. apart around a system of soaker hoses. Divide plants in flats with a sharp, clean knife, giving each a good root system. Half fill each hole with diluted fertilizer, plant the seedling high, and press the soil down around the stem firmly enough so the plant resists a tug. Water with a diluted fertilizer solution.

HOW TO PROVIDE CARE AND MAINTENANCE

To promote rapid, unchecked growth, for the next 2 or 3 weeks water often enough to sustain the soil moisture. After that, water deeply when you water the flower garden. Thin the seedlings if they become crowded. After the first flush of bloom, fertilize, and repeat every 3 to 5 weeks through August.

ADDITIONAL ADVICE

Kochia self-sows in warm climates and can be a nuisance. To prevent spreading, cut the plants back before the seeds have time to mature in the fall.

Busy Lizzie

*I*mpatiens is the best flower for brightening shaded corners and woodlands. These carefree plants come into bloom in early May and sustain lavish displays of showy, open-faced flowers with no effort on your part. When cool air and moisture return to Virginia after mid-September, impatiens just covers itself with blooms that last until frost comes. The colors range from sparkling white to red, orange, salmon, melon, and orchid, and there are spotted forms and bi-colors. The foliage is dark-green, bronze, or variegated. For containers and hanging baskets choose the Super Elfin series. Under 10 in., they branch freely, allowing many more flowers per plant, and stay close to the ground with spread of 12 in. or more. For the front of the border, choose medium heights, 10 to 12 in. tall. For bedding, choose the tall Blitz series, 14 to 16 in. high. Try impatiens with coleus or caladiums in matching colors—they are beautiful together. There are double-flowered impatiens; the flowers are exquisite, but not as showy as the standard types. Impatiens is a great follow-on plant for bulbs planted in corners that become shady as trees leaf out.

WHEN TO PLANT

Set out seedlings after the air has warmed—April in Zone 8, mid-May in Zones 6 and 7. Impatiens can be started from seed indoors 6 to 10 weeks before planting time, but it is a bother to grow, and I do not recommend it.

WHERE TO PLANT

Tall and filtered shade are best for impatiens. Modern cultivars tolerate 4 or 5 hours of direct sun, especially morning sun, and especially when they are mulched and growing in humusy, moist soil. In hot, sandy areas of Virginia, grow impatiens in containers in shady corners.

HOW TO PLANT

Prepare the bed by digging in 2 in. of coarse sand or chicken grit, 2 in. of humus, and a slow-release 5-10-5 fertilizer. In clay soil, add a small handful of gypsum and of superphosphate for each plant. Mark planting holes for seedlings 6 to 8 in. apart around a system of

soaker hoses. Divide plants in flats with a sharp, clean knife, giving each a good root system. Half fill each hole with diluted fertilizer, plant the seedling high, and press the soil down around the stem firmly enough so the plant resists a tug. Water with a diluted fertilizer solution. Apply a 3-in. mulch starting 3 in. from the stems.

HOW TO PROVIDE CARE AND MAINTENANCE

To promote rapid, unchecked growth, for the next 2 or 3 weeks water often enough to sustain the soil moisture. Water early in the day or after the sun has gone by, and avoid wetting the foliage. After that, to keep the plants compact, water impatiens only enough to keep it from wilting. Fertilize rarely, if at all, and very lightly.

ADDITIONAL ADVICE

Seedlings of impatiens fresh from the nursery are much more susceptible to cold than are the mature plants in fall. They will sulk if the ground is icy cold when they are set out, and they will succumb to even a little frost. Flower production often slows in high heat, but it will pick up when the heat lets up. Impatiens does not need deadheading.

OTHER CULTIVARS AND SPECIES

New Guinea impatiens is a very showy, bold, and large-flowered upright hybrid 1½ ft. tall with beautiful leaves. The leaves of some varieties are bronzed or variegated with shades of green, yellow, pink, and red. Like ordinary impatiens, New Guinea impatiens flowers non-stop into late fall. It prefers slightly acidic soil. It blooms well with 4 to 6 hours of direct sun. The bottom branches flower more fully if they are pinched back early.

Coleus

*C*oleus is a brightly patterned foliage plant I use to provide showy colors for shaded areas where few flowers bloom. Seedlings set out in mid-spring grow bigger and more lush and colorful every month until killed by early frosts. A leafy, upright plant 14 to 16 in. or taller, coleus displays combinations and variegations of brilliant red-mahogany, green, yellow, white, blue, rose, and the color combinations get wilder every year. One striking cultivar is 'Concord' which has velvety purple leaves on 24-in. stems. I love 'Highland Fling ' whose leaves are yellow splashed with light green. It is handsome paired with 'Molten Lava', which has red leaves with a red margin. A pretty variety is 'Salmon Lace' which is salmon-edged, green, and cream-white. 'Scarlet Poncho' is red and gold with trailing stems suitable for hanging baskets. Try all the colors together. I like to combine coleus with impatiens in matching or contrasting colors—scarlet-patterned coleus with scarlet impatiens, for example, and lime-green coleus and white impatiens. Young plants and rooted cuttings will bloom in a semi-sunny window indoors all winter long. The only chore associated with coleus is pinching out the bluish flower spikes: that keeps the plants shapely.

WHEN TO PLANT
Coleus grows easily from seed indoors any time, and outdoors after temperatures reach 70 degrees Fahrenheit. Plant seedlings outdoors after the weather warms in mid-May.

WHERE TO PLANT
In warm parts of Zone 7, plant coleus in the bright shade of tall trees or in dappled light; in cool, hilly regions, it can take 4 to 6 hours of direct sun, especially morning sun.

HOW TO PLANT
Protect the seedlings from direct sun and plant after the sun has gone by. Prepare the bed by digging in 2 in. of coarse sand or chicken grit, 2 in. of humus, and a slow-release 10-10-10 fertilizer. In clay soil, add a small handful of gypsum and of superphosphate for each plant. Sow seeds following package instructions, or mark planting

holes for seedlings 6 to 8 in. apart around a system of soaker hoses.
Divide plants in flats with a sharp, clean knife, giving each a good
root system. Half fill each hole with diluted fertilizer, plant the
seedling high, and press the soil down around the stem firmly
enough so the plant resists a tug. Water with a diluted fertilizer
solution. Apply a 3-in. mulch starting 3 in. from the stems.

How to Provide Care and Maintenance

To promote rapid, unchecked growth, for the next 2 or 3 weeks
water often enough to sustain the soil moisture. After that, water
deeply every week unless you have a soaking rain. Thin the
seedlings if they become crowded. Once the plants show signs of
new growth, to encourage branching, pinch out the top 3 to 4 in.
of the lead stem. Deadhead—that is remove flower spikes as they
start up—to prevent the plants from becoming straggly.

Additional Advice

This is a member of the square-stemmed group mint belongs to, and
it grows like topsy as long as it does not go dry. The leaves are thin
and soon wilt when water is lacking.

Other Cultivars and Species

Best for baskets are cultivars of *Coleus blumei* whose leaves include
dashes of white, red, purple, yellow, and green, and *C. pumilus*, a
well-branched, green-edged, dark purple creeping or trailing
species.

Common Foxglove

*T*his spring bloomer is stately as a hollyhock and makes a dramatic linear statement. Two to 5 ft. tall, the straight-up stems are hung with pendulous, thimble-shaped blooms in pink, red, purple, or white with dark spots. Among the foxglove species there are annuals, biennials, and perennials. The dwarfish Foxy strain, beautiful hybrids of the biennial *D. purpurea*, are favorites in Virginia where we grow them as annuals since they flower in early summer from seed sown 5 months before. They're a good size for containers. 'Alba' is taller, an extraordinarily beautiful pure white that makes a fabulous cutting flower. Foxglove is essential to the cottage garden's romantic tangle, absolutely striking planted in clumps of 3 to 5 with columbines, poppies, and zinnias, and gorgeous by itself in a container dripping with small-leaved ivy.

WHEN TO PLANT

Sow seeds in the garden where the plants are to bloom in early spring or early fall—set out seedlings as soon as the soil becomes workable.

WHERE TO PLANT

Plant in part shade. 'Foxy' withstands some wind, but taller cultivars may need staking unless sheltered by a wall or other plantings. If you are starting seeds in the garden, sow them where the plants are to bloom. Foxgloves cannot stand excessive heat, so avoid planting them in hot, windless pockets.

HOW TO PLANT

Prepare the bed by digging in 2 in. of coarse sand or chicken grit, 3 in. of humus, and a slow-release 5-10-5 fertilizer. In clay soil, add a small handful of gypsum and of superphosphate for each plant. Work the soil 8 to 12 in. deep. Sow seeds following package instructions, or mark planting holes for seedlings 6 to 8 in. apart around a system of soaker hoses. Divide plants in flats with a sharp, clean knife, giving each a good root system. Half fill each hole with diluted fertilizer, plant the seedling high, and press the soil down around the stem firmly enough so the plant resists a tug. Water with a diluted fertilizer solution. Apply a 3-in. mulch starting 3 in. from the stems.

How to Provide Care and Maintenance
To promote rapid, unchecked growth, for the next 2 or 3 weeks water often enough to sustain the moisture in the soil. After that, water deeply every week unless you have a soaking rain. Thin the seedlings if they become crowded. After the first flush of bloom, fertilize and repeat every 3 to 5 weeks until the plants go out of bloom.

Additional Advice
Foxgloves require sustained moisture.

Other Cultivars and Species
Rusty foxglove, *Digitalis ferruginea*, is a striking, lanky 6-ft. biennial with coppery yellow flowers that have a furry lower lip. *D. grandiflora* (syn. *D. ambigua*), yellow foxglove, is just 24 in. tall, a refined, creamy-yellow perennial. *D. lutea*, a 3-in. perennial, bears small green-lemon flowers and is lovely in woodlands.

Cosmos

*B*eautiful, drought-tolerant cosmos brings to the late summer garden airy, fresh green foliage and bright, open-faced pastel flowers that bloom until early frosts. Planted in mid- to late spring, by summer's end seeds or seedlings grow into willowy 3- to 4-ft. branches spangled with 2- to 4-in. flowers with crested or tufted centers. Plants of the Sonata series are compacts, 20 to 24 in. tall. Cosmos colors are crimson, rose, yellow, white, pink, and burgundy-red. They last well in arrangements—cutting encourages new growth—and are beautiful in bouquets with dahlias, blue salvia, and aromatic mint. I recommend the Early Wonder series, a mix of big-flowered cosmos in vibrant rose, pink, crimson, and white. For late summer color, plant *C. sulphureus* in orange: it is as clear and bright as orange juice. A spectacular duo is cosmos interplanted with the great big wildly colorful Joseph's-coat *Amaranthus tricolor* 'Molten Fire'. Cosmos self-sows exuberantly: I let a few grow up and transplant them to places left empty by the passing of spring flowers.

WHEN TO PLANT

Sow seeds or transplant seedlings outdoors after the ground has warmed in May. Early-flowering strains bloom from seed in 8 to 10 weeks. Or sow seeds indoors in late April and plan to transplant 2 to 3 weeks later.

WHERE TO PLANT

Cosmos does best in full sun but makes do with 4 to 6 hours a day. Place tall varieties at the back of the flower border. If you are starting seeds in the garden, sow them where the plants are to bloom. Cosmos withstands drying winds but may need staking.

HOW TO PLANT

Prepare the bed by digging in 2 in. of coarse sand or chicken grit, 2 in. of humus, and a slow-release 5-10-5 fertilizer. In clay soil, add a small handful of gypsum and of superphosphate for each plant. Sow seeds following package instructions, or mark planting holes for seedlings 6 to 8 in. apart around a system of soaker hoses. Divide plants in flats with a sharp, clean knife, giving each a good root system. Half fill each hole with diluted fertilizer, plant the seedling high, and press the soil down around the stem firmly enough so the plant resists a tug. Water with a diluted fertilizer solution. Apply a 3-in. mulch starting 3 in. from the stems.

How to Provide Care and Maintenance

To promote rapid, unchecked growth, for 2 or 3 weeks water often enough to sustain the soil moisture. After that, water deeply every week unless you have a soaking rain. Thin seedlings if they become crowded. When the seedlings reach 24 in., to encourage branching, pinch out the top 3 to 4 in. of the lead stem. Repeat as the next set of branches develops. Though cosmos blooms lavishly even without deadheading, I deadhead to avoid a plethora of volunteers next season.

Additional Advice

The plants are delicate—but tough—and need no special attention. They self-sow prolifically—so plan to weed some out next season.

Other Cultivars and Species

For cutting, plant 'Sea Shells', which bears flowers that have creamy-white, shell-pink, or crimson and pink interiors; 'Psyche Mixed', for its semi-double and single flowers; and the variegated white and pink 'Candy Stripe'.

Dwarf Sunflower

*T*he new short, many-branched varieties of sunflower produce dozens of small, sunny-faced flowers that both gardeners and florists have fallen in love with . . . and for good reason. They bloom mid- to late summer, make lasting cut flowers, and are spectacular in the garden. The shortest and earliest to bloom is 'Big Smile', which is 12 to 14 in. tall, and produces flowers from seed in 50 to 60 days. The most adorable is 'Teddy Bear', a 2-footer with 6-in. fully double sunflowers. It is small enough to grow in a container. Thompson & Morgan Inc. (PO Box 1308, Jackson, N.J. 08527-0308) offers it. For cutting, plant pollenless varieties like 'Sunrich', a 3-footer that bears 4- to 6-in. flowers. Standard sunflowers produce a pollen that can be as unwelcome as lily pollen. A very popular new sunflower is 3-in. 'Floristan', a yellow-tipped, rusty-red bi-color which is ready for cutting in 9 or 10 weeks after the seed has been sown.

WHEN TO PLANT

Sow seeds after all danger of frost has gone by, and the air is warming up a little. They will need 5 to 10 days to germinate, but the plants usually grow rapidly.

WHERE TO PLANT

Sow seed in full sun where the plants are to grow. There is not a finicky plant in the bunch as long as there is plenty of direct sun.

HOW TO PLANT

Prepare the bed by digging in 2 in. of coarse sand or chicken grit, 3 in. of humus, and a slow-release 5-10-5 fertilizer. In clay soil, add a small handful of gypsum and of superphosphate for each plant. Work the soil 8 to 12 in. deep. Sow seeds following package instructions, or mark planting holes for seedlings 6 to 8 in. apart around a system of soaker hoses. Divide plants in flats with a sharp, clean knife, giving each a good root system. Half fill each hole with diluted fertilizer, plant the seedling, and press the soil down around the stem firmly enough so the plant resists a tug. Water with a diluted fertilizer solution. Apply a 3-in. mulch starting 3 in. from the stems.

How to Provide Care and Maintenance

To promote rapid, unchecked growth, for the next 2 or 3 weeks water often enough to sustain the moisture in the soil. After that, water deeply every week unless you have a soaking rain. Thin the seedlings if they become crowded. After the first flush of bloom, fertilize and repeat every 3 to 5 weeks through August. If you grow sunflowers for the seedheads, expect to have a little tussle with the birds. When they start visiting, cover the heads with cheesecloth.

Additional Advice

Take sunflowers for cutting in the evening or the early morning. Remove all but the top pair of leaves and plunge the stems into boiling water for 1½ to 2 minutes. Condition the stems by keeping them in water in a tall container overnight. Before placing the stems in an arrangement, recut them. Cured this way, I find they last at least a week and usually 10 days.

Other Cultivars and Species

Helianthus annuus is the old-fashioned, 12-in. species with flower heads 1 ft. across. *H. tuberosus*, the Jerusalem artichoke, is a 12-in. perennial with edible roots that bears small, fluffy flowers. Late blooming, these tall, coarse plants are used in vegetable patches and in wild and grass gardens.

Edging Lobelia

*I*n semi-shade, these delicate-looking plants 6 to 8 in. high—and twice as wide—produce clouds of thin, fragile stems spangled with tiny florets in luminous, intense shades often with a white eye. Some varieties have fresh green foliage, some have decorative bronze foliage. In the cooler reaches of Virginia, Zone 6, edging lobelia growing with some protection from direct sun often goes on blooming into fall. Yet in hot spots, like my Washington, D.C., garden in summer, it disappears with the coming of high heat in June. For edging, choose varieties that grow upright. These usually are offered in white or shades of blue. The Palace series has pretty bronze foliage. One of my favorites is deep blue 'Crystal Palace'. The Moon series is especially heat-resistant. 'Paper Moon' is an exquisite white, a large, neat plant that covers itself with moon-shaped flowers. For hanging baskets, choose plants of the Cascade or Fountain series which bloom profusely and have a trailing habit. These are offered in vivid blue and in white, crimson, rose pink, and lilac. If you fall in love with the intensity of lobelia's colors, look into some of the large, upright perennial blue and red lobelias described below.

WHEN TO PLANT
In spring after the soil has warmed, set out seedlings—April in Zone 8, mid-May in Zones 6 and 7.

WHERE TO PLANT
Plant lobelia in part sun or semi-shade. It blooms well as long as it gets some direct sun, preferably cool morning sun. In cool regions, lobelia adapts to 4 hours and more of direct sun, as long as soil moisture is maintained and the roots are cooled by a mulch.

HOW TO PLANT
Prepare the bed by digging in 1 in. of coarse sand or chicken grit, 2 in. of humus, and a slow-release 5-10-5 fertilizer. In clay soil, add a small handful of gypsum and of superphosphate for each plant. Install a system of soaker hoses. Divide plants growing in flats with a sharp, clean knife, giving each a good root system. Half fill each

hole with diluted fertilizer, plant the seedling high, and press the soil down around the stem firmly enough so the plant resists a tug. Water with a diluted fertilizer solution. Apply a 3-in. mulch between plants.

HOW TO PROVIDE CARE AND MAINTENANCE

To promote rapid, unchecked growth, for the next 2 or 3 weeks water often enough to sustain the moisture in the soil. Continue to maintain soil moisture, especially as the weather heats up. Cut back and fertilize after every flush of blooming to encourage continued flowering.

ADDITIONAL ADVICE

The seedlings will sulk if the ground is icy cold when they are set out. Wait to plant until 2 weeks after that last frost date: in the Williamsburg area that's April 14; Culpepper, April 17; Richmond, May 4; Washington, D.C., March 25. It self-sows in good conditions.

OTHER CULTIVARS AND SPECIES

Lobelia cardinalis, the cardinal flower, is a tall, brilliant-red perennial found in wet, shaded places. 'Queen Victoria' is one of many handsome cultivars now offered for planting in the garden. *L. siphilitica* 'Blue Peter' is a long-lasting garden variety. It is known as the blue cardinal flower. *L. × gerardii* is a very tall, multi-stemmed purple-blue cross between the two above species.

Everlasting

*T*here are two everlastings I like especially—the colorful little strawflower, *Helichrysum bracteatum*, and velvety-gray licorice plant, *H. petiolare*. Both are easy-to-grow, low-maintenance plants with lots of uses. The one I cannot do without is the licorice plant, whose asymmetrical branching and dainty leaves I love in hanging baskets. A trailer/climber, it throws stems in all directions—up, down, sideways—and provides a frilly, silvery background for the flowers growing around it. Its own flowers are pale and unimportant. I love licorice plant as a filler in the garden, too, and use it for filler around the leggy bottoms of low-growing bushes in my small rose garden. *H. bracteatum*, the strawflower, gets to be about 30 in. tall and is grown in the cutting garden for its crisp, colorful little flowers and for dried winter arrangements. The blooms are about 2^1/$_2$ in. across and are cut for drying before they are fully expanded. The colors are bright-yellow, pale-pink, orange, red, and white.

WHEN TO PLANT

Sow seeds after the soil has thoroughly warmed—April in Zone 8, mid-May in Zones 6 and 7. Or sow seeds indoors in late March or early April; then transplant to the garden in mid-May.

WHERE TO PLANT

Plant *H. bracteatum*, the strawflower, in full sun and set plants to stand 15 in. apart. Plant *H. petiolare*, the licorice plant, in semi-sun and set plants to stand 24 in. apart.

HOW TO PLANT

Prepare the bed by digging in 2 in. of coarse sand or chicken grit, and a slow-release 5-10-5 fertilizer. In clay soil, add a small handful of gypsum and of superphosphate for each plant. Work the soil 8 to 12 in. deep. Divide plants in flats with a sharp, clean knife, giving each a good root system. Half fill each hole with diluted fertilizer, plant the seedling high, and press the soil down around the stem firmly enough so the plant resists a tug. Water with a diluted fertilizer solution. Apply a 3-in. mulch starting 3 in. from the stems.

How to Provide Care and Maintenance

To promote rapid, unchecked growth, for the next 2 or 3 weeks water often enough to sustain the soil moisture. After that, water deeply every week unless you have a soaking rain. Once the plants show signs of new growth, to encourage branching, pinch out the top 3 to 4 in. of the lead stem.

Additional Advice

The seedlings will sulk if the ground is icy cold when they are set out. Wait to plant until 2 weeks after that last frost date.

Garden Verbena

V̶erbena × hybrida is a spectacular basket plant and a fabulous shoreside performer. It is a fast-growing, vigorous, free-blooming creeper/trailer with branches 8 to 18 in. long. From summer until frost it produces heads of small, bright florets in white, red, pink, yellow, or purple. The leaves are oval or lance-shaped, serrated, and dark-green. These hybrids are used very effectively in hot Washington, D.C., as follow-on ground cover for municipal beds where bulbs grow in spring. Another verbena species, *V. bonariensis*, is grown in Virginia gardens for its appeal to butterflies. It is bushy, 3 to 4 in. high, with upright, flowering stems and sweet-scented purple or lilac flowers. It is also rather leggy, so we plant several close together and hide their bare bottoms by interplanting with silvery artemisia. The flowers are good for cutting.

When to Plant

Verbena × hybrida may be started from seed sown indoors in early spring or outdoors when the weather warms. Because the seed germinates slowly, I recommend buying seedlings. *V. bonariensis* is offered as a container plant in spring; plant when the weather warms.

Where to Plant

Plant *Verbena × hybrida* where it will get full sun or sun until afternoon. It tolerates drought, wind, and searing sun. Plant *V. bonariensis* where it will get full sun. It tolerates poor, dry soil.

How to Plant

Prepare the soil by digging in 2 in. of coarse sand or chicken grit, 2 in. of humus, and a slow-release 5-10-5 fertilizer. In clay soil, add a small handful of gypsum and of superphosphate for each plant. Work the soil 8 to 12 in. deep. Sow seeds following package instructions. Make planting holes for seedlings of the hybrids 6 to 8 in. apart around a system of soaker hoses. Space planting holes for *V. bonariensis* 1 ft. apart. Half fill each hole with diluted fertilizer, plant the seedling high, and press the soil down around the stem firmly enough so the plant resists a tug. Water with a diluted fertilizer solution. Apply a 3-in. mulch starting 3 in. from the stems.

How to Provide Care and Maintenance

To promote rapid, unchecked growth, for the next 2 or 3 weeks water the verbenas often enough to sustain the soil moisture. After that, water when you water the flower garden. Thin the seedlings if they become crowded. When *V. bonariensis* is growing vigorously, encourage branching by pinching out the top 3 to 4 in. of each stem. After each flush of bloom, remove spent flowerheads and fertilize.

Geranium

*S*ome of our most-loved garden and porch plants are members
of this tribe that blooms spring through fall. The showiest geraniums are the zonals. Their globe-shaped red, salmon, fuchsia, pink, or
white blooms provide brilliant flowers for window boxes and planters.
The leaves are horseshoe-shaped, usually banded with a maroon or a
bronze zone. The big potted geraniums offered at garden centers in
spring and fall are grown from cuttings. Choose these for baskets and
planters. The little seed-grown plants with colorful zoning don't seem
to get very big: I think of them as useful for fronting small flower beds.
Another beautiful form of *Pelargonium* is the trailing ivy-leaved type
with stiff, waxy foliage cascading on stems 3 to 4 in. long. These
geraniums are planted for their foliage: the blooms are single or semi-
double but modest—white to deep-rose with darker markings. My
favorite geraniums right now are the Balcon types which bear masses
of flowerheads composed of dainty, single florets on slender stems that
stand out from trailing, deeply cut foliage. Another quite different
geranium group has crinkly leaves that are scented. The flowers are
sparse, but the scents make them popular porch and house plants.

WHEN TO PLANT

After the air has warmed, set out rooted cuttings or seedlings. You
can start seeds for the small forms indoors 10 to 12 weeks before
planting time, but unless you can provide controlled temperatures
and fluorescent lights, this may prove a frustrating exercise.

WHERE TO PLANT

All geraniums prefer western exposure in summer with some protection from the heat of afternoon. They sustain hot, dry, windy
exposures in containers, but they will begin to flourish when nights
cool down.

HOW TO PLANT

Prepare the soil for geraniums by digging in 2 in. of coarse sand or
chicken grit. In clay soil, add a small handful of gypsum and of
superphosphate for each plant. Geraniums do well in soil whose
pH is 5.5 to 6.5, neutral to slightly acid. Half fill each hole with

water, plant the seedlings high, and press the soil down around the stem firmly enough so the plant resists a tug. Water well. Apply a 3-in. mulch starting 3 in. from the stems.

How to Provide Care and Maintenance

Allow the soil surface to dry between deep waterings. Water moderately but don't allow the plants to dry out completely. Once the plants show signs of new growth, to encourage branching, pinch out the top 3 to 4 in. of the lead stem and side branches and repeat once more. Deadhead to encourage flowering.

Additional Advice

Softwood cuttings root readily in winter, and in early spring you may set in water in a sunny window.

Other Cultivars and Species

For a patio centerpiece, I recommend the zonal geranium varieties that have white-splashed leaves and flowers in either white, bright-red, or hot pink.

Jasmine Tobacco

OTHER COMMON NAME: Flowering Tobacco

*W*hite nicotiana is a wonderful flower for partly shaded areas. The flowers are lovely, though somewhat lost in the foliage, but I love the lily-like fragrance that rises from nicotiana in the evening. Set out in mid- to late spring, by autumn nicotiana grows into a 15- to 24-in. plant with long tubular blossoms and big leaves that are a fresh green. It blooms in my garden until mid-October, and some years it lasts even longer. The only really fragrant varieties I have encountered are the white nicotianas. 'Fragrant Cloud' has large white flowers that
perfume the air in late afternoon. Though not markedly fragrant, the 'Nikki' series offers a welcome variety of colors. Pink, rose, maroon-red, and crimson are available, and there is a pretty, green-white called 'Lime Green'. The flowers of the older nicotiana cultivars open in the evening—hence the evening perfume—but these newer plants stay open all day. 'Sensation Mixed' varieties stay open all day and have some fragrance.

WHEN TO PLANT

Sow seeds indoors 6 to 8 weeks before the last frost date: in the Williamsburg area that's April 14; Culpepper, April 17; Richmond, May 4; Washington, D.C., March 25. The time to plant seedlings is after the soil has warmed—April in Zone 8, mid-May in Zones 6 and 7.

WHERE TO PLANT

In really warm areas of Zone 8, plant nicotiana in part shade; in cool, hilly regions, it can take full sun, especially morning sun. Young seedlings are damaged by heavy rains, so avoid planting nicotiana where it will be susceptible to floods from gutters or watering gusts of wind.

HOW TO PLANT

Nicotiana transplants well, but the seedlings must be hardened off gradually. Move flats into the light over a week's time before plant-

ing. Prepare the bed by digging in 2 in. of humus and a slow-release 5-10-5 fertilizer. In clay soil, add a small handful of gypsum and of superphosphate for each plant. Work the soil 8 in. deep. Plant around a system of soaker hoses. Divide plants in flats with a sharp, clean knife, giving each a good root system. Half fill each hole with diluted fertilizer, plant the seedling high, and press the soil down around the stem firmly enough so the plant resists a tug. Water with a diluted fertilizer solution. Apply a 3-in. mulch starting 3 in. from the stems.

How to Provide Care and Maintenance

To promote rapid, unchecked growth, for the next 2 or 3 weeks water often enough to sustain the soil moisture. After that, water deeply every week unless you have a soaking rain. Once the plants show signs of new growth, to encourage branching pinch out the top 3 to 4 in. of the lead stem. After the first flush of bloom, fertilize, and repeat every 3 to 5 weeks through August.

Additional Advice

Species and hybrids will self-sow, sometimes in their original colors, occasionally several colors on one plant. Remove spent flower stalks towards midsummer to promote flowering and to prevent the plants from setting seed.

Other Cultivars and Species

Woodland tobacco, *Nicotiana sylvestris*, another annual species, is hard to find but worth a search. It bears clusters of white flowers that are intensely fragrant at night.

Marigold

*T*he marigolds fill the garden with bursts of petals the colors of the sun, from yellow-white to gold to burnt orange. They start easily from seed and are drought-resistant, heat-tolerant and problem-free. They bloom non-stop until frosts and have beautiful, lacy foliage with a sharp, not universally popular, aroma. There are two main groups: big, round, fluffy types that flower in 12 weeks or so, and small dainty marigolds that bloom in as little as 6 weeks.The fluffy types are African or Aztec marigolds, *Tagetes erecta*. The blooms are 2 to 4 in. across on plants between 10 in. and hedge height. Their colors are yellow to gold, orange and pumpkin-orange. 'Odorless' and the new almost-white marigolds belong to this group. The dainty types, which are often blotched mahogany-red, are French marigolds, cultivars of *T. patula*. They're enduring plants up to 12 in. tall bearing flowers 1½ to 2 in. across. They're perfect for edging, ground cover, and window boxes. This group tends to self-sow. "Triploid" marigolds are crosses between these species. They bloom early, are as durable as
the French marigolds, and they are also as full as the Africans—and almost indestructible.

WHEN TO PLANT
When the weather warms—in April in Zone 8, mid-May in Zones 6 and 7—sow seeds in the garden. Or 4 to 6 weeks before the weather warms, start seeds indoors in a sandy potting mix. Then transplant to the garden.

WHERE TO PLANT
Plant all marigolds in full sun, except the white varieties, which prefer part shade.

HOW TO PLANT
Prepare the bed by digging in 2 in. of coarse sand or chicken grit, 2 in. of humus, and a slow-release 5-10-5 fertilizer. In clay soil, add a small handful of gypsum and of superphosphate for each plant. Work the soil 8 to 12 in. deep. Sow seeds following package instructions or mark planting holes for seedlings 6 to 8 in. apart around a

system of soaker hoses. Divide plants in flats with a sharp, clean knife, giving each a good root system. Half fill each hole with diluted fertilizer, plant the seedling high, and press the soil down around the stem firmly enough so the plant resists a tug. Water with a diluted fertilizer solution. Apply a 3-in. mulch starting 3 in. from the stems.

How to Provide Care and Maintenance

To promote rapid, unchecked growth, for the next 2 or 3 weeks water often enough to sustain the soil moisture. After that, water deeply when you water the flower beds. Marigolds can stand a lot of neglect. Thin the seedlings if they become crowded. After the first flush of bloom, fertilize, and repeat every 3 to 5 weeks through August.

Additional Advice

Deadhead to keep blooms coming and drench with liquid fertilizer in August. The little French marigolds often self-sow even in window boxes. A yellow variety volunteered and bloomed year after year in a planter on a Manhattan terrace.

Other Cultivars and Species

Tagetes tenuifolia, the signet marigolds, are stocky plants 2 ft. tall and almost covered with dainty little single flowers. The fine, lacy foliage has a lemon scent. The plant is spreading-erect, perfect for edgings and rock gardens, and it self-sows.

Brassica oleracea (Acephala group)

Ornamental Kale or Cabbage

*T*he big, showy, ornamental cabbages and kales stage winter's best show of color. Twelve to 24 in. high and wide, their jade-green leaves are streaked, splotched, and edged in soft shades of red, purple, and cream. The colors become more vibrant as the temperatures cool in late fall and winter, and they handle temperatures as low as 20 degrees Fahrenheit. We set them out as full-grown plants in September or early October, usually as replacements for mums that have gone out of bloom. These are real cabbages and kales, so when spring comes, they bolt upward into flowerheads and lose their beauty. Ornamental cabbage looks like a flat cabbage, and it also looks like a huge, jade-green rose edged with wine-red, pink, cream—or all three. 'Color Up Hybrid' is a brilliant variety that is splotched and streaked with color for a full 80% of the head. Flowering kale Peacock Hybrid is extra compact—about 12 in. tall—and has amazingly beautiful cream-and-wine leaves that are feathery and extravagantly serrated or notched.

WHEN TO PLANT

Sow seed outdoors in a sunny spot in late spring or early summer—these plants grow best when temperatures are between 65 and 80 degrees Fahrenheit. Or sow seeds indoors in flats 5 to 7 weeks before planting time, which is in September or early October. You can set out seedlings any time after summer's high heat has gone by.

WHERE TO PLANT

Plant the ornamental cabbages and kales in full sun. If you are starting seeds in the garden, sow them where the plants are to mature. They have long roots and are not easy to dig and transplant. If you are planning to move them, transplant them to containers while they are still young seedlings, and grow them there until planting time.

How to Plant

Brassicas thrive in a pH between 6.5 to 7.5. Prepare the bed or planting holes by digging in 2 in. of coarse sand or chicken grit, 2 in. of humus and a slow-release 10-10-10 fertilizer. In clay soil, add a small handful of gypsum and of superphosphate for each plant. Work the soil 9 to 12 in. deep. Space seeds about 1 in. apart. If you are transplanting full-grown plants, set them so their centers are about 24 in. apart and deep enough so they are buried up to their first leaves. Apply a 3-in. mulch starting 3 in. from the stems.

How to Provide Care and Maintenance

To promote rapid, unchecked growth in seeds, water weekly the first 3 weeks unless it rains. After that, water deeply every week, unless you have a soaking rain. When they are half grown, fertilize seedlings with a side dressing of 10-10-10. Do not fertilize again. Overfeeding dulls their colors. Plants that are set out full grown in fall do not need extra water unless there is a fall drought. Do not fertilize them.

Additional Advice

Do not let flowerheads grow up; keep them pinched out.

Ornamental Peppers

*T*he ornamental peppers are pretty, leafy little plants whose fruits add sparkling touches of color to the garden from late summer to mid-fall. Most ornamental peppers are edible hot peppers used in chiles, moles, and other Mexican dishes. Our long, hot summers ripen many of the most colorful chiles from green to red or to yellow, orange, lilac, or purple. More than 100 varieties are available, and more are turning up every year. Many varieties have more than one name and flavor. You will find a huge variety and the latest colors in the catalogs of specialists like *The Pepper Gal*, Box 23006, Fort Lauderdale, FL 33311. The U.S. National Botanic Garden uses the colorful hot peppers in containers paired with matching petunias. They are excellent container plants, indoors or outdoors, pretty with Fantasy petunias in colors matched to the fruits.

WHEN TO PLANT
Sow seeds indoors 7 to 10 weeks before the daytime weather outdoors will reach 70 to 80 degrees Fahrenheit, or set out transplants after the weather has reached that temperature. To get them off to a fast start, on cool nights cover the seedlings with hot caps.

WHERE TO PLANT
Hot peppers like hot weather, so reserve your hottest, sunniest miniclimate for these Latin American señoritas. If you live in a cool, hilly region, look for a spot that has all-day direct sun, along with a white wall that will bounce additional foot candles of sun at your peppers, or a stone surface that will absorb heat during the day and give it off at night.

HOW TO PLANT
Chile peppers thrive in fertile, well-drained soil. Prepare the bed by digging in 2 in. of coarse sand or chicken grit, 2 in. of humus, and a slow-release 5-10-5 fertilizer. In clay soil, add a small handful of gypsum and of superphosphate for each plant. Sow seeds following

package instructions, or mark planting holes for seedlings 6 to 8 in. apart around a system of soaker hoses. Divide plants in flats with a sharp, clean knife, giving each a good root system. Half fill each hole with diluted fertilizer, plant the seedling high, and press the soil down around the stem firmly enough so the plant resists a tug. Water well. Apply a 3-in. mulch starting 2 in. from the stems. When the first blossoms open, give the plants a light application of fertilizer.

How to Provide Care and Maintenance

Thin the seedlings if they become crowded. The peppers need lots of fertilizer early in the season, tapering off later. They will not set fruit if they have too much water or fertilizer as they mature. To promote rapid, unchecked growth, for the 2 or 3 weeks after planting, water often enough to sustain the soil moisture. Water weekly after that until toward the end of summer; then run the plants rather dry—but not dry enough so they wilt.

Additional Advice

Peppers drop many of their new blossoms when a full quota of fruit is beginning to ripen. Harvest some of the peppers and the plants will start to set fruit again—if the weather is hot.

Viola × wittrockiana

Pansies

*I*n Virginia, flats of pansies are offered at garden centers in late August and September, and again in March. We plant them right through October and fill out the beds in spring. Set where they will get direct sun in fall and spring, and protection from the sun when trees leaf out, pansies get to be 6 to 9 in. tall, and bloom until May or June. In cool hill country, they can bloom most of the summer—if they are deadheaded. In my garden pansies have survived our last several winters to become the first flowers of spring. They are spectacular massed in beds. I plant pansies where flowering bulbs will come up in matching or contrasting colors—yellow pansies and miniature daffodils, for example, and white-and-blue pansies with brilliant-red species tulips. For a showy display, plant the large-flowered pansies whose faces are painted in combinations of white, yellow, pink, blue, purple, black, orange, and mahogany-red. For loads of blooms, plant mixed varieties of the hybrids that come in melting solid colors— coral, peach, lavender, yellow, and blue. Yellow is the showiest pansy color.

WHEN TO PLANT

Plant pansies when the weather starts to cool in fall, and in early spring fill out the beds with more plants.

WHERE TO PLANT

In warm parts of Zone 7, plant pansies where the light will become dappled when the trees leaf out in spring. In cool, hilly regions, pansies can take a little more sun.

HOW TO PLANT

Prepare for pansies by digging in 2 in. of coarse sand or chicken grit, 2 in. of humus, and a slow-release 5-10-5 fertilizer. In clay soil, add a small handful of gypsum and of superphosphate for each plant. Work the soil 8 to 12 in. deep. Divide plants in flats with a sharp, clean knife, giving each a good root system. Half fill each hole with diluted fertilizer, plant the seedling high, and press the soil down around the stem firmly enough so the plant resists a tug. Water with a diluted fertilizer solution. Apply a 3-in. mulch starting 3 in. from the stems.

HOW TO PROVIDE CARE AND MAINTENANCE

After the first flush of fall bloom, deadhead and fertilize. Fertilize again when the weather begins to warm up in late winter, and resume deadheading and regular feeding.

ADDITIONAL ADVICE

As spring advances, pansies become leggy. With shearing and constant deadheading you can keep the plants producing and looking well until late May or later.

OTHER CULTIVARS AND SPECIES

Viola tricolor, the little tricolor violet called Johnny-jump-up, is an easy growing relative of the pansy that in spring bears masses of tiny multi-colored blooms with whiskered, pansy faces. The colors are yellow, white, and blue, and the height is 6 to 12 in. *V. odorata* 'Duchesse de Parme' and 'Lady Hume Campbell' are exquisitely perfumed violets. Check the fragrance before buying!

Petunia

*T*he petunias star in window boxes and hanging baskets, and they are superb bedding plants for sunny places. Set out in mid-spring, they develop into leafy mounds loaded with showy, trumpet-shaped flowers, and they bloom on through August as long as you deadhead meticulously. You can promote a new flush of bloom by cutting back old stems. And you can keep the show going by planting new seedlings next to maturing plants every few weeks. Petunias come in many forms. Choose Cascade types and the 'Fantasy' miniatures (which will bloom indoors in winter) for baskets and window boxes. Choose upright forms for bedding. The grandiflora (big-flowered) forms and doubles produce fewer flowers, but they are magnificent. The multifloras (many flowered) cover themselves with small, single blossoms. Planted in mixed colors, they froth up into one of summer's prettiest multicolor displays. Petunias come in every color and many bi-colors. The sparkling whites are just about indispensable for baskets and planters—buy them early. There never seem to be enough. Petunias are quite long-lasting as cut flowers—individual blossoms fade, but others on the branch open. If your summers are very hot, choose F1 Hybrid Single Multifloras.

WHEN TO PLANT

After the soil has warmed—April in Zone 8, mid-May in Zones 6 and 7—plant seedlings grown in 3 or 4 packs. Larger plants may play out very quickly. Start seeds indoors 10 weeks before planting time, if you can provide controlled temperatures, and repot and transplant twice.

WHERE TO PLANT

Petunias need 6 to 8 hours of direct sun to do their best, but will still do well given 4 to 6 hours. Avoid planting petunias where heavy falls of water will hit during a rainstorm. The branches are tender and need protection from heavy winds and showers.

How to Plant

Prepare the bed by digging in 2 in. of coarse sand or chicken grit, 2 in. of humus, and a slow-release 5-10-5 fertilizer. In clay soil, add a small handful of gypsum and of superphosphate for each plant. Petunias do best in soil with a pH in the 6.0 to 7.0 range. For petunias set out as bedding plants, provide a system of soaker hoses. Divide plants in flats with a sharp, clean knife, giving each a good root system. Half fill each hole with diluted fertilizer, plant the seedling high, and press the soil down around the stem firmly enough so the plant resists a tug. Water with a diluted fertilizer solution. Apply a 3-in. mulch starting 3 in. from the stems.

How to Provide Care and Maintenance

To promote rapid, unchecked growth, for the next 2 or 3 weeks soak bedding plants often enough to keep the soil damp, and fertilize them every 3 weeks. Water and fertilize hanging baskets and containers daily throughout the season. When the stems are 6 in. long, pinch out the tips of the central stems. Repeat with every 4 in. of growth until the plants are many-branched. Remove faded petunias and the seed pods behind them as quickly as you can—they form seeds and stop flowering. Trim plants back a third in midsummer to encourage late blooming.

Additional Advice

Petunias self-sow and in warmer regions may produce flowering volunteers by summer's end—just when other petunias may be fading. Plant volunteers next to fading plants.

Other Cultivars and Species

I love the sweet clove scent of fragrant varieties, but they are hard to find. They are most often purple or white, and in their background usually is the large white, night-scented *Petunia axillaris*.

Pink Vinca

OTHER COMMON NAME: Madagascar Periwinkle

*C*atharanthus blooms from early summer until frost, growing bigger, fuller, and more beautiful every week. It also tolerates heat, drought, and pollution. The shiny leaves are dark green, and the flowers are like small, flat phlox, or vinca flowers, in mauve-pink or white, often enhanced by a dark rose or red eye. The whites and crimson-eyed whites just light up the garden. The standard size is 12 to 18 in., but there are smaller plants for containers and small gardens. Plants of the 'Magic Carpet' strain are 6 to 9 in. high, with flowers in white and shades of pink and rose—very heat tolerant. 'Bright Eye' is a white dwarf with a carmine eye. 'Pink Panther' is under 12 in. and has clear, rose-red flowers with a darker eye. Vinca is a low-maintenance flower that never needs deadheading. Cut, the flowers continue to open buds for several days, and the leaves stay fresh.

WHEN TO PLANT

Seeds started indoors bloom in summer and fall. Seed germination can be difficult since the plants are extremely sensitive to cold and over-watering, so I recommend you plant nursery seedlings when they come on the market in late spring.

WHERE TO PLANT

Catharanthus blooms are given at least half a day of sun in my Washington, D.C., garden. In cool regions it can tolerate full sun as long as the soil is well-drained and humusy.

HOW TO PLANT

Prepare the bed by digging in 2 in. of coarse sand or chicken grit, 2 in. of humus, and a slow-release 5-10-5 fertilizer. In clay soil, add a small handful of gypsum and of superphosphate for each plant. Sow seeds following package instructions, or mark planting holes for seedlings 6 to 8 in. apart around a system of soaker hoses. Divide

ANNUALS

plants in flats with a sharp, clean knife, giving each a good root system. Half fill each hole with diluted fertilizer, plant the seedling high, and press the soil down around the stem firmly enough so the plant resists a tug. Water with a diluted fertilizer solution. Apply a 3-in. mulch starting 3 in. from the stems.

How to Provide Care and Maintenance
To promote rapid, unchecked growth, for the next 2 or 3 weeks water often enough to sustain the soil moisture. After that, water deeply every week unless you have a soaking rain. Once the plants show signs of new growth, to encourage branching, pinch out the top 3 to 4 in. of the lead stem. Pinch out the next 2 sets of branches as they develop. After the first flush of bloom, fertilize and repeat every 3 to 5 weeks through August.

Additional Advice
The seedlings will sulk if the ground is cold when they are set out.

Portulaca grandiflora

Rock Rose

Portulaca, a pretty little trailing plant 3 to 6 in. tall with succulent, needle-like leaves, can take almost any amount of heat. A sun lover, planted in mid-spring it spreads and blooms until frosts kill it in October or November. The flowers are single or double, red, pink, yellow, coral, or white. A hardy annual, it usually is grown from seed sown directly in the garden. The strain called Shirley Poppy has been used to hybridize begonia and ranunculus-flowered plants in wonderful shades of pink, rose, and coral pink. Modern portulacas stay open through the day and close at night. The old-fashioned species tended to close their blooms after clouds or bees had visited. Types like 'Cloudbeater' and 'All-Day Mix' don't really keep the promise in their names, but summer days here are mostly sunny, except for brief afternoon thundershowers, so that does not matter much. Portulaca makes a great temporary ground cover for hot, dry slopes and rock gardens. It is ideal for edging driveways and in other places you tend to neglect, and makes pretty hanging baskets.

When to Plant

In mid-spring, sow seeds in the garden. Or 8 weeks before the weather warms, sow seeds indoors in a sandy potting mix. Transplant the seedlings to the garden after the weather warms—April in Zone 8, mid-May in Zones 6 and 7.

Where to Plant

Plant portulaca in full sun—in partial light the flowers do not open. If you are starting the plants in the garden from seed, sow the seeds where the plants are to bloom.

How to Plant

Prepare the bed by digging in 2 in. of coarse sand or chicken grit, 2 in. of humus, and a slow-release 5-10-5 fertilizer. In clay soil, add a small handful of gypsum and of superphosphate for each plant. Sow seeds following package instructions, or mark planting holes for seedlings 6 to 8 in. apart around a system of soaker hoses. Divide plants in flats with a sharp, clean knife, giving each a good root system. Half fill each hole with diluted fertilizer, plant the seedling high, and press the soil down around the stem firmly enough so the plant resists a tug. Water with a diluted fertilizer solution. Apply a 3-in. mulch starting 3 in. from the stems.

How to Provide Care and Maintenance

To promote rapid, unchecked growth, for the next 2 or 3 weeks water lightly with a fine spray often enough to sustain the soil moisture. Thin the seedlings if they become crowded. Portulaca is famous for its tolerance of drought, but the plants are fullest and the flowers most beautiful when some humidity is maintained. After the first flush of bloom, fertilize, and repeat every 3 to 5 weeks through August.

Additional Advice

The seedlings will sulk if the ground is icy cold when they are set out. Wait to plant until 2 weeks after that last frost date: in the Williamsburg area that's April 14; Culpepper, April 17; Richmond, May 4; Washington, D.C., March 25. It often self-sows.

Salvia

OTHER COMMON NAME: Sage

*T*he salvias are easy-growing plants that fill the garden with a wide variety of strong colors all summer and through autumn. There are 3 major groups—blue, red, and herbal. The blue sages are tall plants that bush out and produce masses of lovely, slender laven-der-blue flower spikes. They are gorgeous planted among rose bushes and at the back of a flower border. Heat- and drought-tolerant *S. farinacea* 'Victoria', which is 18 to 20 in. tall, and the slightly taller Wedgewood blue 'Blue Bedder', are among the best. *S. leucantha*, the Mexican bush sage, is a beautiful, tender perennial 3 to 4 ft. tall with fragrant, velvety leaves. We grow it here as an annual. Late summer through frosts it stretches out loads of spikes covered with lavender flowers that have white corollas. The scarlet sage, *S. splendens*, is the parent of today's short, stocky cultivars in designer colors like auber-gine, salmon, lilac and purple, gold and, of course, red. Massed in the sun, these salvias are striking! Try aubergine salvia with coral New Guinea impatiens. Wild! You'll find the aromatic and beautifully var-iegated herbal sages, varieties of *S. officinalis*, discussed in Chapter 6.

WHEN TO PLANT

Ten to 12 weeks before planting time—April in Zone 8, mid-May in Zones 6 and 7—sow seeds indoors in a moist, humusy mix, and grow the seedlings at about 55 degrees Fahrenheit. Or sow seeds in the garden in late fall or in mid-spring.

WHERE TO PLANT

Plants set in full sun give the best performance, though some blue sages flower moderately well with only morning sun, particularly in the warm reaches of Virginia. If you are starting seeds in the garden, sow them where the plants are to bloom.

HOW TO PLANT

Prepare the bed by digging in 2 in. of coarse sand or chicken grit, 2 in. of humus, and a slow-release 5-10-5 fertilizer. In clay soil, add a small handful of gypsum and of superphosphate for each plant. Sow seeds following package instructions, or mark planting holes for seedlings 6 to 8 in. apart around a system of soaker hoses. Divide plants in flats with a sharp, clean knife, giving each a good root system. Half fill each hole with diluted fertilizer, plant the seedling high, and press the soil down around the stem firmly enough so the plant resists a tug. Water with a diluted fertilizer solution. Apply a 3-in. mulch starting 3 in. from the stems.

HOW TO PROVIDE CARE AND MAINTENANCE

To promote rapid, unchecked growth, for the next 2 or 3 weeks water often enough to sustain the soil moisture. After that, water deeply every week unless you have a soaking rain. The sages are drought-resistant but flourish when watered during prolonged dry spells. Thin the seedlings if they become crowded. When blue salvias begin to grow, to encourage branching, pinch out the top 3 to 4 in. of the lead stem. After the first flush of bloom, fertilize and repeat every 3 to 5 weeks through August. After every flush of bloom, remove spent flower stems to promote flowering.

ADDITIONAL ADVICE

The seedlings will sulk if the ground is icy cold when they are set out. Wait to plant until a week or so after that last frost date: in the Williamsburg area that's April 14; Culpepper, April 17; Richmond, May 4; Washington, D.C., March 25.

OTHER CULTIVARS AND SPECIES

Salvia farinacea 'Rhea' is a 14-in. blue salvia that flowers freely and is recommended for planters and for small gardens.

Snapdragon

*S*napdragons are free-flowering, lasting staples of both cutting gardens and flowering borders. I cannot imagine a flower garden without a goodly supply of their lovely pastel spires. In Virginia we call snapdragons annuals, but in my Washington, D.C., garden they usually come back at least one year, and often two, to provide one of spring's loveliest early displays. The survivors get stringy in summer heat, so as soon as snapdragon seedlings come on the market, I plant young 'uns near the veterans. Together they keep the garden blooming until frost. Choose tall sizes, 24 to 30 in., for cutting and for the back of the border. These may need staking. For windy places, choose large-flowered tetraploids like 'Ruffled Super Tetra' for their strong stems. If you like the open-faced snapdragons, look for varieties labeled 'Monarch' and 'Butterfly', hybrids 16 to 18 in. tall. The Princess strain has luscious bi-colors 12 to 15 in. high that also are excellent for cutting. Dwarfs like 'Tahiti', which is 7 to 9 in. high, are gorgeous as seedlings, but they never fill out the way larger snapdragons do. If rust is a problem in your garden, be sure to buy rust-resistant strains.

WHEN TO PLANT

Start seeds indoors in flats 10 to 12 weeks before planting time, or sow seeds in late fall, or in mid-spring. Wait to plant seeds and seedlings until danger of frost is past. Snapdragons often volunteer a few self-sown plants the second season: when they are growing vigorously, dig and transplant them to the garden.

WHERE TO PLANT

In warm parts of Zone 7 and in Zone 8 plant snapdragons in bright, dappled light or where they will get direct morning sun for 4 to 6 hours. In cool, hilly regions, plant snapdragons in full sun. You can start snapdragons from seeds in the garden, but they will take some time to flower, so sow the seeds where the plants are to bloom.

HOW TO PLANT

Prepare the bed by digging in 2 in. of humus and a slow-release 5-10-5 fertilizer. In clay soil, add a small handful of gypsum and of superphosphate for each plant. Work the soil 8 to 12 in. deep. Snapdragons do well in soil whose pH is 5.5 to 7.0. Sow seeds following package instructions, or mark planting holes for seedlings 6 to 8 in. apart around a system of soaker hoses. Divide plants in flats with a sharp, clean knife, giving each a good root system. Half fill each hole with diluted fertilizer, plant the seedling high, and press the soil down around the stem firmly enough so the plant resists a tug. Water with a diluted fertilizer solution. Apply a 3-in. mulch starting 3 in. from the stems.

HOW TO PROVIDE CARE AND MAINTENANCE

For the next 2 or 3 weeks promote rapid, unchecked growth by watering often enough to keep the soil moist. After that, water deeply every week unless you have a soaking rain. Thin crowded seedlings and encourage branching by pinching the tips out when the seedlings are 2 in. high. Then pinch out the tips of the next 2 sets of branches that develop. When cutting or deadheading, cut the stem just above the next branching node. New, flowering stems will develop at the node. After the first flush of bloom, fertilize and repeat every 3 to 5 weeks through August.

ADDITIONAL ADVICE

Though snapdragons often winter over, the seedlings your garden center offers in spring come from a greenhouse environment. Transplanted to icy cold ground they will sulk. So do not be tempted to plant until 2 weeks have passed since the last frost date for your area: in the Williamsburg area that's April 14; Culpepper, April 17; Richmond, May 4; Washington, D.C., March 25.

OTHER CULTIVARS AND SPECIES

For big bouquets, choose 'Double Supreme' hybrids which reach to 36 in. tall and bloom in clear, solid shades of red, pink, rose, and yellow.

Sweet Alyssum

Sweet alyssum is a frothy little edging plant that covers itself with tiny, scented flowers in sparkling white, rosy-violet, or purple from summer through late fall. It is mid-November as I write this, and a few blooms are still visible bordering the beds under the weeping cherry. This is a dainty plant 4 to 8 in. high that grows into a low mound 12 to 18 in. across. In extreme heat in midsummer, a slump in flower production can occur, but the blossoms return when cooler weather arrives. Some beautiful varieties are 'Little Sorrit', 'New Carpet of Snow', 'Noel Sutton', 'Elizabeth Taylor', 'Royal Wedding', 'Creme Beauty', and 'Geranium Pink'. I plant sweet alyssum so that it drips over the edges of hanging baskets, planters, and tubs planted with purplish ornamental peppers. It thrives tucked into moist planting pockets in a dry stone wall. Alyssum also does well near the sea. However you use alyssum, be sure to set at least a few plants by the porch or patio where you can enjoy its sweet scent in late summer.

WHEN TO PLANT

Sow seeds indoors in March or outdoors when the weather begins to warm in April—and be patient. It is slow to germinate. Or plant seedlings from the garden center as soon as the soil has warmed—April in Zone 8, mid-May in Zones 6 and 7.

WHERE TO PLANT

Sweet alyssum can do with a little less than direct sun all day, but it needs at least 4 to 6 hours of direct sun to flower well at all. If you are sowing seeds in the garden, sow them where the plants are to bloom.

HOW TO PLANT

Prepare the bed by digging in 2 in. of coarse sand or chicken grit, 2 in. of humus, and a slow-release 5-10-5 fertilizer. In clay soil, add a small handful of gypsum and of superphosphate for each plant. Work the soil 8 to 12 in. deep. Sweet alyssum does well in soil whose pH is 6.0 to 7.0. Sow seeds following package instructions, or mark planting holes for seedlings 6 to 8 in. apart around a system of soaker hoses. Divide plants in flats with a sharp, clean knife, giving each a good root system. Half fill each hole with diluted fertilizer, plant the seedling high, and press the soil down around the stem firmly enough so the plant resists a tug. Water with a diluted fertilizer solution. Apply a 3-in. mulch starting 3 in. from the stems.

HOW TO PROVIDE CARE AND MAINTENANCE

To promote rapid, unchecked growth, for the next 2 or 3 weeks water often enough to sustain the soil moisture. After that, water deeply when you water the flower garden. Sweet alyssum is versatile as to moisture and withstands heat. Thin the seedlings if they become crowded. After the first flush of bloom, fertilize and repeat every 3 to 5 weeks through August. Shear after each flush of bloom to discourage seed setting and to encourage flowering.

ADDITIONAL ADVICE

Sweet alyssum self-sows and can spread like wildfire to other parts of the garden. Discard volunteers, because chances are these will turn out to be plants that have reverted to the original, less-interesting species, not the beautiful cultivar you planted originally.

OTHER CULTIVARS AND SPECIES

'Cloth of Snow' is a really small form.

Wishbone Plant

OTHER COMMON NAME: Bluewings

This is a bushy little annual, 12 in. high with light-green leaves, bearing masses of bi-colored blooms like tiny snapdragons in blue and white, pink and white, or shades of violet. They are charming fillers for baskets, window boxes, and rock gardens. If you cut off the dead flowers after each flush of bloom, it will flower from early summer until frosts.

WHEN TO PLANT

Start seeds indoors 4 to 6 weeks before planting time and set seedlings out after the soil has warmed—May or June, or buy seedlings already in bloom.

WHERE TO PLANT

Plant torenia in dappled light; in cool, hilly regions, it can take 4 hours of direct sun, especially morning sun. If you are starting seeds in the garden, sow them where the plants are to bloom.

HOW TO PLANT

Prepare the bed by digging in 2 in. of coarse sand or chicken grit, 2 in. of humus, and a slow-release 5-10-5 fertilizer. In clay soil, add a small handful of gypsum and of superphosphate for each plant. Work the soil 8 to 12 in. deep. Divide plants in flats with a sharp, clean knife, giving each a good root system. Half fill each hole with diluted fertilizer, plant the seedling high, and press the soil down around the stem firmly enough so the plant resists a tug. Water with a diluted fertilizer solution. Apply a 3-in. mulch starting 3 in. from the stems.

How to Provide Care and Maintenance

To promote rapid, unchecked growth, for the next 2 or 3 weeks water often enough to sustain the soil moisture. After that, water deeply every week unless you have a soaking rain. Water torenias in baskets or containers daily. After each flush of bloom, shear off the spent flowers and water with a diluted house plant fertilizer.

Zinnia

innia's sparkling colors and broad range of sizes have made it the great summer annual for bedding and for cutting. Set out in early summer, zinnias bloom through early fall as long as they are deadheaded. These are carefree plants, except where there is mildew. If it is a problem, buy mildew-resistant cultivars. All varieties need heat, can stand rather dry soil, and keep their colors in blazing sun. They bloom in 4 to 5 weeks from sowing. Seedlings in bloom are ideal candidates for spaces left empty by the passing of spring flowers. There is a zinnia color for every taste—red, pink, orange, magenta, yellow, white, and bicolors—and forms and sizes for every purpose. There are tiny 6-in. plants with 2-in. flowers, and 30-in. plants with 6-in. flowers. Some have petals quilled like a cactus, some are curled as dahlias, some both. You have a choice of ruffled and flat-petaled forms, doubles and singles. The large-flowered zinnias flower less freely than the small-flowered zinnias and start blooming a little later.

WHEN TO PLANT

Sow seeds outdoors or plant seedlings after the soil has warmed— April in Zone 8, mid-May in Zones 6 and 7. Zinnias will sulk in cold soil. Or start zinnia seeds indoors in flats 3 to 4 weeks before planting time.

WHERE TO PLANT

Plant zinnias in full sun. They may bloom with 4 to 6 hours of sun— but not as fully. They transplant easily, but for a fast start, sow seeds where the plants are to bloom.

HOW TO PLANT

Prepare the bed by digging in 2 in. of coarse sand or chicken grit, 2 in. of humus, and a slow-release 5-10-5 fertilizer. In clay soil, add a small handful of gypsum and of superphosphate for each plant. Work the soil 8 to 12 in. deep. Sow seeds following package instructions. If you are setting out seedlings, mark planting holes 6 to 8 in. apart around a system of soaker hoses. Half fill each hole with diluted fertilizer, plant the seedling high, and press the soil down around the stem firmly enough so the plant resists a tug. Water with a diluted fertilizer solution. Apply a 3-in. mulch starting 3 in. from the stems.

HOW TO PROVIDE CARE AND MAINTENANCE

To promote rapid, unchecked growth, for the next 2 or 3 weeks, water often enough to sustain the soil moisture. After that, water deeply every week unless you have a soaking rain. Thin the crowded seedlings, allowing generous space around each plant. When the seedlings are 6 in. high, encourage branching by pinching out the tips of the lead stems. When cutting or deadheading, cut the stem just above the next branching node. New flowering stems will develop at the node. After the first flush of bloom, fertilize and repeat every 3 to 5 weeks through August.

ADDITIONAL ADVICE

Zinnias last well when the stem ends are stripped of leaves, plunged into boiling water for 30 seconds, then soaked in warm water several hours before being placed in an arrangement.

OTHER CULTIVARS AND SPECIES

For cutting, I like: tall green 'Envy'; 'Border Beauty' hybrids which are dahlia-type semi-double flowers on bushy 20-in. plants; 'Bouquet' hybrids, large, semi-ruffled fully double blooms 3 1/2 in. across on sturdy 22-in. branching plants; 'Candy Cane' Mix, 17-in. plants with semi- and double flowers striped in bright pink, rose, and cerise.

Deciduous Trees

*B*ECAUSE A TREE IS SUCH A LARGE EVENT IN A
LANDSCAPE, every aspect of a well-chosen tree can contribute to your pleasure in having it there—from branching to bark
to foliage and flowers.

The first rule in choosing a tree is: make sure you love it! A tree
is the most important plant purchase you are likely to make. Trees
and the larger shrubs give the garden their defining structure. They
are the linears that anchor the other elements—shrubs, ornamental
grasses, flower beds, paths, lawns, and water gardens. A young tree
requires decades to achieve its mature form. It is painful to wait 15
years for the tree to grow up and then to discover that you have
made a mistake.

A tree is also apt to be costly. So make sure the specimen you buy
is pest resistant, doesn't have a tendency to break apart as it gets
older (as do some early varieties of the Bradford pear), and won't
succumb to diseases, as many older varieties of crab apple will.
Worse even than having the wrong tree, or a tree in the wrong
place, is the experience of nurturing a beautiful tree and then losing
it. It leaves a gap in the heart as big as the gap in the garden.

Choose a tree that prefers the local soil structure and pH. You can
amend the soil for a smallish shrub, knowing the roots are apt to
stay within its borders. But the feeder roots of a tree 40 ft. tall reach
out between 40 and 60 ft. from the drip line, and you can't dig a
hole that big. For hard-to-transplant trees, I recommend amending
the soil of a hole the size of a card table to give it a good start, but
after that it must adapt to what's there.

Current research suggests that trees start to grow again sooner,
and grow stronger and more resistant, if they are subject early to
natural stress. Staking and wrapping aren't necessarily helpful
beyond the first year. Research has shown that a painted-on white-

wash, calcium carbonate with resins in it, is enough to prevent the winter sun from injuring young trunks.

Fertilize at half the rate recommended on the package, starting from the drip line outward to a distance that equals the height of the tree, plus half again its height. (For a 40-ft. tree, that would be 60 ft.).

And be sure to compost the leaves in fall! The nutrients they contain should go to enriching your soil, not clogging a landfill! The fast way to recycle your leaves is to suck them up in a blower-vacuum, and blow the powdery residue out over the garden. Another easy way is to grind the leaves into the blow-vac's holding bag and turn the residue onto your compost heap.

PRUNING TREES

Most trees require very little pruning. Remove branches growing into the center of the tree or crossing other branches. Prune a deciduous tree when it is dormant, just after the coldest part of the season. If the tree bleeds when sap starts to flow, don't be perturbed. When the tree leafs out, the sap will stop running.

Pruning stimulates growth, and you can use that knowledge to improve the productivity of a flowering tree. Prune a flowering tree that blooms in spring on last year's wood, like the dogwoods and the flowering fruit trees, after the flowers have faded. Prune a flowering tree that blooms on current growth—crape myrtle, for example—shortly before growth begins in spring.

It isn't necessary to paint or tar a pruning cut. There's a ring or collar from which each branch grows: find it and cut back to just beyond it, taking care not to damage the ring. From it the plant will develop an attractive, healthy covering for the wounded area.

American Beech

The beech is a tall, beautiful tree that has silver-gray bark and branches that sweep to the ground, literally creating a shaded hiding place for nut-loving squirrels. It is too low to sit under and too shaded even to grow weeds. The leaves come out late in spring and in the fall turn a soft, attractive russet-gold-brown. The American beech, *F. grandifolia*, is an imposing native species that reaches heights of 50 to 70 ft., growing 9 to 12 ft. over a 10-year period. It has high surface roots that are hard to cover, but are attractive when interplanted with small flowering bulbs. This species is rather difficult to transplant. The European beech, *F. sylvatica*, transplants more readily and is successful in all but the warmest parts of the state. Among interesting cultivars of this species are the weeping, green-leaved 'Pendula' and purple-leaved 'Purpurea Pendula'. There is a narrow upright form called 'Fastigiata'.

WHEN TO PLANT

Transplant a young container-grown or balled and burlapped tree with great care in early spring. Take particular care not to break the rootball of the American beech, which does not transplant easily.

WHERE TO PLANT

A beech tree needs lots of space all around and full sun—though it can handle dappled shade when young. A beech needs acid soil, pH 5.0 to 6.5.

HOW TO PLANT

Dig into a hole the size of a card table 2-in. layers of coarse sand or chicken grit and leaf mold or sphagnum peat moss. In clay soil, work into the hole 1 cupful each of gypsum and superphosphate. Unwind the roots circling the ball of a containerized tree and plant it with the crown an inch above ground level. If the tree is balled and burlapped, set it into the hole, cut the rope, slash the burlap, and pull the top part away from the rootball. Make a saucer of earth to hold water. Apply a 3-in. mulch starting 3 in. from the stem.

How to Provide Care

A beech may grow straighter if it's staked its first year after planting. Do not leave a stake on after the tree is established and growing strongly. After planting, pour a bucketful of water into the tree saucer every week unless there's a soaking rain.

Additional Advice for Care

In late winter before growth begins, broadcast $1/2$ the recommended dose of an organic 5-10-5 fertilizer for acid-loving plants from the drip line out to a point at a distance equal to $1^1/2$ times the tree's height. Water it in. Replenish the mulch. In summer or in early fall, cut out branches that will grow into the center of the tree or rub against other branches.

Additional Cultivars and Species

An unusual and interesting cultivar of the European beech is River's purple beech, *F. sylvatica* 'Riversii', a large, spreading tree with a deep-purple color that usually holds in summer.

American Sweet Gum

The American sweet gum is a tall, handsome shade tree with large five-pointed leaves that in fall turn to true yellow, red and purple—a spectacular show most years. In summer, the leaves are a deep, attractive glossy green. The bark is grayish-brown and interestingly corky. At maturity, the tree is about 60 to 75 ft. with a spread that equals two-thirds of the height. In moist soil, it grows rather quickly, 2 to 3 ft. a year. In dry soil, the growth is a little slower. Sweet gum is the perfect choice for an open suburban or country landscape where the soil is acid and moist, land that was previously forested wetland, for example. It makes a superb lawn tree, but its prickly fruit must be removed before mowing.

WHEN TO PLANT

Plant a young container-grown or balled and burlapped tree in early spring while the tree is still dormant. Handle the rootball with care. Under the best of circumstances it takes a while to recover from the move.

WHERE TO PLANT

Sweet gum requires full sun. Set the tree where there will be lots of space all round for the development of its root system. It does best in slightly acid soil, pH 5.5 to 6.5.

HOW TO PLANT

Dig into a hole the size of a card table a 2-in. layer of coarse sand or chicken grit and 3 in. of leaf mold or sphagnum peat moss. In clay soil, work into the hole 1 cupful each of gypsum and superphosphate. Unwind the roots circling the ball of a containerized tree and plant it with the crown an inch above ground level. If the tree is balled and burlapped, set it into the hole, cut the rope, slash the burlap, and pull the top part away from the rootball. Fill the hole, watering in to settle the soil. Make a saucer of earth to hold water. Apply a 3-in. mulch starting 3 in. from the stem.

HOW TO PROVIDE CARE

A tree may grow straighter if it's staked its first year after planting. Do not leave a stake on after the tree is established and growing strongly. After planting, pour a bucketful of water into the tree saucer every week unless there's a soaking rain. If you wish to plant the area around the tree with a living mulch, use only drought-tolerant ground covers, like myrtle, or a slow-growing, small-leaved variegated ivy.

ADDITIONAL ADVICE FOR CARE

In late winter before growth begins, broadcast an organic 5-10-5 fertilizer for acid-loving plants to just beyond the drip line at half the recommended rate and water it in. Replenish the mulch. Repeat in November. Once the plant is well established, switch to a 7-6-19 fertilizer. During the winter, remove branches that will grow into the center of the tree or rub against other branches.

American Yellowwood

OTHER COMMON NAME: Virgilia

The American yellowwood is a small, flowering tree that in mid-spring literally drips foot-long clusters of fragrant, white flowers resembling Wisteria. The bees love it. The leaves start a bright yellow-green, change to bright-green in summer, and then to a not very showy golden-yellow in fall. The bark is silvery, rather like that of the American beech. It is a low-branching tree that grows a little more than a foot a year to 30 to 50 ft., with a spread of 40 to 55 ft. You can use this as a flowering shade tree for the middle of a small lawn or as backing for a flowering shrub border. It is not particularly bothered by drought and is generally trouble-free. One of the few flowering trees that does not require somewhat acid soil, its native habitat is limestone cliffs and ridges, from North Carolina to Kentucky and Tennessee, but it's hardy well to the north of Virginia.

WHEN TO PLANT
Plant a young tree in early spring while the tree is still dormant.

WHERE TO PLANT
Yellowwood requires full sun. It does well not only in alkaline soils but also in soils that are slightly acid.

HOW TO PLANT
Dig into a hole the size of a card table a 2-in. layer of coarse sand or chicken grit. In clay soil, work into the hole 1 cupful each of gypsum and superphosphate. Unwind the roots circling the ball of a containerized tree and plant it with the crown an inch above ground level. If the tree is balled and burlapped, set it into the hole, cut the rope, slash the burlap, and pull the top part away from the rootball. Fill the hole, watering in to settle the soil. Make a saucer of earth to hold water. Apply a 3-in. mulch starting 3 in. from the stem.

HOW TO PROVIDE CARE

A tree may grow straighter if it's staked its first year after planting. Do not leave a stake on after the tree is established and growing strongly. After planting, pour a bucketful of water into the tree saucer every week unless there's a soaking rain.

ADDITIONAL ADVICE FOR CARE

In late winter before growth begins, broadcast an organic 5-10-5 fertilizer to just beyond the drip line at half the recommended rate and water it in. Replenish the mulch. Repeat in November. Once the plant is well established, switch to a 7-6-19 fertilizer. Because the tree weeps abundantly when pruned in winter or spring, cut it back only in summer.

ADDITIONAL CULTIVARS AND SPECIES

Some nurseries offer a pink cultivar, 'Rosea'.

Black Gum

OTHER COMMON NAMES: Sour Gum, Black Tupelo

In fall, this is the most beautiful of all our native trees. The leaves change to a glowing yellow, then to orange, scarlet and purple. The form is pyramidal, and the branches are somewhat drooping. The usual height is 30 to 50 ft., but it grows taller in the wild, especially near water. It bears bluish fruits that are somewhat hidden by the leaves. The black gum looks its best featured at the edge of a lawn or near a stream or a pond where its autumn foliage will be seen. It handles enough pollution to be used as a street tree in the suburbs or a small town, but it has a taproot which makes it difficult to transplant.

WHEN TO PLANT

With great care, plant a young container-grown or balled and burlapped tree in early spring while the tree is still dormant. Do not break the rootball.

WHERE TO PLANT

In cultivation it does best in full sun or bright, dappled shade. The black gum requires moist, well-drained acid soil, pH 5.5 to 6.5, and needs some protection from wind.

HOW TO PLANT

Dig into a hole the size of a card table 2-in. layers of coarse sand or chicken grit and of leaf mold or sphagnum peat moss. In clay soil, work into the hole 1 cupful each of gypsum and superphosphate. Handle the root ball with great care. Plant a containerized tree with the crown an inch above ground level. If the tree is balled and burlapped, set it into the hole, cut the rope, slash the burlap, and pull the top part away from the rootball. Fill the hole, watering in to settle the soil. Make a saucer of earth to hold water. Apply a 3-in. mulch starting 3 in. from the stem.

HOW TO PROVIDE CARE

After planting, pour a bucketful of water into the tree saucer every week unless there's a soaking rain. If you wish to plant the area around the tree with a living mulch, use only drought-tolerant ground covers, like myrtle, ajuga, or a slow-growing, small-leaved variegated ivy. Hostas and small spring flowering bulbs like wood hyacinths are also acceptable ground cover. Until the tree is established and growing strongly, shelter it behind a burlap screen in winter.

ADDITIONAL ADVICE FOR CARE

In late winter before growth begins, broadcast half the recommended dose of an organic 5-10-5 fertilizer for acid-loving plants from the drip line out to a point at a distance equal to 1½ times the tree's height. Water it in. Replenish the mulch. Once the plant is well established, switch to a 7-6-19 fertilizer. In late fall, cut away any branches that grow into the center of the tree or rub against other branches.

Callery Pear

OTHER COMMON NAME: Flowering Pear

*T*he flowering pear is a beautiful, pyramidal tree 30 to 50 ft. high—bigger than most of the flowering fruit trees. In early spring, it covers itself with clusters of small, white blooms. In fall, the glossy, green leaves turn an attractive wine red and persist into November. The fruits are small and russet colored and attract birds. The flowering pear has been widely planted as a street tree. The first flowering pear was 'Bradford', a beautiful tree that unfortunately tends to split as it matures. It is being replaced by disease-resistant 'Capital', a columnar flowering pear that is well suited to narrow sites and streets. The leaves turn a coppery color in fall and are persistent. 'Whitehouse', a larger tree for boulevards and parks, has a strongly developed central stem, abundant flowers before the leaves, and beautiful red-and-purple leaves early in the fall. The flowering pear is a little too big for a small city garden but is handsome in a larger suburban landscape. It is a good espalier subject.

WHEN TO PLANT

Plant a balled and burlapped tree in late winter or early spring before the plant leafs out.

WHERE TO PLANT

A flowering pear flowers most fully and produces the brightest fruits when growing in full sun. However, like most small flowering trees, with 4 to 6 hours of sun or day-long bright, filtered light, it will perform well. The callery pears succeed in soils with a broad pH range, 5.5 to 7.5.

HOW TO PLANT

Dig into a hole the size of a card table 2-in. layers of coarse sand or chicken grit and of leaf mold or sphagnum peat moss. In clay soil, work into the hole 1 cupful each of gypsum and superphosphate. Unwind the roots circling the ball of a containerized tree and plant it with the crown an inch above ground level. If the tree is balled and burlapped, set it into the hole, cut the rope, slash the burlap, and pull the top part away from the rootball. Fill the hole, watering in to settle the soil. Make a saucer of earth to hold water. Apply a 3-in. mulch starting 3 in. from the stem.

HOW TO PROVIDE CARE

A tree may grow straighter if it's staked its first year after planting. Do not leave a stake on after the tree is established and growing strongly. After planting, pour a bucketful of water into the tree saucer every week unless there's a soaking rain. If you wish to plant the area around the tree with a living mulch, use only drought-tolerant ground covers, like myrtle, ajuga, or a slow-growing, small-leaved variegated ivy. Hostas, liriope, mondo grass, and small, spring-flowering bulbs like wood hyacinths are also acceptable ground cover.

ADDITIONAL ADVICE FOR CARE

In late winter before growth begins, broadcast an organic 5-10-5 fertilizer for acid-loving plants to just beyond the drip line at half the recommended rate and water it in. Replenish the mulch. Repeat in November. Once the plant is well established, switch to a 7-6-19 fertilizer. In late winter or early spring cut away branches that will grow into the center of the tree or rub against other branches.

Halesia tetraptera (syn. *carolina*)

Carolina Silverbell

The Carolina silverbell is a lovely native tree that grows wild all the way from West Virginia to Florida and eastern Texas. It is a low-branched tree, 30 to 40 ft. at maturity. From April to early May, it bears clusters of pendant bell-shaped white flowers that flutter in the breeze. In bloom, halesia is a wall of white. In fall, the foliage changes to yellow or yellow-green. This is not a particularly showy tree once it has gone out of bloom, but it's a perfect choice for wood-land borders and looks lovely naturalized on a hillside or by a stream. In a landscaped garden, it shows off to best advantage placed against a background of evergreens.

WHEN TO PLANT

Plant a container-grown or a balled and burlapped tree in fall before Indian summer, or in early spring while the tree is still dormant.

WHERE TO PLANT

The Carolina silverbell can be planted in full sun or in a spot that gives it 4 to 6 hours of sun or all-day filtered light. It does best in slightly acid soil, pH 5.0 to 6.0. It thrives in rich, well-drained soil, and along stream banks and hillsides in light shade. It is excellent for naturalizing.

HOW TO PLANT

Dig into a hole the size of a card table 2-in. layers of coarse sand or chicken grit and of leaf mold or sphagnum peat moss. In clay soil, work into the hole 1 cupful each of gypsum and superphosphate. Unwind the roots circling the ball of a containerized tree and plant it with the crown an inch above ground level. If the tree is balled and burlapped, set it into the hole, cut the rope, slash the burlap, and pull the top part away from the rootball. Fill the hole, watering in to settle the soil. Make a saucer of earth to hold water. Apply a 3-in. mulch starting 3 in. from the stem.

How to Provide Care

After planting, pour a bucketful of water into the tree saucer every week unless there's a soaking rain. If you wish to plant the area around the tree with a living mulch, use only drought-tolerant ground covers, like myrtle or a slow-growing, small-leaved variegated ivy.

Additional Advice for Care

In late winter before growth begins, broadcast an organic 5-10-5 fertilizer for acid-loving plants to just beyond the drip line at half the recommended rate, and water it in. Replenish the mulch. Repeat in November. Once the plant is well established, switch to a 7-6-19 fertilizer. Carolina silverbell blooms on year-old wood. Any pruning that is necessary should be undertaken immediately after flowering.

Crab Apple

*A*pple orchards thrive in the Shenandoah Valley near the West Virginia border where summers aren't quite so hot and fall is crisp and lingers—but the apple tree found in most gardens is the flowering crab apple. These small spreading trees are covered in spring with exquisite apple blossoms, fragrant in some hybrids, and the brilliant fall fruits attract flocks of birds. Older varieties have problems, but there are new and beautiful disease-resistant hybrids. The most picturesque of the crab apples is the 20-ft. tea crab, *M. hupehensis*, with long, wand-like branches, spreading 25 ft. The flowers are fragrant, and the fruits greenish-yellow to red. It has excellent resistance to everything but fireblight. Another healthy and popular beauty is the 18-ft. Japanese flowering crab apple, *M. floribunda*. The branches have a 25-ft. spread and present an exceptionally beautiful silhouette in winter. The buds are deep-pink to red, fading to white as they open, and the fruit is yellow-red. There are literally dozens, and probably hundreds, more sound hybrids available. Before you fall in love with one of them, make sure it's a disease-resistant plant.

WHEN TO PLANT

The best times for planting are in fall before Indian summer, and in early spring while the tree is still dormant.

WHERE TO PLANT

Nearly all crab apples flower most fully and produce the brightest fruits when they're planted in full sun, but they can make do with 4 to 6 hours of sun or all-day filtered light. An exception is 40-ft. 'Dolgo' which does well in shade. Keep a distance of 500 ft. between crab apples and red cedar plants to prevent spreading of red cedar galls. Crab apples do best in slightly acidic soil, pH 5.0 to 6.5.

HOW TO PLANT

Dig a hole 6 in. deeper than the rootball and wider toward the top. Use a spading fork to loosen the sides of the hole. In clay soil, work into the hole 1 cupful each of gypsum and superphosphate and top it with 2 in. of soil. Unwind the roots circling the ball of a containerized tree and plant it with the crown an inch above ground level. If the tree is balled and burlapped, set it into the hole, cut the rope, slash the burlap, and pull the top part away from the rootball. Fill the hole, watering in to settle the soil. Make a saucer of earth to hold water. Apply a 3-in. mulch starting 3 in. from the stem.

HOW TO PROVIDE CARE

A tree may grow straighter if it's staked its first year after planting. Do not leave a stake on after the tree is established and growing strongly. Pour a bucketful of water into the tree saucer every week unless there's a soaking rain. If you wish to plant the area around the tree with a living mulch, use only drought-tolerant ground covers like myrtle, ajuga, or a slow-growing, small-leaved variegated ivy. Small spring-flowering bulbs like wood hyacinths are also acceptable ground cover.

ADDITIONAL ADVICE FOR CARE

In late winter before growth begins, broadcast half the recommended dose of an organic 5-10-5 fertilizer for acid-loving plants from the drip line out to a point at a distance equal to $1^1/2$ times the tree's height. Water it in. Replenish the mulch. Before early June, remove sucker growth and branches growing into the center of the tree.

ADDITIONAL CULTIVARS AND SPECIES

A lovely crab apple for a small garden is 'Narragansett', a recent disease-resistant introduction by the National Arboretum. The long-lasting flower buds are dark carmine, then bright red, opening to white, followed by persistent glossy, cherry-red fruits.

Crape Myrtle

*T*he crape myrtles are small, flowering trees and large shrubs that light up July and August with upright sprays of florets that look like lilacs and often last for many weeks. The colors range from a warm raspberry through melting shades of rose, pink, melon and mauve, and there are also whites. The bark is mottled light tan to gray and very smooth. Now that the National Arboretum has introduced an array of disease- and mildew-resistant hybrid crape myrtles, they're featured in gardens and parks all over the state, except in the coldest places near the West Virginia border. But even a plant that appears to have been killed by winter cold is likely to send up branches that will flower. A small crape myrtle can be grown as a shrubby perennial. Named for Native American tribes, these new varieties have cinnamon-colored exfoliating bark, and the foliage of pink varieties turns showy colors in the fall. Most grow relatively quickly to 15 ft. or so, but they can be kept to shrub-size by cutting the plants back to the ground before they leaf out. Crape myrtles leaf out late, especially when new, and bloom on that season's new wood. To have lots of flowers, prune every year.

WHEN TO PLANT
Transplant container-grown or balled and burlapped trees in spring, or in the fall before Indian summer.

WHERE TO PLANT
Crape myrtles flower most fully growing in full sun. However, like most small flowering trees, they will bloom with 4 to 6 hours of sun or all-day dappled light. Crape myrtles do best in moist, heavy loam and clay soils in the acid range, pH 5.0 to 6.5.

HOW TO PLANT
Dig into a hole the size of a card table 2-in. layers of coarse sand or chicken grit and of leaf mold or sphagnum peat moss. Unwind the roots circling the ball of a containerized tree and plant it with the crown an inch above ground level. If the tree is balled and burlapped, set it into the hole, cut the rope, slash the burlap, and pull the top part away from the rootball. Fill the hole, watering in

to settle the soil. Make a saucer of earth to hold water. Apply a 3-in. mulch starting 3 in. from the stem.

HOW TO PROVIDE CARE

After planting, pour a bucketful of water into the tree saucer every week until August unless there's a soaking rain. Do no fall watering. A tree may grow straighter if it's staked its first year after planting. Do not leave a stake on after the tree is established and growing strongly. If you wish to plant the area around the tree with a living mulch, use only drought-tolerant ground covers, like myrtle, ajuga, or a slow-growing, small-leaved variegated ivy. Hostas and small spring-flowering bulbs like wood hyacinths are also acceptable ground cover.

ADDITIONAL ADVICE FOR CARE

Before growth begins, broadcast an organic 5-10-5 fertilizer for acid-loving plants to just beyond the drip line at half the recommended rate, and water it in. Replenish the mulch. Once the plant is well established, switch to a 7-6-19 fertilizer. Crape myrtle blooms on the current year's growth, so prune away last year's flowering panicles in spring, before growth begins.

ADDITIONAL CULTIVARS AND SPECIES

'Natchez' is a white-flowered tree 21 by 30 ft. or more wide with handsome, exfoliating bark. Pink 'Osage', dark-pink 'Sioux', and lavender 'Yuma' are smaller, slower-growing plants that end up between 12 and 15 ft. tall.

Dogwood

*T*he dogwood is a small, native tree whose layered branches are covered in mid-spring with sparkling white star-shaped flowers (actually pointed bracts), followed in fall by bright-red fruits that attract birds. Cold colors the foliage red-to-plum. The wild dogwood that blooms with the redbuds at the edges of our woodlands is the 20- to 30-ft. *C. florida*. It is Virginia's state flower, and the white, pink or red varieties bloom in almost every garden. Unfortunately, it has problems. It is better to plant the equally beautiful, disease-resistant Chinese dogwood, *C. kousa* var. *chinensis*, or one of the new Rutger hybrids, *C. × rutgeriensis*, crosses between the Kousa and the Florida species. These dogwoods are bigger and bloom later—June in my garden—and perch their flowers on the tops of the branches. Weeping kousas like 'Elizabeth Lustgarten' are breathtaking. As the Chinese dogwood matures, the bark exfoliates attractively. There are some exquisite variegated forms of the Chinese dogwood, such as 'Wolf Eyes'. The tricolor dogwood, *C. f.* 'Welchii', has jade-green leaves splashed cream-white and pink that turn a spectacular rose-red, red-purple in fall.

WHEN TO PLANT

With great care, plant a young container-grown or balled and burlapped dogwood in early spring while the tree is still dormant. Be careful not to break the rootball.

WHERE TO PLANT

Dogwoods are most successful in bright filtered or dappled light and in partial shade, but they tolerate full sun. They don't live very long in urban gardens. The kousas need more sun than the Florida dogwoods, but mine does well in the dappled light of several street trees. They tolerate some drought. Dogwoods require acid soil, pH 5.0 to 6.5, and will do very well on land that was forested.

How to Plant

Dig into a hole the size of a card table 2-in. layers of coarse sand or chicken grit and leaf mold or sphagnum peat moss. In clay soil, work into the hole 1 cupful each of gypsum and superphosphate. Unwind the roots circling the ball of a containerized tree and plant it with the crown an inch above ground level. If the tree is balled and burlapped, set it into the hole, cut the rope, slash the burlap, and pull the top part away from the rootball. Fill the hole, watering in to settle the soil. Make a saucer of earth to hold water. Apply a 3-in. mulch starting 3 in. from the stem.

How to Provide Care

A tree may grow straighter if it's staked its first year after planting. Do not leave a stake on after the tree is established and growing strongly. After planting, pour a bucketful of water into the tree saucer every week unless there's a soaking rain. If you wish to plant the area around the tree with a living mulch, use only drought-tolerant ground covers, like myrtle, ajuga, or a slow-growing, small-leaved variegated ivy. Hostas and small spring-flowering bulbs like wood hyacinths are also acceptable ground cover.

Additional Advice for Care

In late winter before growth begins, broadcast half the recommended dose of an organic 5-10-5 fertilizer for acid-loving plants from the drip line out to a point at a distance equal to $1^1/2$ times the tree's height. Water it in. Replenish the mulch. Repeat in November. Once the plant is well established, switch to a 7-6-19 fertilizer.

Additional Cultivars and Species

The Cornelian cherry dogwood, *C. mas*, is a small tree with modest blooms that opens clusters of yellow flowers in early spring before the leaves. The tart, scarlet fruit, once a food crop, attract birds. The giant dogwood, *C. controversa*, resembles the Florida dogwood, but in the wild reaches 60 ft.

Flowering Cherry

*A*fter the witchhazels bloom at the National Arboretum, a whole bevy of flowering fruit trees come into bloom—all species and hybrids of the genus *Prunus*. The most celebrated are the flowering cherries, but there are plums, apricots, peaches, almonds, nectarines, and cherry laurels. Bred for their blooms, they produce rudimentary fruit appealing only to birds. A very popular flowering cherry is the Higan, or rosebud, cherry, *P. subhirtella* 'Pendula', which blooms early and is a weeping tree with single pink flowers. Even more beautiful is the double weeping cherry, 'Pendula Plena Rosea', ('Yae-Shidare-Higan'), which blooms a little later and stands up to bad weather. The trees that flower at the Tidal Basin in Washington, D.C., are Yoshino cherries, *P. × yedoensis*, which often bloom just in time to catch the last winter storm. The finest of this type is 'Akebono', a pink-flowered, fragrant form that prefers somewhat acid soil and adapts to semi-sun. 'Shidare Yoshino' is a weeping form. 'Ivensii' has fragrant, white flowers on weeping branches. The sargent cherry, *P. sargentii*, which has beautiful bark, can double as a shade tree in a small garden.

WHEN TO PLANT
Transplant container-grown or balled and burlapped trees in early spring.

WHERE TO PLANT
Flowering fruit trees bloom most fully and produce the brightest fruits when they're growing in full sun.

HOW TO PLANT
Dig into a hole the size of a card table a 3-in. layer of coarse sand or chicken grit. In clay soil, work into the hole 1 cupful each of gypsum and superphosphate. Unwind the roots circling the ball of a containerized tree and plant it with the crown an inch above ground level. If the tree is balled and burlapped, set it into the hole, cut the rope, slash the burlap, and pull the top part away from the rootball. Fill the hole, watering in to settle the soil. Make a saucer of earth to hold water. Apply a 3-in. mulch starting 3 in. from the stem.

HOW TO PROVIDE CARE

After planting, pour a bucketful of water into the tree saucer every week unless there's a soaking rain. If you wish to plant the area around the tree with a living mulch, use only drought-tolerant ground covers, like myrtle, ajuga, or a slow-growing, small-leaved variegated ivy. Hostas, liriope, mondo grass, and small spring-flowering bulbs like wood hyacinths are also acceptable ground cover.

ADDITIONAL ADVICE FOR CARE

In late winter before growth begins, broadcast a half-inch of lime-free compost over the soil to a foot or two beyond the drip line and water it in. Prune after flowering. Cut away young branches that will grow into the center of the tree or rub against other branches.

ADDITIONAL CULTIVARS AND SPECIES

The flowering plums bloom before most cherries and some have nice red foliage. *P.* × *blireana*, which is a 20-ft. double pink, has red-dish-purple foliage that turns to green-bronze in summer and red-bronze in fall. The cherry plum, *P. cerasifera* 'Diversifolia', is a purple-leaved tree whose new leaves are brilliant red. The pink flowers are single and cover the branches. The cherry laurel called 'Otto Luykens' laurel is a fine compact form about 4 ft. tall that bears small white flowers in spring. The leaves are long and thin, about 4 in. by 1 in., and it does very well even in quite dense shade. An excellent edging shrub.

Fringe Tree

*I*n mid-spring, just as the leaves are filling out, this lovely little tree wraps itself in a mist of sweetly fragrant, greenish-white flowers that consist of drooping, fringe-like petals 6 to 8 in. long. With the first real cold, the leaves turn luminous yellow-gold and hang on as long as the weather stays fairly moderate. Then, almost overnight, the foliage browns and drops off. The female plants bear bloomy, purple fruit the birds relish. The petals of the flowers on male trees are larger and showier, but the fruit is smaller and somewhat hidden by the foliage. The average height is between 15 and 25 ft. The fringe tree tolerates urban pollution. In the wild, it's often found growing near water. It is very pretty seen at a distance—across a lawn for example, or near a pond or a stream.

WHEN TO PLANT

Set out a young container-grown or a balled and burlapped tree in early spring while the tree is still dormant. Be careful not to break the rootball.

WHERE TO PLANT

The fringe tree flowers most fully growing in full sun. However, with 4 to 6 hours of sun or bright, filtered light all day it still performs well. It does best near water in slightly acid soil, pH 6.0-6.5.

HOW TO PLANT

Dig into a hole the size of a card table 2-in. layers of coarse sand or chicken grit and of leaf mold or sphagnum peat moss. In clay soil, work into the hole 1 cupful each of gypsum and superphosphate. Unwind the roots circling the ball of a containerized tree and plant it with the crown an inch above ground level. If the tree is balled and burlapped, set it into the hole, cut the rope, slash the burlap, and pull the top part away from the rootball. Fill the hole, watering in to settle the soil. Make a saucer of earth to hold water. Apply a 3-in. mulch starting 3 in. from the stem.

HOW TO PROVIDE CARE

A tree may grow straighter if it's staked its first year after planting. Do not leave a stake on after the tree is established and growing strongly. After planting, pour a bucketful of water into the tree saucer every week unless there's a soaking rain. If you wish to plant the area around the tree with a living mulch, use only drought-tolerant ground covers, like myrtle, ajuga, or a slow-growing, small-leaved variegated ivy. Hostas, liriope, mondo grass, and small, spring-flowering bulbs like wood hyacinths are also acceptable ground cover.

ADDITIONAL ADVICE FOR CARE

In late winter before growth begins, broadcast half the recommended dose of an organic 5-10-5 fertilizer for acid-loving plants from the drip line out to a point at a distance equal to 1½ times the tree's height. Water it in. Replenish the mulch. Once the plant is well established, switch to a 7-6-19 fertilizer. Right after flowering, cut away young branches that will grow into the center of the tree or rub against other branches.

ADDITIONAL CULTIVARS AND SPECIES

C. retusus, the Chinese fringe tree, is a large multi-stemmed species with smaller leaves that in May and June covers itself with a fleece of 2- to 3-in. upright florets. This species flowers on the season's new growth, so it should be pruned, if needed, in late winter before growth begins.

Ginkgo

A tall, stately tree ideal for city parks, the ginkgo has easily recognized, fan-shaped leaves and turns a luminous yellow-gold in fall. The lower length of the trunk is usually bare. It tolerates pollution and salt, so it has been used as a street tree in cities—in New York, for example—though that is not its best use. The height growing in a tree box is 30 to 40 ft., but on the Capitol Hill grounds in Washington, D.C., there are several older species that must be close to 100 ft. tall. It is a long-lived tree and is estimated to have been growing on the planet for 150 million years. The strain we have now comes from China, but at one time it grew wild on this continent. Ask for and make sure you get a male ginkgo. The female tree produces a messy, plum-like fruit/seed that smells bad. One of the best-looking cultivars is a broad-headed male called 'Autumn Gold'. There are a number of columnar cultivars. 'Princeton Sentry' PP 2726 is a columnar grafted male with very beautiful fall foliage. 'Mayfield' is another narrow, columnar type.

WHEN TO PLANT

You can plant a ginkgo in fall before Indian summer or in early spring while the tree is still dormant.

WHERE TO PLANT

The ginkgo requires full sun, at least 6 hours a day. It does well in almost any soil, and tolerates pollution and salt.

HOW TO PLANT

Dig a modest planting hole about 6 in. deeper than the rootball and wider toward the top. Work a spading fork into the sides of the hole to loosen compacted soil. In clay soil, work into the hole 1 cupful each of gypsum and superphosphate and top it with 2 in. of soil. Unwind the roots circling the ball of a containerized tree and plant it with the crown an inch above ground level. If the tree is balled and burlapped, set it into the hole, cut the rope, slash the burlap, and pull the top part away from the rootball. Fill the hole, watering in to settle the soil. Make a saucer of earth to hold water. Apply a 3-in. mulch starting 3 in. from the stem.

HOW TO PROVIDE CARE

A tree may grow straighter if it's staked its first year after planting. Do not leave a stake on after the tree is established and growing strongly. After planting, pour a bucketful of water into the tree saucer every week unless there's a soaking rain.

ADDITIONAL ADVICE FOR CARE

In late winter before growth begins, broadcast half the recommended dose of an organic 5-10-5 fertilizer for acid-loving plants from the drip line out to a point at a distance equal to $1^1/_2$ times the tree's height. Water it in. Replenish the mulch. Once the plant is well established, switch to a 7-6-19 fertilizer. Cut away any young branches that will grow into the center of the tree or rub against other branches.

'Heritage' River

*I*n winter, the chalky-white bark of the river birch is a wonderful asset, especially seen against a background of evergreens. As a group, the birches are tall, slender trees with graceful crowns of dainty leaves that move in every breeze and turn to yellow and yellow-green in fall. The most famous is the white, or canoe birch, *B. papyrifera*, but it's hardy only in the cooler parts of Virginia. A better choice for warm regions is the 30-ft. cultivar 'Heritage', a river, or red birch, *B. nigra*. It also is also resistant to the birch bark borer that plagues this group. 'Heritage' has handsome, white bark that exfoliates, exposing inner bark that may be salmon-pink to grayish, cinnamon, or reddish-brown. It grows fairly quickly, especially in moist soil. At the National Arboretum, a good planting of this specimen separates the herb garden from the meadow.

WHEN TO PLANT

The best times for planting are in fall before Indian summer, and in early spring while the tree is still dormant. But container-grown trees set out almost any time in spring or fall succeed. Though the air cools, the earth remains warm and the roots go on growing.

WHERE TO PLANT

Birches thrive in full sun, but they also do well in the dappled shade cast by other trees. The river birch does best in naturally moist soils and can stand a modest amount of flooding from time to time since it originated in swampy bottomlands. It requires soil whose pH is below 6.5.

HOW TO PLANT

Dig a modest planting hole about 6 in. deeper than the rootball and wider toward the top. Work a spading fork into the sides of the hole to loosen compacted soil. In clay soil, work into the hole 1 cupful each of gypsum and superphosphate and top it with 2 in. of soil. Unwind the roots circling the ball of a containerized tree and plant it with the crown an inch above ground level. If the tree is balled and burlapped, set it into the hole, cut the rope, slash the burlap, and pull the top part away from the rootball. Fill the hole, watering in to

DECIDUOUS TREES

settle the soil. Make a saucer of earth to hold water. Apply a 3-in. mulch starting 3 in. from the stem.

How to Provide Care

A birch may grow straighter if it's staked its first year after planting. Do not leave a stake on after the tree is established and growing strongly. After planting, pour a couple of bucketfuls of water into the tree saucer every week unless there's a soaking rain.

Additional Advice for Care

Before growth begins, broadcast half the recommended dose of an organic 5-10-5 fertilizer for acid-loving plants from the drip line out to a point at a distance equal to 1½ times the tree's height. Water it in. Replenish the mulch. Once the plant is well established, switch to a 7-6-19 fertilizer. Cut away any young branches that will grow into the center of the tree or rub against other branches.

Additional Cultivars and Species

In the cooler parts of the state, Zones 6/7, the 50-ft. Japanese white birch, *B. platyphylla* var. *japonica* 'Whitespire', does very well. A superior birch introduced by a former Director of the National Arboretum, John L. Creech, it has distinctive white bark with contrasting black triangles at the base of lateral branches.

Hornbeam

*T*he American hornbeam, *C. caroliniana*, is a small, handsome, slow-growing 20- to 30-ft. tree that grows wild in woodlands all over the East. The bark is gray-blue and fluted, and perhaps for that reason it also is known as "blue beech." It is an excellent choice for naturalizing near streams and rivers, since it tolerates pollution, wet soil, and periodic flooding. The foliage in fall is orange to dark red. It makes an attractive street tree, but it's difficult to transplant. *C. betulus*, the European hornbeam, is a very shearable tree that in Europe is used in high hedges and to create pleached allees. It withstands smoke, dust and drought, and is considered one of the finest medium-to-small shade trees for urban gardens, malls and commercial developments. The papery fruit looks like small lanterns. 'Columnaris' and 'Fastigiata' are narrow forms, and there are variegated and pendulous cultivars.

WHEN TO PLANT

Plant young container-grown or balled and burlapped trees in early spring while the plant still is dormant. The hornbeam is not easy to transplant, so handle the rootball with care.

WHERE TO PLANT

The American hornbeam does well in part or full shade and in somewhat acid soil. The European hornbeam does best in full sun but tolerates part shade. It can manage in soil that is either acid or alkaline.

HOW TO PLANT

Dig into a hole the size of a card table 2-in. layers of coarse sand or chicken grit and of leaf mold or sphagnum peat moss. In clay soil, work into the hole 1 cupful each of gypsum and superphosphate. Handle the rootball with great care. Unwind the roots circling the ball of a containerized tree and plant it with the crown an inch above ground level. If the tree is balled and burlapped, set it into the hole, cut the rope, slash the burlap, and pull the top part away from the rootball. Fill the hole, watering in to settle the soil. Make a saucer of earth to hold water. Apply a 3-in. mulch starting 3 in. from the stem.

HOW TO PROVIDE CARE

A tree may grow straighter if it's staked its first year after planting. Do not leave a stake on after the tree is established and growing strongly. After planting, pour a bucketful of water into the tree saucer every week unless there's a soaking rain. If you wish to plant the area around the tree with a living mulch, use only drought-tolerant ground covers, like myrtle, ajuga, or a slow-growing, small-leaved variegated ivy. Hostas, liriope, mondo grass, and small, spring-flowering bulbs like wood hyacinths are also acceptable ground cover.

ADDITIONAL ADVICE FOR CARE

In late winter before growth begins, broadcast half the recom-mended dose of an organic 5-10-5 fertilizer for acid-loving plants from the drip line out to a point at a distance equal to 1½ times the tree's height. Water it in. Replenish the mulch. Once the plant is well established, switch to a 7-6-19 fertilizer. Prune in late fall or early winter. The European hornbeam can stand heavy pruning.

Sophora japonica

Japanese Pagoda Tree

*A*n airy, exceptionally beautiful tree for parks, the Japanese pagoda tree bears showy panicles of creamy white, somewhat fragrant pea-like flowers in summer. The flowers are followed by drooping clusters of pale-green, winged pods that are persistent and just as beautiful as the flowers. Gardeners who have planted the species often are disappointed to discover that the flowers don't begin to appear until the tree is 10 to 14 years old—but the display is worth waiting for. The bark is pale gray. The tree grows rapidly to 40 to 50 ft. and with maturity is almost as wide. It thrives under heat and tolerates drought and difficult city conditions. Princeton Nurseries has introduced a cultivar, 'Regent', that has a large oval crown of glossy, dark-green leaves; it comes into bloom at 6 to 8 years of age. Another Princeton Nurseries introduction, 'Princeton Upright', has a narrow growth habit suitable for streets and small parks. There is a weeping form, 'Pendula', which seldom flowers, but is attractive nonetheless.

WHEN TO PLANT

Plant a young container-grown or balled and burlapped tree in spring while it still is dormant. It is somewhat tender to cold when young, but when as it matures it will withstand more cold than it's likely to encounter in Virginia.

WHERE TO PLANT

The Japanese pagoda tree flowers most fully when growing in full sun.

HOW TO PLANT

Dig a modest planting hole about 6 in. deeper than the rootball and wider toward the top. Work a spading fork into the sides of the hole to loosen compacted soil. In clay soil, work into the hole 1 cupful each of gypsum and superphosphate, and top it with 2 in. of soil. Unwind the roots circling the ball of a containerized tree and plant it with the crown an inch above ground level. If the tree is balled and burlapped, set it into the hole, cut the rope, slash the burlap, and pull the top part away from the rootball. Fill the hole, watering in to settle the soil. Make a saucer of earth to hold water. Apply a 3-in. mulch starting 3 in. from the stem.

HOW TO PROVIDE CARE

Stake the tree the first year after planting and prune it in the late fall to encourage a central leader. Remove the stake after 1 or 2 years. After planting, pour a bucketful of water into the tree saucer every week unless there's a soaking rain. If you wish to plant the area around the tree with a living mulch, use only drought-tolerant ground covers, like myrtle, ajuga, or a slow-growing, small-leaved variegated ivy. Hostas, liriope, mondo grass, and small, spring-flowering bulbs like wood hyacinths are also acceptable ground cover.

ADDITIONAL ADVICE FOR CARE

In late winter before growth begins, broadcast an organic 5-10-5 fertilizer to just beyond the drip line at half the recommended rate, and water it in. Replenish the mulch. Repeat in November. Once the plant is well established, switch to a 7-6-19 fertilizer.

Japanese Zelkova

*T*his tall, stately shade tree has been used to replace the American elm in streets, parks, and on large properties. It is low-branched and somewhat vase-shaped and grows 2 to 3 ft. a year to a height of 50 to 80 ft. with an equal spread. The leaf somewhat resembles the leaf of the American elm and turns yellow-orange-buff with cold weather. Some years it colors red or maroon-red. The bark resembles that of a cherry tree, smooth and reddish when the tree is young, corky later. Zelkova tolerates some urban pollution. The Princeton Nursery cultivar 'Village Green' grows more rapidly than the species, and the foliage turns a rusty red in fall.

WHEN TO PLANT

Plant a container-grown or balled and burlapped tree in early spring while the tree is still dormant. You can also set a zelkova out in fall, well before Indian summer, but in that case protect it with burlap for winter, because young trees are susceptible to frost damage.

WHERE TO PLANT

The zelkova grows best in full sun but tolerates bright, filtered light when young. It adapts to a broad pH range.

HOW TO PLANT

Dig into a hole the size of a card table a 2-in. layer of leaf mold or peat moss. In clay soil, work into the hole 1 cupful each of gypsum and superphosphate. Unwind the roots circling the ball of a containerized tree and plant it with the crown an inch above ground level. If the tree is balled and burlapped, set it into the hole, cut the rope, slash the burlap, and pull the top part away from the rootball. Fill the hole, watering in to settle the soil. Make a saucer of earth to hold water. Apply a 3-in. mulch starting 3 in. from the stem.

HOW TO PROVIDE CARE

A tree may grow straighter if it's staked its first year after planting. Do not leave a stake on after the tree is established and growing strongly. After planting, pour a bucketful of water into the tree saucer every week unless there's a soaking rain. If you wish to plant the area around the tree with a living mulch, use only drought-tolerant ground covers, like myrtle, ajuga, or a slow-growing, small-leaved variegated ivy. Hostas, liriope, mondo grass, and small spring-flowering bulbs, like wood hyacinths, are also acceptable ground cover.

ADDITIONAL ADVICE FOR CARE

In late winter before growth begins, broadcast an organic 5-10-5 fertilizer to just beyond the drip line at half the recommended rate and water it in. Replenish the mulch. Repeat in November. Once the plant is well established, switch to a 7-6-19 fertilizer. In fall, cut away any branches that will grow into the center of the tree or rub against other branches.

ADDITIONAL CULTIVARS AND SPECIES

The Chinese elm, *Ulmus parvifolia* 'Dynasty', released by the National Arboretum, is a moderately fast-growing tree with the spreading form of the American elm. It has produced attractive, red autumn leaves in Washington, D.C., and is highly resistant to elm problems. It tolerates stressful conditions and is a good street and park tree.

Maple

or the home garden perhaps the most valuable shade tree
is the maple. In spring, it covers itself with colorful buds, and
in fall the leaves turn to yellow, orange and bright red. The species
renowned for fall color in the Northeast is the sugar maple, *A. saccharum*. But here and farther south, the small swamp maple, *A. rubrum*,
is a much better performer and has brighter fall color. It grows at a
moderately fast pace to 40 to 60 ft. in cultivation. It is an excellent
street tree, a good size for suburban gardens, and thrives in moist
places, though it will be smaller. Outstanding cultivars are 'October
Glory' and 'Autumn Flame'. For a smaller garden, a more suitable
plant may be the 25-ft. paperbark maple, *A. griseum*, whose fall color
can be spectacular. It has beautiful bark that peels in strips, revealing
a cinnamon-brown interior. Another very beautiful species used in
landscaping is the shrubby little Japanese maple, *A. palmatum*, whose
deeply cut leaves are red in spring. The species' leaves turn green in
summer, but some varieties remain red, notably 'Bloodgood'.
'Burgundy Lace' is a beautiful, open-branched, smaller plant.

WHEN TO PLANT

Plant a container-grown or balled and burlapped tree in fall before
Indian summer, or in early spring while the tree is still dormant.

WHERE TO PLANT

The larger maples require a place in full sun. The Japanese maple
may burn if it is without some protection from the noon sun in summer. Maples do best in slightly acid conditions and are likely to
thrive in an area that once was forested.

HOW TO PLANT

Dig a modest planting hole about 6 in. deeper than the rootball and
wider toward the top. Work a spading fork into the sides of the hole
to loosen compacted soil. In clay soil, work into the hole 1 cupful
each of gypsum and superphosphate and top it with 2 in. of soil.
Unwind the roots circling the ball of a containerized tree and plant it
with the crown an inch above ground level. If the tree is balled and
burlapped, set it into the hole, cut the rope, slash the burlap, and

pull the top part away from the rootball. Fill the hole, watering in to settle the soil. Make a saucer of earth to hold water. Apply a 3-in. mulch starting 3 in. from the stem.

How to Provide Care

A tree may grow straighter if it's staked its first year after planting. Do not leave a stake on after the tree is established and growing strongly. After planting, pour a bucketful of water into the tree saucer every week unless there's a soaking rain. Even when the tree has matured, in droughts water a maple every week thoroughly. Maples cast a shade too dense to support ground cover other than shade-tolerant lawn grass right under the drip line.

Additional Advice for Care

In late winter before growth begins, broadcast half the recommended dose of an organic 5-10-5 fertilizer for acid-loving plants from the drip line out to a point at a distance equal to 1½ times the tree's height. Water it in. Replenish the mulch. Once the plant is well established, switch to a 7-6-19 fertilizer. Cut away any branches that will grow into the center of the tree or rub against other branches.

Additional Cultivars and Species

A species that makes an excellent street tree is the sycamore, or planetree maple, *A. pseudoplatanus*. It is rather colorless, but it flourishes in salty conditions and endures winds other maples don't tolerate. The mature height is 40 to 60 ft. 'Brilliantissimum' unfolds leaves that are shrimp pink, then yellow, and then green. It requires shade from noon sun.

Oak

*T*he oaks are magnificent spreading shade trees suited to parks and large landscapes. Among species that have considerable success as city street trees are the fast-growing red oak, *Q. rubra*, the pin oak, *Q. palustris*, and the willow oak, *Q. phellos*. In cultivation, the red and the pin oak reach 60 to 70 ft. Both color shades of maroon-red in fall. The fall color of the red oak is a little brighter. One of the best oaks for the city is the willow oak. A smaller tree 40 to 60 ft. in cultivation, its leaves are long, narrow, and in fall turn yellow and then russet red. It has a tap root, but transplants fairly easily, and grows as much as 2 ft. per year. It succeeds even on poorly drained clay soil. The live oak, *Q. virginiana*, a massive, long-lived tree 50 to 80 ft. high, has willow-shaped leaves that drop in spring just before new growth arrives. A superb shade and street tree, it's named for this state, but it's seen only in Zone 8, the very warm part of the state.

WHEN TO PLANT

The best time to plant an oak is in early spring. Set out young, container-grown or balled and burlapped trees that are still dormant. The red oak has a tap root that needs a little more care at planting time than the pin oak, which has a shallow, fibrous root system.

WHERE TO PLANT

Oaks do best growing in full sun and in slightly acid soil. The willow oak succeeds even in poorly drained clay soil.

HOW TO PLANT

Dig a deep planting hole, especially for tap-rooted trees. Make it about 6 in. deeper than the rootball and wider toward the top. Work a spading fork into the sides of the hole to loosen compacted soil. Set the rootball of a container-grown tree in the hole with the crown about an inch above where it was going in the pot. If the tree is balled and burlapped, set it into the hole, cut the rope, slash the burlap, and pull the top part away from the rootball. Fill the hole, watering in to settle the soil. Make a saucer of earth to hold water. Apply a 3-in. mulch starting 3 in. from the stem.

How to Provide Care

Stake the tree, and prune it as it grows to develop a strong, central leader. Do not leave a stake on after the tree is established and growing strongly. After planting, pour a bucketful of water into the tree saucer every week unless there's a soaking rain. If you wish to plant the area around the tree with a living mulch, use only drought-tolerant ground covers, like myrtle, ajuga, or a slow-growing, small-leaved variegated ivy. Hostas, liriope, mondo grass, and small, spring-flowering bulbs like wood hyacinths are also acceptable ground cover.

Additional Advice for Care

In late winter before growth begins, broadcast half the recommended dose of an organic 5-10-5 fertilizer for acid-loving plants from the drip line out to a point at a distance equal to $1^1/2$ times the tree's height. Water it in. Replenish the mulch. Once the plant is well established, switch to a 7-6-19 fertilizer. Cut away any branches that will grow into the center of the tree or rub against other branches.

Additional Cultivars and Species

The swamp white oak, *Q. bicolor*, a timber tree that grows wild in swampy places, is excellent for naturalizing in wet areas. The bur or mossycup oak, *Q. macrocarpa*, has corky branches that give it a picturesque appearance. It is difficult to transplant, but is very adaptable, thrives in alkaline soil, and tolerates urban conditions.

Redbud

hen the wild dogwoods bloom at the edge of Virginia woodlands, the little redbuds growing nearby cover their slim branches with showy, red-purple or magenta buds that open into rosy pink flowers. After it flowers, but sometimes before, this multi-stemmed or low-branching native tree puts forth reddish-purple leaves that change to dark, lustrous green, and sometimes to gold in fall. A mature redbud reaches 20 to 30 ft. in the wild. The fruit is a brown pod. Some lovely cultivated varieties are available. 'Forest Pansy' is a favorite, a strikingly colorful, purple-leaved redbud. 'Flame' is an attractive, double-flowered form. 'Alba' is a lovely, white-flowered cultivar. And there's a lovely new variegated form, 'Silver Cloud', whose leaves are splashed with silvery white throughout summer, then gradually fade to a cool green.

WHEN TO PLANT
Plant a young balled and burlapped or container-grown tree in early spring while it's still dormant, or in fall before Indian summer.

WHERE TO PLANT
Redbuds flower most fully growing in full sun. However, like most small flowering trees, with 4 to 6 hours of sun, or the bright all-day dappled light of an open woodland, they will perform well. Redbud succeeds in alkaline or acid soil, but not in a permanently wet location.

HOW TO PLANT
Dig into a hole the size of a card table 2-in. layers of coarse sand or chicken grit and of leaf mold or sphagnum peat moss. In clay soil, work into the hole 1 cupful each of gypsum and superphosphate. Unwind the roots circling the ball of a containerized tree and plant it with the crown an inch above ground level. If the tree is balled and burlapped, set it into the hole, cut the rope, slash the burlap, and pull the top part away from the rootball. Fill the hole, watering in to settle the soil. Make a saucer of earth to hold water. Apply a 3-in. mulch starting 3 in. from the stem.

How to Provide Care

A tree may grow straighter if it's staked its first year after planting. Do not leave a stake on after the tree is established and growing strongly. After planting, pour a bucketful of water into the tree saucer every week unless there's a soaking rain. If you wish to plant the area around the tree with a living mulch, use only drought-tolerant ground covers, like myrtle, ajuga, or a slow-growing, small-leaved variegated ivy. Hostas, liriope, mondo grass, and small, spring-flowering bulbs like wood hyacinths are also acceptable ground cover.

Additional Advice for Care

In late winter before growth begins, broadcast an organic 5-10-5 fertilizer to just beyond the drip line at half the recommended rate and water it in. Replenish the mulch. Repeat in November. Once the plant is well established, switch to a 7-6-19 fertilizer. Cut away any branches that will grow up to rub against other branches.

DECIDUOUS TREES

Serviceberry

OTHER COMMON NAME: Shadblow

*T*he serviceberries are airy, little trees that grow in open woodlands and bear clusters of delicate ivory-white flowers in very
early spring. The blossoms are followed by persistent, usually black,
berry-like fruits that are rather sweet—and edible—and very attractive
to birds. In fall, the leaves turn to yellow, orange and dark red. The
downy serviceberry, or Juneberry, *A. arborea*, is native to the Piedmont
woods of Georgia and best for the warmer parts of the state. The shadblow, *A. canadensis*, which is found in bogs and swamps from Maine
to South Carolina, is best for the cool hill country near West Virginia
and for wet woodlands. The serviceberries are most effective in
groups at the edge of woodlands or as a backdrop for an island of
shrubs where the fall color will be seen.

WHEN TO PLANT

Plant container-grown or balled and burlapped plants in early
spring while the tree is still dormant, or in fall before Indian
summer.

WHERE TO PLANT

The serviceberry blooms well in full sun and in bright, all-day,
filtered light. It grows in almost any soil, but thrives in moist, well-
drained acid soil, pH 5.0 to 6.5.

HOW TO PLANT

Dig into a hole the size of a card table 2-in. layers of coarse sand or
chicken grit and of leaf mold or sphagnum peat moss. In clay soil,
work into the hole 1 cupful each of gypsum and superphosphate.
Unwind the roots circling the ball of a containerized tree and plant it
with the crown an inch above ground level. If the tree is balled and
burlapped, set it into the hole, cut the rope, slash the burlap, and
pull the top part away from the rootball. Fill the hole, watering in to
settle the soil. Make a saucer of earth to hold water. Apply a 3-in.
mulch starting 3 in. from the stem.

HOW TO PROVIDE CARE

A tree may grow straighter if it's staked its first year after planting. Do not leave a stake on after the tree is established and growing strongly. After planting, pour a bucketful of water into the tree saucer every week unless there's a soaking rain. If you wish to plant the area around the tree with a living mulch, use only acid-tolerant ground covers, like myrtle, or a slow-growing, small-leaved variegated ivy.

ADDITIONAL ADVICE FOR CARE

In late winter before growth begins, broadcast an organic 5-10-5 fertilizer for acid-loving plants to just beyond the drip line at half the recommended rate and water it in. Replenish the mulch. Repeat in November. Once the plant is well established, switch to a 7-6-19 fertilizer.

DECIDUOUS TREES

115

Sourwood

OTHER COMMON NAME: Sorrel Tree

*T*his lovely, native tree veils itself in drooping racemes of fragrant white flowers in summer, late June or July. Then in fall, the foliage colors yellow, red and purple. Attractive seed pods follow the flowers and persist through fall, and deeply furrowed bark makes an attractive winter feature. Sourwood is a slow-growing tree that takes a dozen years to reach 15 ft. or so. In culture, it eventually will grow to between 25 and 30 ft. It is attractive to bees and is a source of a superb honey. Sourwood grows wild along the banks and streams of coastal Virginia, and it's hardy in the farthest northern and western reaches of the state. It is a beautiful tree that naturalizes fairly easily and is well worth the effort needed to establish it in the home landscape. It does not transplant very well or tolerate urban pollution. Be sure to buy a container-grown plant from a reliable nursery, and handle the transplanting with great care.

WHEN TO PLANT

Plant a young container-grown tree in early spring while it's still dormant.

WHERE TO PLANT

Sourwood does well in full sun, but it tolerates bright filtered light all day or part bright shade. It requires acid soil, pH 5.5 to 6.5.

HOW TO PLANT

Dig into a hole the size of a card table a 2-in. layer of coarse sand or chicken grit and 3 in. of leaf mold or sphagnum peat moss. In clay soil, work into the hole 1 cupful each of gypsum and superphosphate. Unwind the roots circling the ball of a containerized tree and plant it with the crown an inch above ground level. Fill the hole, watering in to settle the soil. Make a saucer of earth to hold water. Apply a 3-in. mulch starting 3 in. from the stem.

HOW TO PROVIDE CARE

A tree may grow straighter if it's staked its first year after planting. Do not leave a stake on after the tree is established and growing strongly. After planting, pour a bucketful of water into the tree saucer every week unless there's a soaking rain. If you wish to plant the area around the tree with a living mulch, use only drought-tolerant ground covers, like myrtle, ajuga, or a slow-growing, small-leaved, variegated ivy. Hostas and small spring-flowering bulbs like wood hyacinths are also acceptable ground cover.

ADDITIONAL ADVICE FOR CARE

In late winter before growth begins, broadcast an organic 5-10-5 fertilizer for acid-loving plants to just beyond the drip line at half the recommended rate and water it in. Replenish the mulch. Repeat in November. Once the plant is well established, switch to a 7-6-19 fertilizer.

Magnolia virginiana

Sweetbay Magnolia

OTHER COMMON NAME: Swamp Magnolia

*T*he magnolias are among the oldest trees on the planet. Virginia's sweetbay magnolia is a small, graceful tree suited for a terrace or a modest landscape. In cooler parts of Virginia, it grows relatively fast to a height of 20 ft. or so, but in cities where temperatures are 10 degrees warmer than the suburbs, and in the warmer areas of the state it reaches 60 ft. or more and is evergreen. It does well in wet, even swampy, soils. These magnolias bloom in late spring and early summer. Creamy white and fragrant, the beautiful blossoms appear sporadically until fall. The flowers are followed by cone-shaped fruits that are dark-red with bright-red decorative seeds, and the leaves have a silvery backing. This species adjusts to considerable shade. Two other beautiful magnolias are planted in Virginia—the small star magnolia, *M. stellata*, and the Chinese or saucer magnolia, *M. × soulangiana*, whose flowers are usually purplish on the outside and cream to white inside. Both bloom before the leaves appear, and unless growing in a cool, north-facing location, they tend to open too soon, just in time to be blasted by the last winter storm.

WHEN TO PLANT

Transplant young container-grown or balled and burlapped magnolias with care before new growth begins in early spring.

WHERE TO PLANT

Magnolias bloom best growing in full sun. But like many other trees, with 4 to 6 hours of sun, or all-day filtered light, they will perform well. Magnolias do best in acid soil, pH 5.0 to 6.5.

HOW TO PLANT

Dig into a hole the size of a card table a 2-in. layer of coarse sand or chicken grit and 3 in. of leaf mold or sphagnum peat moss. In clay soil, work into the hole 1 cupful each of gypsum and superphosphate. Unwind the roots circling the ball of a containerized tree and plant it with the crown an inch or two above ground level. If the tree is balled and burlapped, set it into the hole, cut the rope, slash the burlap, and pull the top part away from the rootball. Fill the hole, watering in to settle the soil. Make a saucer of earth to hold water. Apply a 3-in. mulch of leaf mold starting 3 in. from the stem.

How to Provide Care

After planting, pour a bucketful of water into the tree saucer every week unless there's a soaking rain. A tree may grow straighter if it's staked its first year after planting. Do not leave a stake on after the tree is established and growing strongly.

Additional Advice for Care

In late winter before growth begins, broadcast an organic 5-10-5 fertilizer for acid-loving plants to just beyond the drip line at half the recommended rate, and water it in. Replenish the mulch. Repeat in November. Once the plant is well established, switch to a 7-6-19 fertilizer.

Additional Cultivars and Species

The National Arboretum has introduced two cultivars that bloom early, but late enough to escape most late frosts. *M.* 'Galaxy' reaches about 40 ft. and bears handsome, saucer-type flowers, ruby-red shading to magenta-rose toward the tip, and opening to a paler red-purple. *M.* 'Spectrum' is similar, but blooms later, and the flowers are large, dark-purple outside, and white within.

Tulip Poplar

he tulip poplar is a tall, handsome, native shade tree suited to large parks and landscapes. In cultivation the height ranges between 70 and 90 ft. with a spread of 35 to 50 ft. In the wild, it grows rapidly, as much as 15 to 20 ft. in a 6- to 8-year period and can reach 150 to 190 ft.—probably the tallest hardwood in America. It grows wild from Massachusetts to Florida, and westward to Wisconsin and Mississippi. It is named for the greenish-yellow, tulip-like flowers that appear in late spring or early summer. Unfortunately, they're borne high in the branches—and aren't readily visible from below. The leaves are blue-green and look like a maple leaf with its tip squared off. In fall, the leaves turn a rich, handsome golden-yellow that makes a very nice show. The tulip tree can tolerate city conditions and is handsome in a park, but too big for street planting.

WHEN TO PLANT

Plant young, container-grown or balled and burlapped trees in early spring while the tree is still dormant.

WHERE TO PLANT

The tulip tree requires full sun. It does best in slightly acid soil, pH 5.5 to 6.5.

HOW TO PLANT

Dig into a hole the size of a card table a 2-in. layer of coarse sand or chicken grit and 3 in. of leaf mold or sphagnum peat moss. In clay soil, work into the hole 1 cupful each of gypsum and superphosphate. Unwind the roots circling the ball of a containerized tree and plant it with the crown an inch above ground level. If the tree is balled and burlapped, set it into the hole, cut the rope, slash the burlap, and pull the top part away from the rootball. Fill the hole, watering in to settle the soil. Make a saucer of earth to hold water. Apply a 3-in. mulch starting 3 in. from the stem.

How to Provide Care

A tree may grow straighter if it's staked its first year after planting. Do not leave a stake on after the tree is established and growing strongly. After planting, pour a bucketful of water into the tree saucer every week unless there's a soaking rain. If you wish to plant the area around the tree with a living mulch, use only drought-tolerant ground covers, like myrtle, or a slow-growing, small-leaved variegated ivy.

Additional Advice for Care

In late winter before growth begins, broadcast an organic 5-10-5 fertilizer for acid-loving plants to just beyond the drip line at half the recommended rate and water it in. Replenish the mulch. Repeat in November. Once the plant is well established, switch to a 7-6-19 fertilizer. In winter, remove any branches that will grow into the center of the tree or rub against other branches.

CHAPTER THREE

Evergreen Trees

A NUMBER OF ORNAMENTAL CONIFERS AND BROAD-LEAVED EVERGREEN TREES THRIVE IN VIRGINIA. If you have space for only one evergreen, consider planting a holly. The leaves of this broadleaved evergreen are a shiny, rich green year-round, and the berries that redden in the fall are as much appreciated by people as they are by birds. The pyramidal American holly grows wild in this state, and the many ornamental hybrids that have been developed with this species as a parent are almost foolproof here. It is one of few evergreen trees that grows as well in part shade as in sunlight, and it tolerates repeated, severe prunings. By clearing away the lower branches, the taller varieties can be developed as shade trees.

A needled conifer that has some of the holly's virtues is the Carolina hemlock, a pyramidal evergreen with short needles that does better in our climate, especially in urban situations, than the better-known Canadian hemlock. Hemlock grows into a handsome shade tree, and a hemlock hedge can be pruned for decades before the central stems become too thick to be attractive. A hemlock and a holly make a great backdrop for a white-barked river birch, and for azaleas and ornamental grasses.

Other lovely conifers that do well here are varieties of blue spruce, silver fir, lacebark pine, and the beautiful golden hinoki cypress. The tall, longleaf pine that is native to our sandy coastal plain would be preserved if it grew on a property I owned, but it's too tall to be considered a garden ornamental.

For hurry-up screening, nothing beats the leyland cypress. It's a shaggy but graceful evergreen with feathery bluish-green, scale-like foliage, and red-brown bark that is handsome as it gets older. In favorable conditions, it grows as much as 3 ft. a year and can be pruned; so it makes a good hedge plant, and does well by the seashore.

Chapter Three

Growing and Pruning Evergreens

The term evergreen is misleading. Every plant must renew its foliage . . . that's part of its life cycle. The plants we call evergreens, pines for example, lose their leaves at more or less regular intervals, but the intervals between are long. Some evergreens drop their leaves at four-year intervals, such as certain hollies, and some species of pine lose foliage every 15 to 18 months. So when an evergreen shows yellowing needles, chances are that it is a normal part of a cycle and not a problem.

This delayed leaf drop is one of the advantages you gain by planting evergreens: no leaves to gather and grind in the fall. Another advantage is that evergreens are moderate drinkers. And given humusy but very well-drained soil, they will thrive. Pruning isn't necessary unless you want to shape the tree or make it denser.

You can slow or dwarf the development of an evergreen by pruning it in summer after its main spurt of growth. By reducing its leaf surfaces, you are limiting the sugar synthesized and sent to the roots, and that limits next year's growth. Never trim more than a third from an evergreen—it is very detrimental to its health. You should not remove more of the top growth (the leader) than the growth of the last year or two. You can cut the main stem back to the first side shoots, and to encourage dense branching to the ground, begin pruning when the plants are 3 to 5 years old to establish the desired shape early in the plant's development.

Light pruning of the branch ends of hemlocks, junipers, and yews is acceptable throughout the growing season, but not when they are dormant, which is in winter. Yews and junipers can take heavy pruning and fill out again very quickly. Firs, pines, spruces, and other evergreens with growth initiated by candles should be pruned in spring when the candles appear at the branch tips. Cutting back the new candles by one-half to two-thirds will make the tips branch, making the tree grow more dense.

Severe pruning in fall isn't a good idea, because the wounds heal more slowly in seasons of reduced activity. But you can save some pruning of your evergreens, including the hollies, until the holiday season, when they make for wonderful, festive decoration.

American Holly

American holly, which is native to the eastern United States, grows into a handsome pyramidal tree 40 to 50 ft. tall and ripens single red berries in October that persist through winter—unless the birds get them. It is practically indestructible here. Female plants bear lots of berries if there's a male pollinator in the neighborhood—and there usually is. The hollies tolerate pollution, drought and repeated pruning. Another very popular holly is slender 25-ft. Foster's holly #2, *Ilex × attenuata* 'Fosteri'. The leaves aren't very sharply toothed, and the bright-red berries are small, but charming. American and Foster's holly make a handsome pair. For a small city garden, consider *I.* × 'Nellie R. Stevens'. It is a small, pyramidal tree 15 to 25 ft. high, that has toothed leaves and bears masses of berries, especially when pollinated by 'Edward J. Stevens', a large male clone. For hedges, *I. cornuta* 'Burfordii', Burford's Chinese holly, is a good choice. It is a 10-ft. cultivar that produces lots of bright-red berries without a pollinator. It is not reliably hardy in Zone 6. For use as a low shrub and for edging, the narrow-leaved, toothless Japanese plant, *I. crenata*, is ideal. It looks like boxwood and regrows well, even after extremely severe pruning.

WHEN TO PLANT

Plant a container-grown or balled and burlapped holly in early spring, so the new roots can work their way into the surrounding soil before hot weather sets in.

WHERE TO PLANT

Holly does well in either full or part sun, but needs protection from strong winds. It requires acid soil, pH 5.0 to 6.0. Avoid sites that are dry.

HOW TO PLANT

Dig a hole 6 in. deeper than the rootball and wider toward the top. With a spading fork, loosen the sides of the hole. In clay soil, work 1 cupful each of gypsum and superphosphate into the hole and top it with 2 in. of soil. Unwind the roots circling the ball of a containerized tree and plant it with the crown 1 in. above ground level. If the tree is balled and burlapped, set it into the hole, cut the rope, slash the burlap, and pull the top part away from the rootball. Fill the hole, watering to settle the soil. Make a saucer of earth to hold water. Apply a loose 3-in. mulch starting 3 in. from the stem.

HOW TO PROVIDE CARE

After planting, pour a bucketful of water into the tree saucer every week unless there's a soaking rain. The first 2 or 3 winters, protect a young plant with a burlap screen.

ADDITIONAL ADVICE FOR CARE

In late winter of the second year, broadcast half the recommended dose of an organic 10-6-4 or 5-10-5 fertilizer for acid-loving plants from the drip line out to a point at a distance equal to $1^1/2$ times the tree's height. Water it in. Replenish the mulch. Save pruning for winter, and use the cuttings for holiday decorations. Make the cuts inside the area where green leaves are growing.

ADDITIONAL CULTIVARS AND SPECIES

There are some beautiful silver- or yellow-edged—variegated— English hollies, for example, *I. aquifolium* 'Argenteo-marginata' and 'Aureo-marginata'. Shrub-height, berry-bearing hollies like *I.* 'Sparkleberry' lose their leaves in winter and cover themselves with brilliant red berries, and they are striking in the snow.

Blue Atlas Cedar

A mature cedar is perhaps the most beautiful of the large evergreens, especially when featured as a specimen in a large landscape and surrounded by a green lawn. An outstanding cultivar is the blue Atlas cedar, a pyramidal tree 40 to 60 ft. tall with steel blue needles. For a smaller landscape, you might prefer the weeping form which has branches 15 to 20 in. wide that drip icy blue foliage. This cedar will be fine in warm Zones 7 and 8, but it's borderline hardy near West Virginia, Zone 6. A better choice for cool areas is the magnificent cedar-of-Lebanon, *C. libani*, which is like the Atlas cedar in form but is dark green. The most graceful of the cedars is the deodar cedar, *C. deodara*, which is native to the Himalayas and has needles that are light blue or grayish green—silvery at times. Zone 7 is the northern end of its hardiness range. I don't recommend the white cedar or Eastern arborvitae, *Thuja occidentalis*, which is so much a presence in gardens farther north. It just does not keep its color reliably in winter this far south.

WHEN TO PLANT
The cedars are difficult to transplant, so set out a young container-grown cedar in early spring, and handle the rootball with great care.

WHERE TO PLANT
The cedars require lots of space all around as they develop, but they don't do well exposed to icy blasts of wind—so avoid the crest of a hill with a northern exposure. The Atlas cedar tolerates partial shade, but the other species named need full sun. Cedars do best in soil pH 5.0 to 6.5, but the Atlas cedar withstands some alkalinity in the soil.

HOW TO PLANT
Dig into a hole the size of a card table 2-in. layers of coarse sand or chicken grit and leaf mold or sphagnum peat moss. In clay soil, work 1 cupful each of gypsum and superphosphate into the hole. Handle the rootball with care. Set the plant with the crown 1 in.

above ground level. Fill the hole, watering to settle the soil. Make a saucer of earth to hold water. Apply a loose 3-in. mulch of pine needles starting 3 in. from the stem.

How to Provide Care

After planting, pour a bucketful of water into the tree saucer every week unless there's a soaking rain. Keep the tree staked during its first year after planting and provide a burlap screen the first winter. Do not leave a stake on after the tree is established and growing strongly.

Additional Advice for Care

In late winter before growth begins, broadcast half the recommended dose of an organic 5-10-5 fertilizer for acid-loving plants from the drip line out to a point at a distance equal to $1^1/2$ times the tree's height. Water it in. Replenish the mulch. Prune away dead wood any time of year. Make the cuts inside the area where green needles are growing.

Carolina Hemlock

The hemlocks are pyramidal evergreens with graceful, feathery, slightly drooping branches. The needles are aromatic, quite short, and have 2 white bands beneath. The cones are small and coppery brown. A species that thrives in this area is the Carolina hemlock, which reaches 45 to 65 ft. It is a great evergreen for screening because it can be sheared repeatedly and kept to hedge height. It grows well almost everywhere in Virginia except the warmer Zone 8 areas near the border of North Carolina. It is a good shore tree, succeeds on stony hill sites, but does not stand much pollution, or hot, dry conditions.

WHEN TO PLANT
Plant a young balled and burlapped, or container-grown, hemlock in fall before Indian summer, or in early spring, while the tree is still dormant.

WHERE TO PLANT
The Carolina hemlock does well in full sun or in partial shade. It needs some shelter from icy winds and cold blasts and prefers cool, acid soil, pH 5.0 to 6.5.

HOW TO PLANT
Dig into a hole the size of a card table 2-in. layers of coarse sand or chicken grit and leaf mold or sphagnum peat moss. In clay soil, work 1 cupful each of gypsum and superphosphate into the hole. Unwind the roots circling the ball of a containerized tree and plant it with the crown 1 in. above ground level. If the tree is balled and burlapped, set it into the hole, cut the rope, slash the burlap, and pull the top part away from the rootball. Fill the hole, watering in to settle the soil. Make a saucer of earth to hold water. Apply a loose 3-in. mulch of pine needles starting 3 in. from the stem.

HOW TO PROVIDE CARE

After planting, pour a bucketful of water into the tree saucer every week unless there's a soaking rain. If you wish to plant the area around the tree with a living mulch, use only drought-tolerant ground covers, like myrtle, ajuga, or ivy. Hostas and small spring-flowering bulbs like wood hyacinths are also acceptable ground cover. A burlap screen for winter protection is a good idea for the first year or two.

ADDITIONAL ADVICE FOR CARE

In late winter before growth begins, broadcast half the recommended dose of an organic 5-10-5 fertilizer for acid-loving plants from the drip line out to a point at a distance equal to $1^{1}/_{2}$ times the tree's height. Water it in. Replenish the mulch. Prune away dead wood any time of year. Do not cut beyond the area where green needles are growing.

ADDITIONAL CULTIVARS AND SPECIES

The cultivar 'Pendula', a weeping form of the Canadian hemlock, *T. canadensis*, is an exceptionally handsome, dark green, shrub-like evergreen that does well in shaded situations. The dwarf form of the Carolina hemlock is 'Compacta'.

Golden Hinoki Cypress 'Crippsii'

The false cypresses are tall, pyramidal evergreens with flat foliage that is white on the undersides and scalelike, distinctly different from the needled evergreens. The Hinoki species are compact pyramidal trees that grow slowly to a height of 60 to 75 ft. and have dark, glossy green leaves. The bark is interesting and highly textured. A reddish brown, it sheds in long, narrow strips. 'Crippsii' is broadly pyramidal with downturned branch tips that are a rich, golden yellow. The mature height is about 30 ft. These are gorgeous trees for a larger landscape.

WHEN TO PLANT

Plant a young container-grown tree in fall before Indian summer, or in early spring, while the tree is still dormant.

WHERE TO PLANT

The Hinoki cypress requires full sun and does best with some protection from wind.

HOW TO PLANT

Dig into a hole the size of a card table 2-in. layers of coarse sand or chicken grit and leaf mold or sphagnum peat moss. In clay soil, work 1 cupful each of gypsum and superphosphate into the hole. Handle the rootball with some care and set the tree with the crown 1 in. above ground level. Fill the hole, watering in to settle the soil. Make a saucer of earth to hold water. Apply a loose 3-in. mulch of pine needles starting 3 in. from the stem.

How to Provide Care

After planting, pour a bucketful of water into the tree saucer every week unless there's a soaking rain. If you wish to plant the area around the tree with a living mulch, use only drought-tolerant ground covers, like myrtle, ajuga, or a slow-growing, small-leaved variegated ivy. Hostas and small, spring-flowering bulbs like wood hyacinths are also acceptable ground cover. For the first few winters, protect the plant from blasts of icy air with a burlap screen.

Additional Advice for Care

In late winter before growth begins, broadcast half the recommended dose of an organic 5-10-5 fertilizer for acid-loving plants from the drip line out to a point at a distance equal to $1^1/_2$ times the tree's height. Water it in. Replenish the mulch.

Additional Cultivars and Species

'Filicoides' is a slow-growing bush or small tree with frond-like branches and foliage that is green. It is a good container plant.

Lace-bark Pine

*T*he pines have large cones and thin, rather soft needles 2 to 5 in. long, growing in bundles of two to five. It is one of the most important of the evergreen groups and includes some dwarf, compact forms that are very useful in landscaping, as well as tall, pyramidal trees. The lace-bark pine is a beautiful, multiple-stemmed species that grows 30 to 50 ft. tall. A major and unique asset is bark that exfoliates and becomes mottled. When the tree is young, the stems are a mixture of green with white and brown. As the trunks mature, they show a great deal of chalky white. It is beautiful set off by the green of a lawn. For a garden by the shore, a better choice is the Japanese black pine, *P. thunbergiana*, which does well in sandy soil and has great salt tolerance. It is a small tree, 30 ft. or so, with dark-green needles. For the city, the Austrian pine, *P. nigra*, is an excellent plant as it can withstand urban conditions and adapts to many soil types. It is a big tree, 50 to 60 ft. tall in cultivation.

WHEN TO PLANT

Plant a young pine, container-grown or balled and burlapped, in early spring.

WHERE TO PLANT

Pines require full sun. The pines do well in a variety of soils, especially sandy soils.

HOW TO PLANT

Dig into a hole the size of a card table 2-in. layers of coarse sand or chicken grit and of leaf mold or sphagnum peat moss. In clay soil, work 1 cupful each of gypsum and superphosphate into the hole. Plant the tree with the crown 1 in. above ground level. If it's balled and burlapped, set it into the hole, cut the rope, slash the burlap, and pull the top part away from the rootball. Fill the hole, watering to settle the soil. Make a saucer of earth to hold water. Apply a loose 3-in. mulch of pine needles starting 3 in. from the stem.

How to Provide Care

After planting, pour a bucketful of water into the tree saucer every week unless there's a soaking rain.

Additional Advice for Care

In late winter before growth begins, broadcast half the recommended dose of an organic 5-10-5 fertilizer for acid-loving plants from the drip line out to a point at a distance equal to $1^{1}/_{2}$ times the tree's height. Water it in. Replenish the mulch. To encourage density, or to change the shape of the plant, cut back new candles by half.

Additional Cultivars and Species

Dwarfs of *P. mugo*, the mugo pine, are attractive, dark green little bundles of needles used in shrub borders and as edging in urban gardens. The mugo pines do well by the shore.

Leyland Cypress

$\mathcal{T}$he leyland cypress is a graceful, asymmetrical evergreen with bluish-green, scalelike, feathery foliage and red-brown bark. In cultivation, it grows amazingly quickly—3 ft. a year—to 60 or 70 ft., and is often used for screening. It sometimes is paired with a desirable, slow-growing evergreen, then cut down to give the star space when it attains a desired height. The leyland cypress withstands heavy pruning, which makes it an excellent hedge plant. 'Blue Pyramid', which grows to 20 to 25 ft., makes an attractive hedge. Some colorful cultivars of the leyland cypress have been developed. The new growth of 'Castlewellan Gold', a narrow upright form about 20 ft. tall, is tipped yellow-gold and turns to bronze in winter. 'Naylor's Blue' is a narrow cultivar 30 to 40 ft. at maturity whose bright, gray-blue foliage is most intensely colored in winter. The leyland cypress does well by the seashore.

WHEN TO PLANT

Plant a container-grown or balled and burlapped tree in fall before Indian summer, or in early spring.

WHERE TO PLANT

The leyland cypress grows best in full sun but does very well with 4 to 6 hours of sun, or all-day filtered light. It adapts to a variety of soils.

HOW TO PLANT

Dig a hole 6 in. deeper than the rootball and wider toward the top. With a spading fork, loosen the sides of the hole. In clay soil, work 1 cupful each of gypsum and superphosphate into the hole and top it with 2 in. of soil. Unwind the roots circling the ball of a container-ized tree and plant it with the crown 1 in. above ground level. If the tree is balled and burlapped, set it into the hole, cut the rope, slash the burlap, and pull the top part away from the rootball. Fill the hole, watering to settle the soil. Make a saucer of earth to hold water. Apply a loose 3-in. mulch of pine needles starting 3 in. from the stem.

How to Provide Care

After planting, pour a bucketful of water into the tree saucer every week unless there's a soaking rain. If you wish to plant the area around the tree with a living mulch, use only drought-tolerant ground covers, like myrtle, ajuga, or a slow-growing, small-leaved variegated ivy. Hostas, and small, spring-flowering bulbs like wood hyacinths are also acceptable ground cover.

Additional Advice for Care

In late winter before growth begins, broadcast half the recommended dose of an organic 5-10-5 fertilizer from the drip line out to a point at a distance equal to $1^1/2$ times the tree's height. Water it in. Replenish the mulch. Prune to maintain size or form before growth begins in early spring.

Oriental Spruce

*T*he spruces are big, symmetrical, conical evergreens that produce large cones and have thin, rigid needles 1/2 to 1 1/4 in. long with 4 sides and sharp points. You can feel the edges if you roll the needle between your fingers. They are aromatic—think of a Christmas tree. This species, the Oriental spruce, grows slowly to about 60 ft., and is one of the best and most adaptable for a small property. The symmetry of the form makes it an excellent choice for a formal landscape. There are some attractive cultivars. 'Gracilis' is a very slow-growing form with bright-green needles, just 15 to 20 ft. tall at maturity. The Oriental spruce does not do well in the warmer reaches of Virginia, Zone 8, close to the North Carolina border. The Norway spruce, *Picea abies*, can stand more heat, but it's not as attractive.

WHEN TO PLANT

Plant balled and burlapped or container-grown spruce in fall before Indian summer or in early spring. Because the spruces have spreading root systems, quite large specimens can be transplanted successfully.

WHERE TO PLANT

The Oriental spruce performs best in full sun, but it does well with 4 to 6 hours of sun, or all-day filtered light. Spruce prefers soil in the somewhat acid range, pH 5.0-6.0.

HOW TO PLANT

Dig a hole 6 in. deeper than the rootball and wider toward the top. With a spading fork, loosen the sides of the hole. In clay soil, work 1 cupful each of gypsum and superphosphate into the hole and top it with 2 in. of soil. Unwind the roots circling the ball of a containerized tree and plant it with the crown 1 in. above ground level. If the tree is balled and burlapped, set it into the hole, cut the rope, slash the burlap, and pull the top part away from the rootball. Fill the hole, watering to settle the soil. Make a saucer of earth to hold water. Apply a loose 3-in. mulch of pine needles starting 3 in.

from the stem.

How to Provide Care

After planting, pour a bucketful of water into the tree saucer every week unless there's a soaking rain.

Additional Advice for Care

In late winter before growth begins, broadcast half the recommended dose of an organic 5-10-5 fertilizer for acid-loving plants from the drip line out to a point at a distance equal to $1^{1/2}$ times the tree's height. Water it in. Replenish the mulch. To encourage density, or to change the shape of the plant, cut back new candles by half.

Juniperus virginiana

Red Cedar

*T*he junipers are an enormously varied tribe of conifers ranging from 60-ft. trees and 50-ft. shrubs to ground-hugging plants from a few inches to 2 ft. high, like the creeping Juniper, *J. horizontalis* 'Wiltonii' described in *Ground Covers*. Some junipers bear sharp awl-shaped needles, and others have scalelike leaves. The male cones are yellow, like catkins, and the female fruit are berry-like cones. This species, the red cedar, is a dense 40- to 50-ft. tree, sometimes pyramidal and sometimes more columnar, with scalelike leaves. The wood is reddish and aromatic, and the bark is a handsome, cinnamon color and exfoliates. A native of eastern and northern North America, the red cedar thrives in climates all the way from Canada to central Florida. The many handsome, cultivated varieties are best featured as lawn specimens, massed for windbreaks, and used as tall hedges. There are many cultivars. 'Burkii', one of several blue-leaved red cedars, grows to be about 30 ft. tall and turns towards purple in winter.

When to Plant
Set out container-grown or balled and burlapped plants in spring or fall. The junipers have a spreading root system that transplants easily.

Where to Plant
Plant in full sun. The tree accepts some shade when young, but will fail unless it grows into full sun. The red cedar does well in acid and in alkaline soils, but other species prefer soil in the pH 5.0 to 6.5 range.

How to Plant
Dig into a hole the size of a card table 2-in. layers of coarse sand or chicken grit and of leaf mold or sphagnum peat moss. In clay soil, work 1 cupful each of gypsum and superphosphate into the hole. Unwind the roots circling the ball of a containerized tree and plant it with the crown 1 in. above ground level. If the tree is balled and burlapped, set it into the hole, cut the rope, slash the burlap, and pull the top part away from the rootball. Fill the hole, watering to

settle the soil. Make a saucer of earth to hold water. Apply a loose 3-in. mulch of pine needles starting 3 in. from the stem.

HOW TO PROVIDE CARE

After planting, pour a bucketful of water into the tree saucer every week unless there's a soaking rain. If you wish to plant the area around the tree with a living mulch, use only drought-tolerant ground covers, like myrtle, ajuga, or a slow-growing, small-leaved variegated ivy. Hostas and small spring-flowering bulbs like wood hyacinths are also acceptable ground cover.

ADDITIONAL ADVICE FOR CARE

In late winter before growth begins, broadcast half the recommended dose of an organic 5-10-5 fertilizer for acid-loving plants from the drip line out to a point at a distance equal to $1^1/2$ times the tree's height. Water it in. Replenish the mulch. Prune away dead wood any time of year, but remember that cut beyond the area where green needles are growing won't sprout new needles.

ADDITIONAL CULTIVARS AND SPECIES

Many graceful, shrub-height junipers are used in landscaping. Some are gold-leaved; some are blue. There is one for every purpose and for every taste. The Pfitzer junipers are wide-spreading, graceful, slightly drooping forms.

Silver Fir

*T*he firs are pyramidal conifers, rather like the spruces we bring indoors for Christmas. Fir needles are long, soft, two-sided, and flatter than those of the spruces. They usually have two white bands beneath. Most firs are big forest trees that live at high altitudes and do poorly in hot, dry cities. The silver, or white, fir has some tolerance for long, hot summers like those in Washington, D.C., and it resists city conditions, heat, cold and drought. In silhouette, the tree looks like a blue spruce, but it's more refined. It reaches 30 to 50 ft. in cultivation and has silvery, blue-green needles 2 to 3 in. long with two pale, bluish bands underneath. The cones are 3 to 5 in. long and greenish when new, shading to purple. A beautiful cultivar is 'Violacea' which has silvery blue needles. For the southern highlands of Virginia, a better choice is the Fraser, or southern balsam fir, *A. fraseri*. It is native to the mountains of West Virginia, North Carolina, and Tennessee.

WHEN TO PLANT

Plant a container-grown or balled and burlapped tree in early spring.

WHERE TO PLANT

The silver fir prefers full sun, but tolerates all-day bright filtered light. Firs do best in slightly acid soil, pH 5.0 to 6.0. The silver fir can live on almost bare rock, but it does poorly in heavy clay soils.

HOW TO PLANT

Dig into a hole the size of a card table 2-in. layers of coarse sand or chicken grit and of leaf mold or sphagnum peat moss. In clay soil, work 1 cupful each of gypsum and superphosphate into the hole and top it with 2 in. of soil. Unwind the roots circling the ball of a containerized tree and plant it with the crown 1 in. above ground level. If the tree is balled and burlapped, set it into the hole, cut the rope, slash the burlap, and pull the top part away from the rootball. Fill the hole, watering to settle the soil. Make a saucer of earth to hold water. Apply a loose 3-in. mulch of pine needles starting 3 in. from the stem.

HOW TO PROVIDE CARE

After planting, pour a bucketful of water into the tree saucer every week unless there's a soaking rain. If you wish to plant the area around the tree with a living mulch, use only drought-tolerant ground covers, like myrtle, ajuga, or a slow-growing small-leaved variegated ivy. Hostas and small, spring-flowering bulbs like wood hyacinths are also acceptable ground cover.

ADDITIONAL ADVICE FOR CARE

In late winter before growth begins, broadcast half the recommended dose of an organic 5-10-5 fertilizer for acid-loving plants from the drip line out to a point at a distance equal to $1^1/_2$ times the tree's height. Water it in. Replenish the mulch. To encourage density, or to change the shape of the plant, cut back new candles by half.

Flowering Bulbs

*T*HE FLOWERING BULBS DEVELOP FROM ONIONLIKE ROOT SYSTEMS that are sleek, with brown wrappers called tunics. Most bloom a few months after they are planted, and many come back year after year. They are planted in mixed flower beds, positioned to come up between and through clumps of perennials, naturalized in wildflower areas, and used to carpet the ground under deciduous shrubs and trees where they will have time to ripen before overhead foliage cuts them off from the sun.

Most bulbs need 6 to 8 hours of direct sun, though they will bloom the first season even without it. But after blooming, the leaves must get enough direct sun to feed the rootbulb before the foliage dies. Otherwise, the bulbs won't likely flower a second year. Ideally, while the yellowing leaves go through their unsightly ripening cycle, they will be screened by the rising foliage of nearby plants.

I've grouped the bulb flowers in this chapter according to their time of bloom.

PLANTING BULBS

Catalogs offer bulbs at discounted prices if you order early. If you receive your bulb order before planting time, store the bulbs in the crisper (but not near apples), or in a cool garage or cellar.

To encourage your bulbs to perennialize, plant them in very well-drained soil. Make sure they receive ample moisture during active growth, but allow them to run rather dry once they have gone dormant. Fertilizing them in late fall and again in late winter increases the possibility they will bloom a second year.

When you plant bulbs, place the bottom (the flat end) at a depth that equals twice the bulb's height. That places small bulbs 3 to 5 in. deep, and large bulbs 5 to 8 in. deep. In heavy soil the planting may

Chapter Four

be a little shallower, and in light sandy soil, a little deeper. When in doubt, plant deep—large bulbs planted close to the surface tend to start bulblets and then forget to bloom.

If you share your garden with squirrels, voles, or other rodents, you will soon learn that they love bulbs. To keep them from getting the major share, line the bulb planting holes with small, sharp gravel, then plant the bulbs and top them with another inch of gravel before filling the hole. Or, cover an area planted in bulbs with hardware cloth and anchor it with rocks.

For spring bulbs to flower the next year, remove spent flower-heads and let the foliage yellow 8 to 12 weeks, then cut it off at the base. Better yet, let the foliage die to the ground before removing it. Do not bind it over to finish ripening. That cuts off the light and oxygen needed to nourish next year's flowers. Rather, plan the garden so the developing leaves of companion and follow-on plants will rise and screen the ripening foliage.

If you wish to dig and replant your bulbs, let the foliage partially yellow, then lift the rootballs and let them dry. Clean them, and store them at 45 to 55 degrees Fahrenheit, never above 63 degrees Fahrenheit. Or, heel the rootballs into an out-of-the-way spot in the garden, and dig and replant the bulbs in the early fall.

Late Winter/ Early Spring Bulbs

*T*he first touch of color comes to the garden in late winter, provided by small bulbs and tubers planted the fall before. Just a few inches high, they appear in February when the witchhazels begin to bloom at the National Arboretum. The snowdrops (*Galanthus*), early crocus, golden winter aconite (*Eranthus*), squill (*Scilla tubergeniana*), and dwarf beardless *Iris reticulata* pop up first. Miniature daffodils like 'Tete a Tete' bloom soon after—then along come glory-of-the-snow (*Chionodoxa luciliae*), the grape hyacinths (*Muscari*), dainty *Cyclamen coum*, and the short species tulips, *Tulipa saxatilis*, *T. tarda*, *T. turkistanica*. The lovely little striped squill (*Pushkinia scilloides*) adds a touch of blue. The ferny foliage of *Anemone blanda* comes up early and remains to flower and backdrop the later-blooming bulbs. Each of the small early bulbs adds only a scrap of color to the winter landscape, so make them showy by planting them in drifts of 20 to 100. They will perennialize if they are fertilized annually. I plant these little heralds of spring in the flower beds, under shrubs, in rock gardens, edging a woodland path, and near the entrances to the house.

WHEN TO PLANT

Plant these little bulbs in September and October. Bulbs planted late tend to have shorter stems and to bloom later. Store bulbs waiting to be planted in the refrigerator crisper or in a cool garage or cellar. Do not store apples in the same crisper.

WHERE TO PLANT

The first year, bulbs will bloom growing in shade. Planted in a sunny, sheltered location, they will bloom early and perennialize. They do best in sites whose soil is dryish in summer and in winter. To create naturalized drifts, choose a sunny, well-drained site and dig an irregularly-shaped planting bed. Throw the bulbs out by the handful and plant where they fall.

FLOWERING BULBS

How to Plant

Dig beds or planting holes 8 to 12 in. deep and mix in 2 in. each of chicken grit and humus, and an application of 9-9-6 Holland Bulb Booster. In clay soil, add gypsum and superphosphate, 1 tablespoon for each hole, 5 lbs. for each 100 sq. ft. Most bulbs thrive in neutral soil. To foil rodents, line and top the plantings with sharp gravel or cover the soil with hardware cloth. Plant small bulbs 1 or 2 in. apart, 3 to 5 in. deep, larger bulbs 2 to 3 in. apart, 5 to 8 in. deep, pointed tips up. Mulch with 2 in. of pine needles, oak leaves, wood chips, or with shredded bark.

How to Provide Care and Maintenance

Most bulbs require ample moisture during the season of active growth, from the moment the first pip breaks ground. But once they are dormant, they do not require watering—in fact, it can be detrimental. After flowering, but before the foliage disappears, spread 9-9-6 Holland Bulb Booster over the bulb plantings at the prescribed rate.

Additional Advice

Large bulb flowers are deadheaded after they have bloomed, and the foliage is allowed to yellow before it is removed. The small bulbs, however, are allowed simply to fade away after blooming. Most come back, at least for a season or two. In good conditions, some will spread.

Early/Mid-spring Bulbs

Spring's big wave of bulb color comes in April and May. The heavily perfumed hyacinths open with early daffodils and late crocus, followed by early-, mid-, and late-season tulips and Dutch irises. Grassy, dainty white *Leucojum aestivum* blooms toward mid-spring along with the fascinating *Fritillarias*, the spring starflower, *Ipheion uniflorum* 'Wisley Blue', and silver bells, *Ornithogalum nutans*. In May the wild or wood hyacinth (*Hyacinthoides hispanica* syn. *Scilla campanulata*) blooms under our star magnolia and the Chinese dogwood. Lily-of-the-valley (*Convallaria majalis*), one of the world's great perfume flowers, is offered with the bulbs and flowers at this season. Though our Zone 7 is the bottom of its heat hardiness range, it grows in dappled light in Washington, D.C., and thrives in Northern Virginia suburban gardens. The clover-like leaves of wood sorrel, *Oxalis adenophylla*, weave mounds of fresh green or iridescent burgundy foliage through the bulb plantings, and remain to background the annuals that take their places after the bulb foliage has ripened and been discarded. Large spring bulbs are impressive grouped in tens in flower borders and naturalized in drifts of 20 or more. Many perennialize.

When to Plant

Plant these bulbs between October and early December, before the first annual frost date, which is October 19 in Washington, D.C.; October 16 in Culpepper; November 13 in Richmond; October 28 in Williamsburg. Store bulbs waiting to be planted in the refrigerator crisper or a cool garage or cellar. Do not store apples in the same crisper.

Where to Plant

The first year, bulbs will bloom growing in shade. Planted in a sunny, sheltered location, they will bloom early and perennialize. They do best in sites whose soil is dryish summer and winter. To create naturalized drifts, choose a sunny, well-drained site and dig an irregularly-shaped planting bed. Throw the bulbs out by the handful and plant where they fall.

HOW TO PLANT

Dig beds or planting holes 8 to 12 in. deep and mix in 2 in. each of chicken grit and humus, and an application of 9-9-6 Holland Bulb Booster. In clay soil, add gypsum and superphosphate, 1 tablespoon for each hole, 5 lbs. for each 100 sq. ft. Most bulbs thrive in neutral soil; for lily-of-the-valley provide pH under 6.0. To foil rodents, line and top the plantings with sharp gravel or cover the soil with hardware cloth. Set large bulbs 2 to 3 in. apart, 5 to 8 in. deep. Plant tulips 10 to 12 in. deep. Mulch with 2 in. of pine needles, oak leaves, wood chips, or with shredded bark.

HOW TO PROVIDE CARE AND MAINTENANCE

Most bulbs require ample moisture during the season of active growth, from the moment the first pip breaks ground. But once they are dormant, they do not require watering—in fact, it can be detrimental. After flowering, but before the foliage disappears, spread 9-9-6 Holland Bulb Booster over the bulb plantings at the prescribed rate.

ADDITIONAL ADVICE

For the bulbs to flower the next year, blossoms must be cut off as they fade, and the stems, especially the foliage, must ripen 8 to 12 weeks before it is removed. Tulip foliage may be removed when it is yellow halfway down. Daffodils are likely to rebloom and to multiply indefinitely without deadheading.

Summer Bulbs

The bulbs that bloom in summer come into flower after nights warm up—mid- to late June—and many bloom until mid-September. There are cold-hardy types and tropicals. The hardy bulbs are planted in fall or early spring. The most compelling are the hybrid lilies (*Lilium*). Some are 7 ft. tall, headily perfumed, and carry 40 to 50 trumpet-shaped flowers. The Asiatic varieties bloom in June, followed by the trumpets, then the Orientals. Another extraordinary hardy bulb is the giant flowering onion (*Allium giganteum*) which blooms in July. The tropical bulbs are planted in spring, and they come into bloom eight to ten weeks later. Exotics like the exquisite spider lily (*Lycoris,*) the Peruvian daffodil (*Hymenocallis narcissiflora*, syn. *Ismene calathina*), and the fragrant peacock orchid, (*Acidanthera bicolor*), are perfect for containers. Clumps of poppy anemones, the short, handsome canna hybrids, crocosmia, gladiolas, and the summer hyacinth (*Galtonia*) are planted where they can screen the yellowing of the spring bulbs. In shade, plant the color-splashed caladiums. To have fragrance all summer long, plant six tuberoses (*Polianthes tuberosa*) every two weeks. For edging, plant the little rain lily (*Zephyranthes*). Group the big bulbs in sets of five or ten.

WHEN TO PLANT

Plant cold-hardy bulbs in fall or early spring. Plant tropicals in mid-spring, and plan to winter them indoors and to replant them the following spring. Store bulbs waiting for planting in the refrigerator crisper, or in a cool garage or cellar. Do not store apples in the same crisper.

WHERE TO PLANT

The first year, bulbs will bloom growing in some shade. Six hours of direct sunlight are necessary to bring most to flower the second season, and the foliage must have time to ripen before it is removed. Otherwise, treat these as annuals and discard them after flowering. The summer-flowering bulbs thrive in the garden and also in containers. Do not plant lilies in recently limed soils.

HOW TO PLANT

Dig planting holes 8 in. to 1 ft. deep and mix in 2 in. each of chicken grit and humus and a small handful of 9-9-6 Holland Bulb Booster. In clay soil, add a small handful of gypsum and of superphosphate for each bulb. Most bulbs thrive in soil whose pH is 6.0 to 7.0, but most lilies require acid soil, so avoid planting them where lime has recently been applied. Set small bulbs 1 or 2 in. apart, 3 to 5 in. deep; set larger bulbs 2 to 3 in. apart, 5 to 8 in. deep. Plant with the pointed tips up. Mulch with 2 in. of pine needles, oak leaves, wood chips, or with shredded bark.

HOW TO PROVIDE CARE AND MAINTENANCE

Perennial bulbs: fertilize the perennial bulbs in late fall and again in late winter by scratching into the soil a handful of 9-9-6 Holland Bulb Booster. Bulbs benefit from ample moisture during their season of active growth, that is, from the moment the first pip breaks ground. Cold-tender bulbs: in autumn lift, clean, and store the cold-tender bulbs indoors in a cool, dry, airy place. Exact storage conditions are recommended by suppliers.

ADDITIONAL ADVICE

Bulbs meant to perennialize benefit from deadheading. Lilies need to be moved every 3 or 4 years to a new, lime-free location that has been enriched with compost and fertilizer.

OTHER CULTIVARS AND SPECIES

Crinum moorei bears clusters of beautiful 4-in., long-tubed, funnel-shaped rose-red flowers topping a tall, bare flower stalk that grows from the neck of a big bulb. It is an imposing accent plant in large beds or islands and, above all, a great container plant. It survives winter only in Virginia's warmest regions.

Fall/Winter Bulbs

*B*ulbs that come into bloom in fall and early winter have a special place in the gardener's heart. The silky petals and tender colors look so fragile, but they endure fall rains and wind storms. Fall-blooming crocuses naturalize readily under shrubs and trees, the saffron crocus (*Crocus sativus*) for one, and yellow-throated *C. kotschyanus* (syn. *C. zonatus*), and showy, durable, lavender-blue *C. speciosus*. Lavender *Colchicum autumnale* and yellow *Sternbergia lutea*, whose leaves last until well into spring, open beautiful, big, crocus-like flowers in September. In late summer and autumn, baby cyclamens (*Cyclamen hederifolium*) spread their marbled leaves and open tiny white to rose-pink flowers. Some early blooming daffodils, like 4-in.-high Tenby daffodils (*Narcissus asturiensis*) and 'Grand Soleil d'Or', bloom here in November some years, and in late winter others. To be effective, plant the small bulbs in groups of at least 20, or 50 to 100.

WHEN TO PLANT

Plant the small, fall-flowering bulbs in late summer. The early daffodils will probably bloom in late winter. Store bulbs that are waiting to be planted in the refrigerator crisper or a cool garage or cellar. Do not store apples in the same crisper.

WHERE TO PLANT

Fall-flowering bulbs prefer to bake in rather dry soil during the dormant summer months. Most, and particularly the colchicums, bloom well growing in sun or part sun. Deadheading the larger bulbs and fertilization of all fall-flowering bulbs in late fall help maintain their vigor.

HOW TO PLANT

Dig beds or planting holes 8 to 12 in. deep and mix in 2 in. each of chicken grit and humus, and an application of 9-6-6 Holland Bulb Booster. In clay soil, add gypsum and superphosphate, 1 tablespoon for each hole, 5 lbs. for each 100 sq. ft. Most bulbs thrive in neutral soil, but the hardy amaryllis requires a pH between 6.0 and 6.5. To foil rodents, line and top the plantings with sharp gravel. Plant these bulbs at a depth that is 3 times their height, pointed tips up. Plant sternbergia and hardy cyclamens with 1/2 in. of soil on top. Mulch with 2 in. of pine needles, oak leaves, wood chips, or with shredded bark.

How to Provide Care and Maintenance

Fertilize the bulbs when the foliage appears by scratching into the soil a handful of 9-9-6 Holland Bulb Booster. Most bulbs require ample moisture during the season of active growth, that is, from the moment the first pip breaks ground, but they do best when they run dry during dormancy. On the northern edge of their hardiness zones, protect the bulbs with a light winter mulch.

Additional Advice

Deadheading the fall and winter flowering bulbs helps them to store up energy for next year's blooming.

Other Cultivars and Species

Italian arum, *Arum italicum* 'Pictum', produces big, arrow-shaped, white-marbled leaves that emerge when the garden is running empty in fall, and persist all winter. In early spring, greenish-yellow flowers, rather like a narrow calla lily, rise, followed by a bunch of attractive red berries that persist through summer.

Ground Covers

*L*AWN GRASSES CARPET THE EARTH BEAUTIFULLY, and in the cool upland regions they prove to be the ground cover of choice. But they require mowing seven months a year, and brown out unless watered during our often extensive summer droughts. Many homeowners are cutting back on the size of their lawns; not eliminating the lawn completely, but replacing its outlying areas with ground covers and naturalized plantings needing some care during spring and fall, with very little in between.

You can use any fast-growing plant that naturalizes as ground cover—daylilies in the sun, water-loving ornamental grasses in wet places, hostas in shade, and many vines. "Real" ground covers are low-growing, multiply rapidly, and grow so dense that they keep out weeds and invasive native plants. Like grass, they create a unified field that harmonizes the various elements in the landscape, such as shrub borders, flower beds, and specimen trees. Some of the most attractive ground covers are the plants on the pages that follow, but not every one of these plants is perfect for every site.

The plant that replaces a lawn in my Washington, D.C., garden is pachysandra. It is wonderfully green and elegant in cool, wet, spring weather, and I love it dearly. But summer by summer, patches succumb to some awful wilt. Since I've always been opposed to spraying and carrying on (if a plant doesn't grow, it goes), I fill areas the pachysandra has vacated with ground covers that don't have problems. Ajuga and the vincas are evergreen most winters, and they bring beautiful flowers to the party. Plumbago, though deciduous and needing three years to take off, is part of the group because I love the electric blue flowers. Cool-looking variegated ivies and lamium are carpeting the areas left bare under the flowering fruit trees.

Diversifying ground cover plants is a safeguard against disaster if one of the plants runs into difficulties. And my richly varied "lawn" accommodates drifts of the little winter-flowering bulbs which are followed by fast-growing aromatic herbs—Greek oregano and thyme, for example. I blow-vac the fallen leaves in autumn, and prune the ground covers in spring to renew their vigor. The cats have taught me not to plant catnip or cat mint.

PLANTING GROUND COVERS

To get ground covers off to a good start, it is essential to do a thorough job of soil preparation. If you will be planting in an area covered by turf or wild plants, in early fall, or in early spring after the soil has dried, remove the turf. Cover the soil with 2 or 3 in. of compost or decomposed leaves, and broadcast a slow-release 10-5-5 fertilizer over the area, along with limestone and gypsum. Rototill 8 in. deep three times over a two-week period. If you are installing an invasive ground cover such as ajuga, bury a 6-in. metal barrier to keep it from overrunning neighboring plantings.

The next part of the job is to set out the ground cover plants in even rows. Start by digging a row of evenly-spaced planting pockets 4 to 14 in. apart across the top of the bed, then set the plants in the pockets and firm them into place. If you are planting on a slope, firm the plants into their holes so the backs are a little lower than the fronts. Position row two planting pockets zig-zag style between those of the row above. Row three will repeat row one, and row four will repeat row two. When the planting is complete, fill empty spaces with 3 in. of an organic mulch.

On a steep slope where erosion is likely to be a problem, it's a good idea to plant through a porous landscape fabric. Push the ends of the fabric into the ground and weight them with rocks. To plant, make rows of X-shaped slits in the fabric, and use a trowel to insert the plants through the slits. Landscape fabric stops, or at least slows, the rooting of the ground cover branches, so plant densely.

Maintain the mulch until the ground cover has grown so dense that it shades out weeds. Plan on at least two years for the plants to grow enough to cover well

Arctostaphylos uva-ursi

Bearberry

OTHER COMMON NAME: Kinnikinick

*B*earberry is one of the most beautiful of all low-growing ground covers. It is not used nearly as often as it should be because it is hard to transplant and slow to spread. A rugged, low-growing trailing evergreen 6 to 12 in. tall, 2 to 4 in. wide—in time it can spread to 15 ft. The leaves are shiny and dark green in summer, bronze-red in cold weather. In spring, they are tipped with clusters of tiny pink or white flowers that are followed by lasting red berries that birds love. Cold isn't a problem, but heat can be. Bearberry is reliably heat-hardy only as far south as Zone 6, the cool upland regions of Virginia. But experienced Zone 7 gardeners recommend it for full sun in Northern Virginia and for light shade farther south. Bearberry is used as a soil stabilizer on sandy banks beside highways and at the shore. It survives without much water in poor sandy, or gravelly, soil, and hot sun. I find it especially attractive as ground cover for hillside terraces, and I love to see it rambling over stony slopes.

WHEN TO PLANT

In very early spring, set out container-grown plants from your garden center or catalog. If local people do not carry bearberry, you will find it in catalogs like *Ray and Peg Prag's Forest Farm Nursery*, in Williams, Oregon. Do not dig bearberry in the wild—it is protected in many states.

WHERE TO PLANT

Bearberry does best where it receives some direct sun and some shade. Though it succeeds in neutral and even in limestone soils, it prefers well-drained, infertile soil with an acid pH 4.5 to 5.5. That makes it an ideal ground cover for land that was forest and wooded areas.

HOW TO PLANT

Since bearberry is difficult to transplant and the plants are fairly costly, put all the effort necessary into soil preparation to avoid being disappointed in the results. Dig generous planting holes. Unless the existing soil is sandy, dig in a layer of 3 in. of sand or chicken grit along with 2 to 3 in. of rotted leaf mold, chopped dried leaves or peat moss. In clay soil, mix in a handful of gypsum and another of superphosphate for each plant. Set the plants 12 to 24 in. apart. Water well. Apply a permanent mulch of pine needles, or rotted leaf mold.

HOW TO PROVIDE CARE AND MAINTENANCE

Water a new planting every week or two the first season. Once the plants are established, local rainfall should be enough to keep bearberry healthy and growing, except during our mid- and late August droughts. Replenish the mulch in late winter until the plants have spread widely enough to shade out weeds.

ADDITIONAL ADVICE

Pruning is rarely needed. Do not fertilize.

OTHER CULTIVARS AND SPECIES

Arctostaphylos uva-ursi 'Big Bear' is large and tinged with red in winter. 'Wood's Red' is a dwarf with unusually large red fruits. 'Massachusetts' is very tolerant of wet conditions. 'Emerald Carpet' has pink flowers and tolerates shade.

Ajuga genevensis, A. reptans

Carpet Bugleweed

*A*juga is the most colorful of the 4- to 8-in. ground covers. The plants form rosettes of leaves 3 to 4 in. long that grow in thick mats. Some forms are green-leaved; others are splashed with cream or pink or have a metallic sheen. In mid- to late spring, ajuga carpets the earth with short, squarish flower spikes that are blue or lavender. There are pink and cream-white varieties, but I think you will find the blues more appealing. In Virginia, ajuga is evergreen. With the coming of cold the leaves take on an attractive bronze-plum tint. When winter is really severe, the leaves flatten and some turn brown. Cold that persists without snow cover, which can happen in Northern Virginia, damages the leaf tips, but the plants soon fill out in spring. I can recommend three species of ajuga. For quick cover, try fast-growing *Ajuga reptans* and its cultivars. If you have patience, try the large erect species, *A. pyramidalis* 'Metallica Crispa', which spreads more slowly and blooms later, but is more beautiful. Green *A. genevensis*, another erect species, is best where crown rot is a problem in warm, muggy weather. It is the slowest species, but it tolerates more direct sun if it is given plenty of moisture.

WHEN TO PLANT

Set out rooted plantlets in early spring or early fall, the best seasons for starting ajuga. Rooted plantlets of *A. reptans* can be cut from the parent plants and replanted any time during the growing season. The other species are best multiplied by dividing the roots in early spring before growth starts.

WHERE TO PLANT

Where summers are muggy, as in Washington, D.C., ajuga does best in tall, bright shade. It handles dense shade, but there it will have smaller leaves, fewer flowers, and the plant will spread slowly toward sunlit areas. In cool upland areas, ajuga can handle full sun. The colored varieties are showiest growing where they receive some direct sun.

HOW TO PLANT

Ajuga can be started from seed sown in flats in late summer for fall planting, or in November for spring planting. Rooted plants are fairly expensive, but you can minimize the cost by choosing the rapid-spreading species *A. reptans* and setting the plants 6 to 12 in. apart. They will soon fill in. Unless your area is sandy, dig into the soil 2 in. of sand or chicken grit, along with an application of a slow-release 10-10-10 fertilizer. Ajuga does best in soil whose pH range is between 6.0 and 7.0. In clay soil, mix in a handful of gypsum and another of superphosphate for each plant. Plant the slower-spreading ajuga species 3 in. apart and be prepared to divide the plants—or prune them back—the following summer. Mulch between the plants to keep weeds under control until the bed fills in.

HOW TO PROVIDE CARE AND MAINTENANCE

Water a new bed every week the first season, unless rain is plentiful. In early spring, scratch a slow-release fertilizer into the soil beside young plants. In the following years, when you fertilize your lawn, water in a granular 10-10-10 fertilizer. Though it is drought resistant, ajuga growing in full sunlight in warm areas of Zone 7 and 8 may need watering during long, hot, dry spells. Keep an eye on the bed in very hot weather, and water it any time the plants show signs of wilting.

ADDITIONAL ADVICE

Remove fallen leaves in autumn to offset the possibility of crown rot. If the problem develops, apply a fungicide recommended by your local garden center.

OTHER CULTIVARS AND SPECIES

Leaves of *Ajuga reptans* 'Burgundy Glow' are cream, pink, rose, and green. 'Atropurpurea' has bronze-purple leaves. Green-leaved 'Purple Torch' has pink flower spikes. 'Alba' has creamy white flowers. 'Pink Beauty' has green leaves and showy pink flower spikes.

Creeping Juniper

*T*his is a creeping form of the plant we know as a tree or a shrub. The foliage is 4 to 6 in. high, and the branches grow horizontally about a foot a year until they spread to 8 to 10 ft. Evergreen and carefree, creeping juniper performs beautifully in sandy soils at the shore, makes a great small lawn, and is a favorite for bordering paths and driveways. I like it planted among rocks and edging masonry walls. Junipers are either male or female plants: the females bear pea-sized gray-blue or green berry-like cones. Some varieties are dark green; others are shaded soft gray-green or blue-green, and there are gold- and silver-tipped forms. In cold weather, many varieties color plum to purple. One of the finest of the flat creeping junipers is 'Blue Rug', *Juniperus horizontalis* 'Wiltoni'. 'Mother Lode' is a 2- to 3-in.-high golden form that is exceptionally handsome. 'Sun Spot' is a smaller plant, 1 to 1½ in. high, whose foliage is spotted yellow throughout the branches. *J. conferta* is excellent on sand dunes and by the shore.

WHEN TO PLANT

Set out container-grown junipers almost any time. The branches of mature junipers will eventually root. To multiply your holdings, in early spring, sever rooted branches and replant them.

WHERE TO PLANT

Creeping junipers need 6 hours of direct sun, even in hot, dry locations. In shade they get thin and ratty. *J. conferta*, the shore juniper, and its cultivars, can handle salt, so they can be planted in areas reached by salt spray. *J. horizontalis* does best in soil with a pH of 5.0 to 6.0, but can handle slightly alkaline soils.

HOW TO PLANT.

Juniper colors most intensely in infertile sandy loam that is somewhat moist. Dig into the planting bed 2 in. of coarse sand or chicken grit to provide good drainage and an equal amount of humus. In clay soil, mix in a handful of gypsum and another of superphosphate for each plant. Set the plants about 3 ft. apart in generous planting holes and spread the roots out over the hole. After planting, water thoroughly. Furnish a permanent 3-in. mulch of pine needles, bark chips, or rotted leaf mold until the plants shade the ground so completely weeds cannot get started—that will take 2 or 3 seasons.

How to Provide Care and Maintenance
Water a new planting every week or two the first season. Since juniper is drought-resistant, once the plants are established, local rainfall should be enough to keep the plants growing except during our mid- and late August droughts. Do not fertilize unless the soil is extremely poor. Replenish the mulch in late winter.

Additional Advice
Creeping junipers may be pruned back in midsummer where branches are beginning to overlap—but they rarely need it.

Other Cultivars and Species
Juniperus horizontalis 'Douglasii', Waukegan juniper, is a rapid-growing trailing form with steel-blue foliage that turns grayish purple in winter. It is a good choice for sandy soils. 'Blue Chip' is a handsome form that keeps its bluish color even in summer.

Dead Nettle

*L*amium is a beautiful, fast-spreading creeper that thrives in partial shade. The trailing stems grow 8 to 10 to 12 in. during the season. The dark-green, oval leaves are blotched or striped-silver or white. Between late spring and midsummer, small hooded flowers appear. This ground cover is evergreen most years in my Washington, D.C., garden. When hit by drought or intense cold without snow cover, I lose much of the bed, so I do not recommend lamiums as cover for large expanses. But yellow archangel, *Lamium* (or *Lamiastrum*) *galeobdolon*, is a blessing in shady places under small trees and tall shrubs. In my garden it produces a froth of silvery leaves under a young star magnolia and in the shade of a purple plum where the light is so dim even hostas and impatiens do poorly. In summer, it throws 1- to 2-ft. stems toward sunnier reaches of the garden, and they root at the nodes. When these stems die in very cold winters, the rooted parent plants remain and regrow in the spring.

WHEN TO PLANT

In early spring, plant root divisions or seedlings. To multiply your holdings, dig rooted plantlets and replant at once in moist, humusy soil. Terminal cuttings taken during the growing season root easily in water and can be planted once the heat of summer has gone by.

WHERE TO PLANT

Lamiums succeed in partial shade. *L. galeobdolon* does better in real shade than *L. maculatum*. Both tolerate more light in the cool upland areas of our region.

HOW TO PLANT

Lamiums do well in almost any soil, but they spread most rapidly in light, well-drained loam. Dig into the planting bed 2 in. of coarse sand or chicken grit and an equal amount of humus, so the soil retains the moisture that encourages rapid growth. In clay soil, mix in a handful of gypsum and another of superphosphate for each plant. Set the plants 1 in. apart. Water well. Mulch between the plants to keep weeds at bay until the plants shade the ground so completely weeds cannot get started.

HOW TO PROVIDE CARE AND MAINTENANCE

Its first month or two, water weekly or bi-weekly, unless there is a good supply of rain. To keep the bed growing vigorously, water lamium as often as you do garden flowers. If lamium dries out repeatedly, the bed will die back to scatterings of rooted plantlets that will then need months to re-establish vigorous growth. Fertilize every 2 or 3 years in early fall or late winter by adding 1/2 in. of compost or an application of 20-10-10 fertilizer.

ADDITIONAL ADVICE

If the plants become straggly toward midsummer, cut them back to 6 to 8 in. to keep the growth full and within bounds. In spring, remove winter-damaged stems and scatter a light application of 20-10-10 fertilizer or compost through the bed. Replenish the mulch if weeds begin to take hold. In late fall, remove dead stems and clear away fallen leaves.

OTHER CULTIVARS AND SPECIES

L. galeobdolon 'Variegata', variegated yellow archangel, has yellow flowers and stands up well to our climate. 'Herman's Pride' is a less-aggressive spreader. *L. g.* var. *compacta* is compact and useful in small areas. *L. maculatum* 'Beacon Silver' has purple-pink flowers and is the most beautiful. 'White Nancy' has white flowers.

Ivy

Ivy is the toughest, greenest, most reliable evergreen ground cover for our area. Where others have failed because of sun or lack of it, because of heat or drought, or too much rain, ivy will almost surely survive—and even thrive. Once established, it grows vigorously. English ivy, *Hedera helix*, the large-leaved form used most often, is a running or climbing woody vine that sends out stems 25 to 50 ft. and sometimes 90 ft. long. It succeeds in shade under trees, though the stems will run toward better light, and it competes well with tree roots. Thickly planted, it makes a dense "lawn" 6 to 8 in. high. Allowed to run, it develops a shrubby form and, if supported, climbs. There are some lovely variegated forms of *H. helix*: 'Aureo-variegata' is variegated yellow; 'Argenteo-variegata', is variegated white and is almost as beautiful as Algerian ivy, *H. canariensis*, a showy form too tender for winters here. My favorite ivies are the small-leaved varieties. They grow slowly, but they are lovely when trained to cascade over walls and in hanging baskets and garden urns.

WHEN TO PLANT

Plant ivy in early spring or fall. Garden centers sell flats of rooted cuttings for ground cover and larger potted plants for use in containers. To encourage ivy to root, peg the end of a stem to the soil, and when it shows new growth, cut it off and replant.

WHERE TO PLANT

Ivy succeeds in shade and in hot sun. It does well almost anywhere, but spreads most rapidly in non-acid soils in the pH 6.0 to 8.0 range. It prefers rich, fairly moist, well-drained organic soil, but it also does quite well in sandy soil by the shore.

HOW TO PLANT

Dig into the planting bed 2 in. of coarse sand or chicken grit and an equal amount of humus so the soil will drain well and retain the moisture that encourages rapid growth. In clay soil, mix in a handful of gypsum and another of superphosphate for each plant. To cover an extensive area, buy flats of rooted cuttings and set them 6 in. apart. Prune straggly stems back to 6 in.. Then soak the ground

with water containing a 20-10-10 fertilizer. Provide a permanent mulch of pine needles or rotted leafmold to control weeds. The vines can take two or three seasons to cover the area.

How to Provide Care and Maintenance

The first growing season water the plants weekly—even daily— if the weather is very hot and dry. The second year keep the soil moderately damp until the plants are well established and running. Water during droughts. Do not fertilize established beds unless the foliage yellows. Shear the planting back every 3 or 4 years to maintain foliage density.

Additional Advice

Ivy-clad walls and trees look wonderful, but the density of foliage at the soil line can create problems. After a period of heavy rains, followed by either great heat or great cold, the base leaves retain moisture that can cause damage from freezing, or in hot, wet weather, rot. The solution is to remove the base foliage. Keep established ivy pruned—it can be invasive.

Other Cultivars and Species

Hedera helix 'Baltica' has small, white-veined leaves and tolerates hot, direct sun. 'Bulgaria' is a large-leaved variety considered especially drought resistant. '238th Street' has 1^{1}/2-in., heart-shaped leaves veined in yellow and is a pretty container plant that can also succeed indoors.

Japanese Pachysandra

$\mathcal{P}$achysandra is a beautiful, rather formal, low-growing evergreen ground cover that does best in light shade. Though it cannot be walked on, pachysandra makes a handsome lawn. It succeeds under tall shrubs and trees, even under maples, beeches, and sycamores where roots are shallow and competitive. This plant is not fast-spreading in my Washington, D.C., garden, but in rich, humusy ground it fills in in a year or two. The only care needed is a periodic trim. The plant consists of upright rosettes of rich-green, scalloped, or saw-toothed leaves on fleshy stems 8 to 10 in. tall. In spring, there is a flush of light-green new growth and small green-white flower spikes appear. They can reappear in fall when Indian summer warmth follows a cold snap. I think the most beautiful variety of Japanese pachysandra is *Pachysandra terminalis* 'Green Carpet', a deep-green cultivar with wide, compact, rather smooth leaves. 'Variegata' and 'Silver Edge' are beautifully edged with a thin margin of white, but tolerate less direct sun and are less vigorous. Our native Alleghany pachysandra, *P. procumbens*, can stand more heat than the Japanese species. It is used southward where Japanese pachysandra is not hardy, but it is small and less attractive.

WHEN TO PLANT

In early spring or fall, set out flats of rooted stems from your garden center or mail-order catalog. Cuttings of new growth taken in summer will root in damp sand tented with plastic. Mist often for 6 weeks. When they resist a gentle tug, transplant to half-and-half sand and peat moss.

WHERE TO PLANT

Pachysandra does best in bright shade of tall trees and in day-long dappled light, but it can handle 2 hours of direct summer sun daily. Where direct sunlight hits pachysandra all day long after the leaves fall, the plants suffer. Acid soil, 4.0 to 5.5, suits pachysandra, so it is a good choice for areas that are wooded. It grows less well in alkaline conditions. It needs rich, moist soil if it is planted where it receives direct sun.

HOW TO PLANT

Provide a planting bed that retains moisture by digging into the soil a layer 2 in. deep of peat moss or chopped leaves along with a 1-in. layer of acidic compost, or add an application of a 10-10-10 slow-release fertilizer labeled as suitable for azaleas and gardenias. In clay soil, mix in a small handful of gypsum and another of superphosphate for each plant. Set rooted cuttings 4 to 6 in. apart and water thoroughly. Provide a 3-in. mulch of pine needles or rotted oak leaves to keep weeds away while the plants fill out.

HOW TO PROVIDE CARE AND MAINTENANCE

For the first season, water your planting weekly. Where pachysandra competes with the roots of trees and shrubs, be sure to water it well during dry spells. In late fall or winter, apply a 10-10-10 fertilizer. Maintain the mulch until the plants have spread sufficiently to shade out weeds. Remove fallen autumn leaves. Though they provide nutrients as they decay, in Washington, D.C.'s muggy summers, my pachysandra is troubled with diseases that are most easily controlled in beds that have plenty of air and light.

ADDITIONAL ADVICE

Diseases such as root rot and fusarium leaf blight will attack very lush stands of pachysandra. Thinning and cutting helps control the problems. If patches of wilted leaves appear and the soil is reasonably moist, treat the area with a fungicide. Euonymus scale can be a problem. To avoid it, before growth begins in late winter, spray with a dormant oil.

OTHER CULTIVARS AND SPECIES

Pachysandra terminalis 'Kingwood' has leaves that are more deeply serrated along the margins. It holds its color very well. *P. t.* 'Green Sheen' has a glossy luster and a more formal look.

Lilyturf

*L*iriope looks like a graceful clump of tall, coarse grass 1/2 to 3/4 in. wide and 12 to 18 in. high. In late summer and early fall, it produces flower spikes rather like grape hyacinth. The flowers may be bluish, purple, lilac, or white, and are followed by shiny black fruits that persist through early winter. A tough and resistant semi- or evergreen plant, lilyturf is ideal for edging and as ground cover. Once established, it is almost impenetrable. For edging flower beds and garden paths, I like the light look of variegated liriopes. 'Gold Banded' has yellow-striped leaves and lilac flowers; 'John Burch' is similar, but has crested lavender flowers. 'Silvery Midget', a little plant 6 in. tall, has silver-streaked foliage and violet flowers. For edging tree boxes, and in large expanses of ground cover, I prefer green varieties, like *Liriope muscari* 'Green'. Creeping lilyturf, *L. spicata*, spreads rapidly by underground stolons and is excellent as a bank holder and to cover very large areas. It is a slightly smaller species with 1/4-in. leaves and pale violet or white flowers.

WHEN TO PLANT

In early spring or early fall, buy container-grown root divisions or seedlings at your garden center or from a catalog—or plant seeds that have soaked for a few hours in warm water. They will need several seasons to fill out. Well-established clumps can be divided in early spring before growth begins.

WHERE TO PLANT

Liriope does best in bright shade under tall trees, but even in dense shade it will spread, though more slowly. These plants are not particular as to soil pH, and succeed in hot, dry locations, but will not tolerate wet spots. Liriope withstands muggy weather and high humidity, and spreads rapidly as long as the soil doesn't dry out.

HOW TO PLANT

Liriope does well in almost any soil, even my high-alkaline soil.
Dig into the planting bed 2 in. of coarse sand or chicken grit to provide good drainage, and an equal amount of humus so the soil will
retain the moisture that encourages rapid growth. Enrich the bed
with a handful of super phosphate and a slow-release 10-10-10 fertilizer. In clay soil, mix in a handful of gypsum and another of
superphosphate for each plant. Set the plants 6 to 8 in. apart. Water
thoroughly after planting. Provide a permanent mulch of coconut
hulls, bark chips, or shredded redwood bark to keep weeds at bay
until the plants shade the ground so completely that weeds cannot
get started.

HOW TO PROVIDE CARE AND MAINTENANCE

Keep the planting watered during droughts the first summer. In late
winter, cut the foliage to the ground to allow for fresh growth, and
replenish the mulch.

ADDITIONAL ADVICE

In continuing wet weather there may be evidence that slugs and
snails are chewing the edges of the leaves. When the soil dries,
sprinkle diotomaceous earth around each plant. Repeat the treat-
ment until all evidence of fresh snail activity ceases.

OTHER CULTIVARS AND SPECIES

Liriope muscari 'Lilac Beauty' and shade-loving 'Christmas Tree' have
exceptionally handsome lavender flowers. Slow-growing 'Monroe's
White' has cream-white flowers. Lovely light 'Silvery Sunproof' has
leaves that are almost white in full sun. *L. spicata* 'Silver Dragon'
is a variegated form with lavender flowers. Dwarf mondo grass,
Ophiopogon japonicus 'Nana', and 'Silver Mist', the variegated form,
are fast-spreading dwarf lilyturfs.

Moneywort

OTHER COMMON NAME: Creeping Jenny

*G*reat in shaded areas with moist soil, lysimachia is a vigorous perennial with round, dark green leaves that stay green all year in most of Virginia. In spring and summer, it bears masses of small, bright-yellow, cup-shaped flowers along the stems. They provide quick cover and can become invasive. *Lysimachia nummularia* naturalizes readily along stream borders, wet banks, and at the edge of damp woodlands. It rambles along the ground, rooting as it goes, and forming a ruffled carpet 1 to 2 in. high of bright-green, penny-shaped leaves. It can stand water up to 2 in. deep. The golden-leaved variety, *L. n.* 'Aurea', creates an interesting color contrast. The plants are 4 to 8 in. tall, and the rounded 1-in.-long leaves start out yellowish in spring—then turn toward lime-green in summer. In the shade the foliage fairly glows. The flowers are yellow and faintly fragrant, blooming in early summer.

WHEN TO PLANT

Buy container-grown plants any time after the last frost in spring and before the first frost in autumn. Multiply your holdings in early spring or in early fall by digging up and replanting rooted sections of the stems.

WHERE TO PLANT

Lysimachias do best in shade, and they will succeed and multiply even in deep shade, as long as the soil is damp. The plants spread aggressively in moist conditions.

HOW TO PLANT

Lysimachias prefer somewhat neutral soil. If the planting bed is in or near woodlands, chances are it will be somewhat acidic, so apply lime to raise the pH. If the bed is not naturally moist, increase the humus content by digging in a 2-in. layer of peat moss or chopped leaves, along with a 1-in. layer of compost, or add an application of a slow-release fertilizer. In clay soil, mix in a handful of gypsum and another of superphosphate for each plant. Set the plants 12 to 18 in. apart. Water thoroughly. Provide a permanent mulch of coconut hulls or well-rotted leaf mold to keep weeds at bay until the plants cover the ground completely.

How to Provide Care and Maintenance

Water a new planting every week unless the ground is naturally moist. Fertilize a new planting early the spring after you set out the plants by scratching a slow-release 10-30-10 fertilizer into the soil beside young plants.

Additional Advice

Prune the plants back in late winter if they are becoming matted. Once established, these plants do well on their own without fertilization or spraying. Neither pests nor diseases seem to come their way—but they will suffer if the soil surface is dry for days at a time. Maintain mulch until the plants spread enough to shade out weeds.

Other Cultivars and Species

Lysimachia congestiflora is a rambling, densely flowered plant. *L. c.* 'Eco Satin Stain' has yellow flowers with a red throat that appear from May to October. *L. punctata* blooms on stems 18 to 24 in. tall, studded with bright yellow flowers. It is lovely growing in sweeps.

GROUND COVERS

Periwinkle

OTHER COMMON NAME: Myrtle

*S*mall-leaved *Vinca minor* and large-leaved *V. major* are beautiful ground covers that in mid-spring bear periwinkle-blue flowers. There are pink-wine and white-flowered varieties, but none I find as attractive as the blues. The trailing branches are lovely carpeting banks, rocky slopes, and in lightly shaded places under tall shrubs and trees. The stems root every few feet, but unlike ivy, vinca does not cling to masonry, so it is ideal for edging walls and terraces. Small-leaved *V. minor* develop tufts 3 to 6 in. high and trailing stems 2 to 3 ft. long with dainty, shiny, dark-green leaves. It makes a handsome lawn but tolerates little foot traffic. *V. major* has larger leaves, is a paler green and produces 3- to 4-ft.-long trailing branches. The most popular variety is *V. m.* 'Variegata' which has jade-green leaves edged with creamy white that are beautiful trailing over the edges of hanging baskets and planters. I use it as a ground cover under the weeping cherry and train it to spill over a brick wall. In winters in Zone 7, I lose all but the central tufts, so I cut back the dead stems and it soon fills out.

WHEN TO PLANT

In early spring or fall, you will find flats of rooted cuttings of *V. minor*, and four packs of *V. major* at garden centers. To multiply your holdings, divide and replant rooted stems as growth resumes in early spring, or during wet weather in late summer and fall.

WHERE TO PLANT

In Virginia, vinca does best in bright shade under tall shrubs or trees and in the partial shade created by a building.

HOW TO PLANT

Vinca needs well-worked, fertile, loamy soil with good drainage. It does well in soil that has rather high alkalinity—a pH ranging between 6.0 and 7.5. Dig into the planting bed 2 in. of coarse sand or chicken grit to provide good drainage, and an equal amount of humus so the soil will retain the moisture that encourages rapid growth, along with an application of a slow release 10-10-10 fertilizer. In clay soil, mix in a handful of gypsum and another of super-phosphate for each plant. Set rooted cuttings or plantlets 6 in. apart. Water thoroughly. Mulch with shredded coconut hulls, fir bark, or rotted leaf mold.

HOW TO PROVIDE CARE AND MAINTENANCE
Do not allow vinca to dry out, especially the first season. To encourage *V. major* growing in baskets and containers to bush out, pinch the tips of the stems back right after planting, and 4 or 5 times more during the growing season. In early spring before growth starts, mow or by hand-cut a vinca lawn to keep the bed thick. Fertilize the bed by scratching a slow-release 10-10-10 fertilizer into the soil beside young plants.

ADDITIONAL ADVICE
During droughts, water vinca deeply whenever you water the flowers. When you fertilize your lawn, water in 10-10-10 fertilizer.

OTHER CULTIVARS AND SPECIES
Vinca minor 'Alba' has creamy-white flowers. It is less vigorous than the species. 'Atropurpurea' has burgundy-colored flowers. 'Bowlesii' has deep-blue flowers and often reblooms a little in summer and fall. 'Sterling Silver' and 'Variegata' have green leaves edged with white and blue flowers. 'Aureo Variegata' has green leaves edged with white and bears white flowers.

Plumbago

OTHER COMMON NAME: Plumbago Larpentae

*O*ne of the bluest of all blue flowers is borne in late summer and fall by this leafy ground cover. The plants form sprawling 6- to 8- to 12-in.-high mats of lasting, glossy leaves. Then from midsummer to frosts, peacock-blue flowers appear at the tips of new growth. The flowers are attractively set off by a rusty-red calyx and bracts. With cold the foliage turns bronze-red. Then with frost it dies, leaving behind a tangle of not very attractive brown stems. Plumbago takes a year or two to get under way, but once established, it throws new growth in every direction, overwhelming lower-growing ground covers such as pachysandra and myrtle. In spite of that, I keep small patches of plumbago in a bed of mixed ground covers because the extraordinary blue flowers are so handsome in the fall. I recommend it for small areas, but not for large expanses. It needs to be cut back after frost wilts the leaves to keep the bed tidy, healthy, and to promote the new growth on which flowers will appear the next season. You pretty well have to cut it back by hand.

WHEN TO PLANT

In early spring, set out rooted divisions or container plants from your garden center or catalog. Multiply your holdings by dividing and replanting rooted cuttings in early spring: as the plants ramble, they root.

WHERE TO PLANT

Plumbago handles more cold than we experience in Virginia, and tolerates high heat. It succeeds under tall deciduous trees but grows more vigorously in bright shade or dappled light. I find plumbago tolerates our droughts, but cannot stand soil that is soggy in winter. Avoid planting it in damp, low-lying areas where the soil alternately freezes and thaws.

HOW TO PLANT

Dig into the planting bed 2 in. of coarse sand or chicken grit and an equal amount of humus, so the soil will retain the moisture that encourages rapid growth, along with an application of a slow-release 10-10-10 fertilizer. In clay soil, mix in a handful of gypsum and another of superphosphate for each plant. Set rooted divisions $1^1/2$ to 2 in. apart. Water well. Mulch with salt hay, straw, or peat moss to keep weeds at bay until the plants shade the ground so completely that weeds cannot get started. That will take 2 or 3 seasons.

HOW TO PROVIDE CARE AND MAINTENANCE

Fertilizing is not necessary unless the soil is extremely poor, but plumbago benefits from the addition of $1/2$ in. or so of compost in late fall or winter every 2 or 3 years. After the foliage dies in the late fall or early winter, cut the planting back by hand. Plumbago blooms on new growth. If you do not cut it back, you will get lots of foliage but you will miss out on its really beautiful flowers.

ADDITIONAL ADVICE

Plumbago spreads by underground roots. It gets matted down in time, and every 3 or 4 years it benefits from dividing.

OTHER CULTIVARS AND SPECIES

Ceratostigma willmottianum, Chinese plumbago, is a shrubby form usually 2 to 3 in. tall, but it can reach 5 in. The flowers are violet-blue, and it is quite beautiful. However, it is reliably hardy only as far south as Zone 8, which in Virginia is the shore area near the North Carolina border.

WHEN IT COMES TO THIS SUBJECT, Virginians are within easy reach of one of the most informative herb gardens in America—the two-acre U.S. National Herb Garden at the National Arboretum in Washington, D.C. Founded in 1980, it was a gift of The Herb Society of America. The many uses of herbs throughout the ages are represented by a series of small herb gardens for special uses. The plants in the Dioscorides Garden were first recorded by that famous Greek physician in 60 A.D. There are collections of dye herbs, early American and Indian herbs, medicinal and culinary herbs, industrial and fragrance herbs, Oriental herbs and beverage herbs. In the center of this grouping are planted herbal trees and shrubs.

Another fascinating area is the classical knot garden, intricately pruned and laid out as fashionably as any garden of sixteenth-century England. And I especially recommend the Historic Rose Garden in spring, when some of the wonderful old roses that parented the modern rose are blooming.

The plants I've recommended in this chapter are important culinary herbs, those that cooks love to have fresh from the garden. I've added lavender, a favorite perfume herb, whose fresh flower buds I like in Mediterranean casseroles and salad dressings. These herbs and many others grow very well in Virginia and survive our mild winters. Parsley stays green through most winters in my garden, being a biennial that begins to deteriorate as the weather warms. It may be harvested in moderation, so in March I plant parsley seedlings or seeds around the plants from the previous spring. Dill dies away in D.C.'s high summer heat, and when the heat dissipates, I replace it with seedlings. The other herbs here tolerate heat—not too surprising since many came originally from the Mediterranean area, which enjoys very hot summers.

Chapter Six

Most herbs need at least 6 hours of sun daily. Since much of our garden is shaded by street trees, the sunny places are given to the flowers, and I plant the herbs in among them. Basil and dill take some shade. I often use low-growing herbs such as parsley, thyme, Greek oregano, and sage as edgers, and in flower boxes and strawberry jars. The sprawling thymes and white-splashed pineapple mint are lovely in hanging baskets with white petunias and pink geraniums.

GROWN AND HARVESTING HERBS

Seeds of the perennial culinary herbs, and lavender, are slow to germinate and have disappointed me often. So I plant these and many other herbs the easy way by setting out seedlings after the soil has dried and warmed in mid-spring. Dill and basil start easily enough from seed.

You'll find kitchen herbs have more flavor if harvested just before you use them. To encourage branching, harvest the main stem of herbs that have a central leader early on, and keep side branches picked so the plant will bush out. When the plants fill out, pick the tender tip sprigs of the youngest branches. Keep herb flowers pinched out as they develop since they're edible, and make charming garnishes. Rinse herbs only if they're muddy, and avoid this entirely by keeping them mulched. Herb foliage stays fresh for a week or so, stored in the crisper in a vegetable bag or in a closed container lined with a damp paper towel.

Never strip a plant of all its foliage or it will have trouble maintaining itself. In summer's high heat—especially in warm regions—herbs go into semi-dormancy. During this season, you should pick herbs sparingly, as the plants are unable to replace the missing foliage and will look awful and be slow to recover.

Ocimum basilicum

Basil

*T*he basils are vigorous, upright annuals or short-lived perennials 1 to 2¹/₂ ft. tall. They survive high heat, but are blackened by frost. Basil's light-green, somewhat puckered leaves have the cool strong bite of mint (a close relative), with hints of anise, clove, and thyme. Minced, it is used with raw tomatoes, in salads, in pasta sauces and pesto, and with lamb, fish, and beef. The leaves freshen the breath and perfumed 'Holy Basil' is used dried in potpourri. The flower spikes make fragrant fillers for bouquets. For flavoring, plant two each of common sweet basil and of 'Holy Basil' in a mixed flowering border in the herb or kitchen garden. In window boxes and for edging, use tiny bush basils like 'Spicy Globe', which grows between 6 and 12 in. tall. The purple-leaved basils aren't very flavorful, but they add fragrance and rich color to flower beds and bouquets. The opal basils and 'Purple Ruffles', an All-American winner, are the most beautiful. Pick sprig tips at will when the leaves still are young. Big harvests for making pesto can begin when the flower spikes begin to form. Basil leaves dry in a minute or two in a microwave.

WHEN TO PLANT

Sow basil seeds in the garden after the soil has warmed and night temperatures are above 50 degrees Fahrenheit, or start seedlings indoors 4 to 6 weeks before. Or set out a few seedlings in mid-spring; then beginning in late spring follow with 2 or 3 successive sowings of seeds of other varieties.

WHERE TO PLANT

Plant basil in full sun or in part sun. It grows easily almost anywhere, as long as it has moisture and 6 hours of sun.

HOW TO PLANT

Prepare the bed by digging in 1 in. of coarse sand or chicken grit, 1 in. of humus, and a slow-release 10-5-5 fertilizer. In clay soil, add a small handful of gypsum and of superphosphate for each plant. Work the soil 8 to 12 in. deep. Basil does well in soils whose pH is between 6.0 and 7.0. Sow seeds thickly, then remove the weakest seedlings to leave plants standing 6 to 8 in. apart. If you are planting seedlings, set them 6 to 8 in. apart. Water well with diluted fertilizer. Apply a 3-in. mulch starting 3 in. from the stem.

How to Provide Care and Maintenance

Pinch out branch tips and flowers early and often to encourage leaf production. To promote rapid, unchecked growth, for the next 2 or 3 weeks, water often enough to sustain the soil moisture. After that, water deeply every week unless you have a soaking rain. Fertilize every 3 to 5 weeks through August. If you have planted seeds, weed around the seedlings until they have grown large enough to shade weeds out. At mid-season, cut the plants back by about half.

Additional Advice

Frost blackens basil, so protect thriving plants from early frosts. They will go on through Indian summer. In late summer, buy young basil seedlings, repot in a generous clay container, and grow a couple indoors for winter use. They will thrive in a cool, sunny spot. Mist and water often.

Other Cultivars and Species

'Opal Basil' has purplish leaves with green markings, bears pink-mauve flowers, and has a bland, but fair, flavor. 'Dark Opal Basil' has little green markings, red stems, and a sweet, anise-like flavor. 'Red Rubin Purple Leaf Basil' is a European selection that holds its color well.

Chives

*C*hive plants produce mounds of 12-in.-high, hollow, dark-green stems that are grassy and thin as a pencil lead. The chopped foliage imparts a mild onion flower and is used as a flavoring agent and garnish for salads, dips, stews, and casseroles. A sprinkling of chopped chives puts a flavorful finishing touch to one of the world's great cold soups, vichysoise. Beginning in June, attractive little round-as-a-ball, lavender-pink flowers appear, and these, too, are edible and taste mildly of onion. Chives are pretty little plants that are attractive tucked into a flowering border or edging an herb or a vegetable garden. Three or four plants will probably be more than enough. Harvest chives with a pair of sharp scissors. Cut no lower than 2 in. from the crown and never take more than a third of the plant at a time. Chopped chives freeze easily and keep well.

WHEN TO PLANT

You can sow chive seeds in the early fall or in early spring, but they are slow to germinate. I prefer to set out clumps of chive seedlings in early fall or in early spring. To multiply your holdings, divide well-established older plants in spring or early fall.

WHERE TO PLANT

Chives will be most productive growing in full sun, but they can take a little filtered shade. If you are starting chives from seeds, plant them where they are to grow.

HOW TO PLANT

Prepare the bed by digging in 2 in. of coarse sand or chicken grit, 1 in. of dried manure, and a slow-release 5-10-10 fertilizer. In clay soil, add a small handful of gypsum and of superphosphate for each plant. Work the soil 8 to 12 in. deep. Chives do best in soils between pH 5.5 and 6.5. Set plants into the garden 6 to 8 in. apart. Water with diluted fertilizer. After the first flush of bloom, fertilize again, and repeat every 3 to 5 weeks through August.

HOW TO PROVIDE CARE AND MAINTENANCE

To promote rapid, unchecked growth, for the next 2 or 3 weeks water often enough to sustain the soil moisture. After that, water deeply during droughts. If you have planted seeds, weed around the seedlings until they have grown large enough to shade weeds out. Harvest flowerheads to prevent the formation of seeds that may self-sow, and which will slow the development of new foliage. Harvest chives foliage sparingly in summer's high heat.

ADDITIONAL ADVICE

In early spring, fertilize with a handful of 5-10-10 slow release fertilizer. Divide chives every 3 to 4 years in early spring. In late summer, you can pot chives in a clay container and bring a clump indoors for very modest winter harvests. They will live through winter in a cool, sunny spot. Water often enough to keep the plants from drying out, but don't let them sit in a puddle.

OTHER CULTIVARS AND SPECIES

A. tuberosum, garlic, or Chinese, chives are flat-leaved and taller and have attractive flowers. You will find these listed in the flower section of catalogs and at garden centers.

Dill

*D*ill is a willowy annual 1 to 3 ft. tall that tops itself with foliage as fine as asparagus fern. It looks a lot like fennel, *Foeniculum*, and tastes of parsley-carrot-lemon-anise. The foliage is called "dill weed." Flowerheads resembling green Queen-Anne's-lace develop as the season warms, and they are edible and eventually produce seeds that are dried and used primarily for pickling. Snipped fresh dill weed is excellent with potatoes, green beans, salads, and in chicken soup. Dill is attractive enough to be planted in a mixed flowering border, and it lends grace to the herb and the kitchen garden. In choosing a place for dill, take into account that it may die out when high heat arrives. Dill dwarf varieties do well in containers. Half a dozen standard-size plants will probably meet your needs. Make a second sowing late in spring to have fresh dill for fall and to harvest for drying. Use scissors to harvest dill tips once the plant is established and growing well. Don't rinse dill weed—it tends to rot. When the plants begin to flower, allow a few blooms to set seed for later harvest. Dill weed and dill seed dry quickly on screens.

WHEN TO PLANT

Plant dill seeds, or seedlings, after the ground has warmed in early spring. Repeat in 10 days to 2 weeks to keep young dill coming. Or start seeds indoors in individual peat pots 6 to 8 weeks before the last frost. Dill does not transplant easily.

WHERE TO PLANT

Because dill's taproots transplant poorly, sow seeds or plant seedlings in the garden where the plants are to grow. Dill needs sun but suffers and usually dies in prolonged, intense heat. In cities and along the southern coast, a little filtered shade can keep dill going longer. Avoid planting dill where walls or white-painted surfaces will reflect the heat.

HOW TO PLANT

Prepare the bed by digging in 2 in. of coarse sand or chicken grit, 1 in. of dried manure, and a slow-release 10-5-5, or your regular grass fertilizer. In clay soil, add a small handful of gypsum and of superphosphate for each plant. Work the soil 8 to 12 in. deep. Dill prefers soil in the acid range, pH 5.5 to 6.5. Sow seeds thickly and plan to thin out the weakest seedlings to leave plants standing 6 to 8 in. apart. If you are planting seedlings, take care not to disturb the root-ball as you plant. Water with diluted fertilizer. Apply a 3-in. mulch starting 3 in. from the stem. Fertilize every 3 to 5 weeks through August.

How to Provide Care and Maintenance

Pinch out tip sprigs regularly to encourage branching. To promote rapid, unchecked growth, for the next 2 or 3 weeks, water often enough to sustain the soil moisture. After that, water deeply every week unless you have a soaking rain. Weed around the plants until they have grown large enough to shade weeds out. Keep the flower heads picked until the end of the season; then allow a few to set seed. If the soil around the dill plants is cultivated, dill often self-sows. Harvest sparingly in high heat.

Additional Advice

Since dill almost surely will disappear when high heat comes, don't fuss over it. Let it go and plan to replant seedlings when summer cools off a bit in early September. When the seedheads show signs of yellowing or browning, but before the seeds are fully ripe or the seedheads dry, gather the seeds into a paper bag and dry them on screens.

Other Cultivars and Species

Fernleaf dill is a lovely, blue-green 18-in. dwarf excellent in containers. It was a 1992 All-American Winner. 'Bouquet' is a compact, bushy variety with big leaves and a excellent flavor. 'Mammoth' is an aromatic 4-ft. dill that is good for pickling. 'Dukat', or 'Tetra-dill', which is related to 'Mammoth', has a more delicate and rather sweet flavor.

Origanum vulgare

Italian Oregano

The hardy Italian oregano, and its close relative, cold-tender sweet marjoram, are small-leaved sprawling or creeping relatives of mint. In summer, they bear panicles of faintly fragrant whitish, pink, or lavender florets. The leaves of Italian oregano, *O. vulgare*, have a bold, peppery bite like that of thyme, and add a nice flavor to salad dressings, tomatoes, and Mediterranean dishes. Dried, the leaves are used to flavor pizza and pasta sauces. I include stems of fresh oregano in bouquets. The plant is upright but somewhat sprawling and is attractive planted in a mixed, flowering border. For use fresh, I prefer the small leaves of Greek oregano, *O. vulgare* spp. *hirtum*, (*O. heracleoticum*) which grow into a pretty green mat, and the tender perennial called sweet marjoram *O. majorana*, which is grown in Virginia as an annual. One of each will meet your needs for fresh oregano and provide leaves to dry for winter. The leaves are ready to harvest when the flower buds begin to break. Air dry the branches, then strip the leaves, bottle, and cap.

WHEN TO PLANT

You can start oregano from seed, but the seedlings will not all have satisfactory flavor. Instead, buy seedlings whose flavor you enjoy, and set them out in mid-spring after the soil has warmed. Multiply Italian oregano by dividing established plants in spring or by digging up and replanting rooted branches any time.

WHERE TO PLANT

Oregano will be most productive growing in full sun. Partially shaded, it also grows well. It can take a lot of heat and resists drought. Italian Oregano will invade nearby garden space with long, trailing stems that root. So, either prune it back every spring or plant it where it can go wild.

How to Plant

Prepare the bed by digging in 2 in. of coarse sand or chicken grit, 1 in. of compost, and a slow-release 10-10-10 fertilizer, or your regular lawn fertilizer. Do not fertilize again; in very rich soils these plants lose their pungency. In clay soil, add a small handful of gypsum and of superphosphate for each plant. Work the soil 8 to 12 in. deep. Set plants into the garden 6 to 8 in. apart and water well. Tie a few of the longest stems to stakes to create a supply of leaves that won't need rinsing.

How to Provide Care and Maintenance

To promote rapid, unchecked growth, for the next 2 or 3 weeks water often enough to sustain the soil moisture. After that, water only when you water the flower beds. Keep the flower spikes pinched out and cut the plants back after their first flush of growth in mid-spring. Harvest only sparingly in summer's high heat. Every 2 or 3 years use rooted stems of Italian oregano to start new plants since the parent will begin to deteriorate.

Additional Advice

To have fresh Italian oregano indoors in winter, in late summer pot in clay-rooted stems or buy a new seedling and grow it indoors in a cool, sunny spot. Water often to keep the plant from drying out. Oregano growing in the garden can be harvested lightly in winter.

Other Cultivars and Species

'Kent Beauty' is an ornamental oregano with attractive pink flowers and modest flavor. *Origanum vulgare* 'Compactum Nanum', a creeper about 2 ft. high, is used between stepping stones. To encourage lateral growth, pinch out the tops when the plants are 2 in. tall. It is not much for flavor.

Lavender

OTHER COMMON NAME: English Lavender

*L*avender is a sprawling little evergreen 2 to 4 ft. tall, whose sweet, lasting scent has made it a favorite source of fragrance for thousands of years. The stems and needle-like, gray/green leaves are intensely, lastingly perfumed, as are the florets that pack the skinny stems in June and often again in August. The flowers are either lavender, deep-purple, blue-gray, pink, or white. Lavender buds are used not only as scent but also to add a sweet mint-anise-rosemary flavor to Herbes de Provence, honey, dessert butters, savory sauces, grilled fish and steaks, marinades for game, and for stews and soups. The lavender recommended for scent and flavor is the English type, Lavandula angustifolia subspecies angustifolia, also known as true lavender,
L. vera, and as *L. officinalis*. I plant lavender so it will sprawl across paths where we will brush against it, releasing its welcome aroma. It's attractive in an herb garden, perfect for a rock garden, and lovely as ground cover under fruit trees. Plant at least half a dozen. Harvest lavender stems just before the buds begin to open, hang them upside down to air dry, then strip off the buds.

WHEN TO PLANT

Plant lavender in early spring, in late summer, or early fall. Lavender seed is very slow to germinate, so I strongly recommend that you set out sturdy seedlings from your local garden center. If you really want to start your own lavender from seed, look for cata-log offerings of specially treated seeds.

WHERE TO PLANT

Lavender requires full sun, and it really takes off when growing on a gravelly or a sandy slope. Lavender can stand a touch of noon shade, but not much. Lavender grows well in large tubs and planters and survives winters outdoors as far North as Zone 5. It thrives in a big tub, but is not suited to indoor growing.

How to Plant

Prepare the bed by digging in 2 in. of coarse sand or chicken grit, 1 in. of composted, non-acid humus, and a slow-release 5-10-5 fertilizer. In clay soil, add a small handful of gypsum and of super-phosphate for each plant. Work the soil 8 to 12 in. deep. Lavender prefers soil that has a pH above 6.0. Unless your soil is pH 7.0 or higher, apply lime every second or third year. Set the plants to stand 8 to 10 in., or more, apart. They develop a spread of 15 to 30 in. Water well. Apply a 3-in. mulch starting 3 in. from the stem.

How to Provide Care and Maintenance

To promote rapid, unchecked growth, for the next 2 or 3 weeks water often enough to sustain the soil moisture. After that, water deeply every week unless you have a soaking rain.

Additional Advice

In early spring to encourage new growth, prune 1 to 2 in. from branch tips. Lavender often reblooms in late summer if the first set of flowering stems has been harvested.

Other Cultivars and Species

The beautiful purple/pink French, or Spanish, lavender, *L. stoechas*, makes a pretty pot and basket plant. The deep-purple 'Hidcote' is colorful, and 'Munstead', a 1 ft. tall plant, has gray foliage that sets off dark-lavender spikes attractive to bees and butterflies. 'Lavender Lady' is a gray-green dwarf that flowers in late summer from spring-sown seed.

Lemon Grass

A mature lemon grass plant looks like a fountaining ornamental grass 2 to 3 in. high and around. The individual stalks are round, like the stems of scallions, but tougher. Peeled to the tender core and chopped, lemon grass imparts a flavor combining lemon and perfumed ginger to stews, rice, sweets and tea. Indian cuisine couples it with turmeric to make mild curries, and in the Orient, it is used with garlic, ginger, coriander and fish sauce. It is an important ingredient in Thai and Southeast Asian cuisine. The species is *Cymbopogon critatus*. If you don't find it at your local garden center, look in catalogs specializing in herbs, like Nichols Garden Nursery, in Albany, Oregon. Lemon grass is attractive in a flower bed. A single plant will meet your needs. During the growing season take side shoots at will without stripping the plant. In mid-autumn, cut fresh, young shoots 2 to 4 in. above the soil surface, strip away the coarse outer stalks, chop them into 2-in. sections, spread them on screens, and let them dry for 10 days or so. Then bottle and cap.

WHEN TO PLANT
Set out a rooted clump of lemon grass about 2 weeks after the last frost date for your area: in the Williamsburg area that's April 14; Culpepper, April 17; Richmond, May 4; Washington, D.C., March 25.

WHERE TO PLANT
Plant lemon grass where it will get at least 6 hours of direct sun daily. Do not plant it where it will be shaded by taller perennials or annuals as they grow up around it.

HOW TO PLANT
Prepare the bed by digging in 2 in. of coarse sand or chicken grit, 2 in. of non-acid humus, and a slow-release 10-10-5 fertilizer. In clay soil, add a small handful of gypsum and of superphosphate for each plant. Work the soil 8 to 12 in. deep. Lemon grass prefers soil with a neutral pH—around 7.0. Plant so that it will have 2 in. of space all around. Water well. Apply a 3-in. mulch starting 3 in. from the stem.

How to Provide Care and Maintenance

To promote rapid, unchecked growth, for the next 2 or 3 weeks water often enough to sustain the soil moisture. After that, water deeply every week unless you have a soaking rain. If lemon grass needs water, the leaves will change from lush green to a muted olive shade.

Additional Advice

In mid-fall, cut the foliage off at the base and divide the clump in 2 or 4 sections. Pot the sections in a sandy soil mix, and bring them indoors to a cool room or a cool greenhouse. Water the soil often enough to keep the roots from drying out completely. When you see signs of new growth, or after the last frost, water the pots, and keep them in a warm, sunny place until it is time to replant them outdoors.

Other Cultivars and Species

Two other garden herbs whose leaves impart lemony accents to food are the hardy (and invasive) perennial lemon balm, *Melissa officinalis*, and lemon verbena, *Aloysia triphylla* (formerly *Lippia citriodora*) which survives winters in the warmest reaches of Virginia, the southern coastal area next to North Carolina.

Mint

he many species of mints are 1 to 3 ft. tall, square-stemmed, strongly growing (very invasive!) perennials whose leaves release a piney scent when brushed against or minced. In summer, they bear attractive spikes of tiny purplish, white, pink, mauve, or lilac florets which are edible. I let some form of *M. arvensis*, which has broad, hairy leaves, grow wild in our kitchen flower bed and keep it in check by harvesting the tallest stems for bouquets. For its sweet, spicy flavor, I grow dainty-leaved spearmint, *M. x piperita*, in porch containers. I harvest and dry lots at the end of the season for mint tea. I plant the beautiful, cream-splashed, less invasive, pineapple mint, *M. suaveolens* 'Variegata', as an edger. Flavor is not its main virtue. Harvest tip sprigs and dry them on screens, or in a microwave oven—or air-dry branches, then strip the leaves, bottle, and cap.

WHEN TO PLANT

In early spring or in late summer, set out root divisions of mints whose flavor you have tasted and like. *M. × piperita* and other hybrids do not come true from seed. To multiply your holdings, dig up and replant rooted branches or root divisions in spring or early fall. Six-inch tip cuttings root readily in potting soil in either spring or early fall.

WHERE TO PLANT

The various mints flourish in full sun or in filtered or bright shade under tall trees. Mint is invasive. The best way to keep the underground roots somewhat under control is to plant mint in bottomless, 2-lb. coffee tins.

HOW TO PLANT

Prepare the bed by digging in 2 in. of coarse sand or chicken grit, 1 in. of dried manure, and a slow-release 10-10-5 fertilizer. In clay soil, add a small handful of gypsum and of superphosphate for each plant. Work the soil 8 to 12 in. deep. Mints do best in slightly acid soil, pH 5.5 to 6.5. Set plants into the garden 6 to 8 in. apart if your goal is ground cover—otherwise grow the plants in containers or in poor or clay soil. Water with diluted fertilizer. Apply a 3-in. mulch starting 3 in. from the stem.

HOW TO PROVIDE CARE AND MAINTENANCE

To promote rapid, unchecked growth, for the next 2 or 3 weeks, water often enough to sustain the soil moisture. Water the small-leaved mints when you water the flower beds; water the big-leaved varieties during droughts. The sprawling mints get muddied during rainstorms. Stake a few branches to have clean leaves available for cooking. Harvest only sparingly in summer's high heat.

ADDITIONAL ADVICE

Mints winter over in the garden, but those growing in tubs and planters may not make it unless their containers are 14 in. wide and deep, or larger. Potted up and brought indoors, mints do not survive long, even under grow lights. Every 4 years divide mint and replant.

OTHER CULTIVARS AND SPECIES

M. × piperita var. 'Citrata', bergamot mint, orange bergamot, or lemon mint is the herb that flavors Earl Gray tea. It is a tender plant, hardy only in Virginia's warmest southern reaches.

Parsley

*A*bout 12 in. tall, parsley is a pungent, winter-hardy biennial composed of succulent stems ending in green leaves. Its second summer, green flowerheads resembling Queen-Anne's-lace grow up, attract butterflies, and then the plant deteriorates. Parsley's earthy flavor has overtones of carrot and celery and makes all the other flavors work together. It is the preferred garnish of international cuisine and joins chervil, tarragon, and chives in fines herbes, and thyme, bay leaf, and sometimes marjoram and orange zest in bouquet garni. It is a key ingredient in classic recipes for frog's legs and escargots. Rich in chlorophyll, fresh parsley kills odors and sweetens the breath. There are two main types of parsley: mossy, curly parsley, which is quite beautiful and minces easily, and flat, open Italian parsley, *P. c.* var. *neapolitanum*, which has a richer flavor. Half a dozen plants will supply your needs. Parsley is handsome as an edging and thrives in window boxes. Harvest individual stems from the base, but never take more than a quarter to a third of one plant at a time. Rinse curly parsley foliage in many changes of cold water before using. To keep parsley for winter, mince it, seal into a paper-lined container, and freeze.

WHEN TO PLANT

In very early spring, set out sturdy seedlings. In late August, sow a dozen parsley seeds around the original planting to have parsley for fall and winter cutting. The original plants will produce the following spring, but soon will go to seed, so repeat the paired plantings every year.

WHERE TO PLANT

Parsley grows best in full sun, but does fairly well with 6 hours of sun daily.

HOW TO PLANT

Prepare the bed by digging in 1 in. of coarse sand or chicken grit, 2 in. of humus, and a slow-release 10-10-10 fertilizer, or your regular lawn fertilizer. In clay soil, add a small handful of gypsum and of superphosphate for each plant. Work the soil 8 to 12 in. deep. Parsley does best in neutral soil, around pH 7.0. Set plants into the garden 8 to 10 in. apart and water well.

How to Provide Care and Maintenance

To promote rapid, unchecked growth, for the next 2 or 3 weeks water often enough to sustain the soil moisture. After that, water deeply every week unless you have a soaking rain. After planting parsley seeds, weed around the seedlings until they have grown large enough to shade weeds out. Harvest only sparingly in summer's high heat. Never strip a parsley plant of more than a quarter or a third of its branches at one time.

Additional Advice

Parsley is evergreen so you can harvest the plants sparingly all winter, but regrowth is very slow.

Other Cultivars and Species

'Clivi' is a mossy dwarf, ideal for window boxes. 'Krausa Parsley' is a moss variety recommended for flavor. 'Triple Curled' is a thickly-ruffled parsley. 'Giant Italian' is a 3-in.-tall deep-green parsley with a full, mellow flavor excellent fresh or dried. *P. c.* var. *tuberosum* is a turnip parsley, grown for its edible root, as well as for the pungent leaves.

Rosemary

*I*n Virginia gardens, rosemary grows into an elegant plant like a needled evergreen, but it rarely gets to be more than 2 ft. tall before winter destroys it. The pungent needles impart a hot, sweet, piney flavor tinged with nutmeg. Hot olive oil infused with rosemary makes a delicious cooking oil and is excellent in salad dressings. Fresh minced rosemary flavors vegetables, marinades, barbecues, chicken, fish, potatoes, fruit salads, rhubarb, oranges, and cookies. It is used in exquisite polentas, spoon breads, and biscuits. Dried, it is used to scent potpourris. Rosemary branches tied into a circlet make a fragrant base for an herb wreath. Plant this aromatic herb near windows and garden seats, anywhere among flowers, and in the herb garden. Two or three plants will meet your needs for use fresh and for drying. In most garden catalogs only the species, *Rosmarinus officinalis*, is offered among the herb plants, but many attractive forms are listed among flowers. Harvest tip sprigs of rosemary at will. To use fresh, strip the leaves and chop them in a mini food-processor. The leaves dry quickly, either in a microwave oven, or on a screen.

When to Plant

Set out seedlings in mid-spring. Rosemary seeds need nights at a constant 75 degrees Fahrenheit to germinate, and even then germination is slow and uncertain. Three months and more after you have given up, seeds sometimes will sprout.

Where to Plant

Rosemary will be most productive growing in full sun, but it can take a little filtered shade. It withstands high heat and some drought and can be planted where it may be neglected.

How to Plant

Prepare the bed by digging in 2 in. of coarse sand or chicken grit and a slow-release 10-10-10 fertilizer, or your regular lawn fertilizer. In clay soil, add a small handful of gypsum and of superphosphate for each plant. Work the soil 8 to 12 in. deep. Rosemary does best in

neutral soil. Set plants into the garden 6 to 8 in. apart and water well. Keep the area weeded or add a 2-in. mulch starting 3 in. from the stem. Do not overdo the mulch.

How to Provide Care and Maintenance

Harvest 1 or 2 in. from young branch tips often to encourage the plant to bush out. To promote rapid, unchecked growth, for the next 2 or 3 weeks water often enough to sustain the soil moisture. After that, water only during droughts.

Additional Advice

To have fresh rosemary in winter, in late summer pot your plant in clay, or buy a new seedling, and grow it indoors in a cool, sunny spot. Water often to keep the plant from drying out, but do not let it sit in a puddle. To keep rosemary alive indoors, maintain the moisture in the soil.

Other Cultivars and Species

The ornamental rosemaries grouped with flowers in catalogs are lovely little shrubs whose leaves are pungent but not the best for cooking. *R. o.* 'Benenden Blue' has handsome blue flowers; 'Lockwood de Forest' has brighter leaves and bluer flowers; 'Kenneth Prostrate' and 'Huntington Carpet' are superior creeping forms; 'Golden Prostratus' is variegated.

Sage

*T*he sages are upright perennial herbs whose grayish leaves have the texture of crepe and impart a biting flavor combining pine, camphor, and citrus. Minced fresh sage is used in salad dressings, with tomatoes, in sauces for pasta, with pork chops, chicken, and vegetables. The flavor of fresh sage becomes more potent the longer it cooks—so use it with caution. Dried sage enhances fatty meats like sausage and is used in stuffing for poultry. The best species for flavoring is *Salvia officinalis*, a small shrub 18 to 24 in. tall that sprawls unless staked, and in summer bears violet, blue, or white flower spikes. Three or four plants will provide plenty of foliage for fresh use and for drying. I plant *S. officinalis*, and some of the ornamental sages mentioned below, toward the front of flowering borders and in the herb and the kitchen gardens. Sage is pretty in a planter, drooping gracefully over the edge. Harvest tender tip sprigs of sage at will. They will keep for a week and more stored in a vegetable bag in the crisper. Sage leaves dry well in a microwave oven, on screens, or tucked into a wreath.

WHEN TO PLANT

For early harvests, in mid-spring set out root divisions or seedlings. To harvest a lot of sage for drying, sow seeds in mid-spring. By late summer the crop will be ready. To multiply your holdings, divide well-established older plants in spring or early fall.

WHERE TO PLANT

Sage will be most productive growing in full sun, but it benefits from a little filtered shade at noon, especially in warmer reaches of Virginia. It can take a lot of heat and resists drought, so it is one of the herbs that can be planted where it might be neglected.

HOW TO PLANT

Prepare the bed by digging in 2 in. of coarse sand or chicken grit, and a slow-release 10-10-10 fertilizer, or your regular lawn fertilizer. In clay soil, add a small handful of gypsum and of superphosphate for each plant. Work the soil 8 to 12 in. deep. Sage does best in neutral soil, around pH 7.0. Set the plants 6 to 8 in. apart and water well. If the leaves sprawl to the ground, stake the plants or the foliage will have to be washed, and that will rob the leaves of some of the essential oils that give them flavor. Apply a 3-in. mulch starting 3 in. from the stem.

How to Provide Care and Maintenance

To promote rapid, unchecked growth, for the next 2 or 3 weeks water often enough to sustain the soil moisture. After that, water deeply when you water the flower beds. If you have planted seeds, weed around the seedlings until they have grown large enough to shade weeds out.

Additional Advice

In late summer, buy a new sage seedling, or pot up one of the garden plants in a clay container and grow it indoors for winter use. It will live at least for a time if you provide a cool, sunny spot, and if you water often enough to keep it from drying out. Sage growing in the garden can be harvested sparingly in winter.

Other Cultivars and Species

A few of the beautiful, colorful sages have flavor, though less than that of the culinary varieties. 'Tricolor' is the showiest. It grows 6 to 10 in. high and has leaves splattered with deep pink, silver gray, cream, and purple. *S. o.* 'Icterina' has beautiful gray leaves splashed with gold.

Herbs

Satureja hortensis, S. montana

Summer Savory and Winter Savory

The two savories are low-growing aromatic herbs with glossy, narrow, dark-green leaves. In summer they bear spikes of dainty flowers. The flavor is peppery, rather like thyme, pine, or a sweet camphor. Minced fresh leaves add a pleasant tang to soups, meat casseroles, sauces, and salads, and they add zip to the cabbage family and bean dishes. Dried savory flavors liqueurs and vinegars, pork products, poultry, fish, and cheese. Summer savory, *Satureja hortensis*, is an annual herb 12 to 18 in. high. The flavor is milder and finer than that of winter savory, best for use fresh. The flowers are pink-lavender or white. The perennial winter savory, *S. montana*, is the one to use for drying. It is hardy here, a woody little evergreen that bears white or blue flowers and grows well even in rocky nooks and crannies. One plant of summer and one of winter savory will provide lots of leaves for fresh use and for drying. The savories thrive in small planters and large pots. Young plants sometimes will live through winter indoors in a sunny window. Harvest tip sprigs of summer savory at will. In August, harvest young sprigs of winter savory, hang them upside down until dry, strip the leaves, bottle and cap.

WHEN TO PLANT

In mid-spring, set out root divisions of winter savory and sow seeds or plant seedlings of summer savory. To multiply winter savory, in spring hill up a little humusy soil around the plant: new shoots ready to transplant will appear in 4 to 6 weeks.

WHERE TO PLANT

Plant savory in full or partial-sun. Sow seeds of summer savory where they are to grow. Savory tolerates drought, so it can be planted in an area where it may be neglected.

How to Plant

Prepare the bed by digging in 2 in. of coarse sand or chicken grit, and a slow-release 10-10-10 fertilizer or your regular lawn fertilizer. In clay soil, add a small handful of gypsum and of superphosphate for each plant. Work the soil 8 to 12 in. deep. Savory does best in neutral soil. Unless your soil is pH 7.0 or higher, apply lime every second or third year. Set plants into the garden 6 to 8 in. apart and water well.

How to Provide Care and Maintenance

To promote rapid, unchecked growth, for the next 2 or 3 weeks water often enough to sustain the soil moisture. After that, the plants will tolerate considerable drought. If you have planted seeds, weed around the seedlings until they have grown large enough to shade weeds out. Harvest branch tips sparingly in summer's high heat.

Additional Advice

To have fresh savory in winter, buy a seedling of winter savory and grow it indoors in a cool, sunny spot. Water often to keep the plant from drying out, but do not let it sit in a puddle.

Other Cultivars and Species

S. m. 'Nana' or 'Pygmaea' is a dwarf winter savory about 4 ft. tall, that looks charming in a wall garden.

Tarragon

arragon is a leafy, flavorful plant 1 to 2 ft. tall that in my garden comes back every 3 or 4 years. I suspect D.C. summer heat weakens it and winter finishes it off. Small, tightly-curled, whitish-green flowers appear in summer. The long, slim leaves have a delicate flavor, combining sweet anise and camphor and something unique to this plant. It is used in French and international cuisine and is an essential ingredient in fines' herbes for stocks and broths, Green Goddess Dressing, Sauce Bearnaise, and excellent with mushrooms, chicken, and fish. Tarragon wine vinegar is a favorite. The dried leaves scent potpourris and toilet water, and dried branches add a haunting sweetness to winter arrangements. Tarragon belongs in every herb collection, but only if you can find a rooted cutting of French tarragon. Taste before buying! Tarragon is best in an out-of-the-way place since it is rather weedy, or in the herb or vegetable garden. It thrives in containers. One or two plants will satisfy your needs. Harvest tip sprigs as needed in spring, more sparingly in summer heat. The leaves are thin and dry quickly in a microwave oven or on a screen.

WHEN TO PLANT

Set out seedlings in early spring. Since it can't be counted on, expect it to behave as an annual and plan to replant it every year.

WHERE TO PLANT

Tarragon will be most productive growing in full sun, or it will make do with 4 to 6 hours of sun. It can take a lot of heat and resists drought, so you can plant it in a place that is likely to be overlooked now and then.

HOW TO PLANT

Prepare the bed by digging in 2 in. of coarse sand or chicken grit, 1 in. of dried manure, and a slow-release 10-10-10 fertilizer, or your regular lawn fertilizer. In clay soil, add a small handful of gypsum and of superphosphate for each plant. Work the soil 8 to 12 in. deep. Tarragon does best in neutral soil, around pH 7.0. Set plants into the garden 6 to 8 in. apart and water well. Apply a 3-in. mulch starting 3 in. from the stem.

HOW TO PROVIDE CARE AND MAINTENANCE

Harvest tip sprigs often in spring to promote growth of tender branches—their leaves are the tastiest. To promote rapid, unchecked growth, for the next 2 or 3 weeks water often enough to sustain the soil moisture. After that, water deeply when you water the flower beds.

ADDITIONAL ADVICE

In late summer, pot tarragon in a clay container and bring a plant indoors for winter use. It will live for a time indoors in a cool, sunny spot, if you water often enough to keep it from drying out.

OTHER CULTIVARS AND SPECIES

Tarragon is a relative of true wormwood, *Artemisia absinthium*, which has medicinal uses, and of *A. abrotanum*, southernwood, which is a beautiful foliage plant with finely divided aromatic leaves lovely in the garden and in bouquets.

Thymus vulgaris

Thyme

he thymes are small, prostrate evergreen perennials with trailing branches 6 to 10 in. long. In early summer, they bear fuzzy clusters of florets in pale pink, white, or lilac. The tiny, dark-green leaves have a sharp flavor like an earthy mint that combines well with bay leaf, parsley, and onion in stuffings for pork, lamb, and in salads, soups, stews, and in creole dishes and gumbos. Parisians sprinkle thyme on steaks for broiling and herb fans brew it to make tea. The sweetest culinary thymes are *Thymus vulgaris* and its cultivars. Because the plants are not reliably winter hardy here, they sometimes are called 'summer thyme'. 'Wedgewood English' is an excellent taller form. The flavor of 'Orange Balsam' has a hint of citrus. Most thymes grow well between stepping stones and surging over garden walls
and in rock walls and they are pretty in hanging baskets. Two or three thymes will meet your needs. Harvest tip sprigs at will to use fresh. The leaves are so small they do not need to be minced—just bruised to release the flavor. Dry thyme branches on screens, strip the leaves, bottle, and cap.

WHEN TO PLANT

For early harvests, in early spring set out root divisions or seedlings. To harvest a lot of thyme for drying, sow seeds in mid-spring. By late summer, the crop will be ready. To multiply your holdings, divide well-established older plants in spring or early fall.

WHERE TO PLANT

A little noon shade is acceptable in the hottest parts of Virginia, but the flavor is best when thyme is growing in full sun. It dies out if it does not have enough sun. Thyme tolerates considerable drought and abuse, so it is one of the herbs that can be grown where it is likely to be neglected.

HOW TO PLANT

Prepare the bed by digging in 2 in. of coarse sand or chicken grit, and a slow-release 5-10-10 fertilizer. In clay soil, add a small handful of gypsum and of superphosphate for each plant. Thyme prefers soil that has a pH above 6.0. Unless your soil is pH 7.0 or higher, apply lime every second or third year. Work the soil 8 to 12 in. deep. Set plants into the garden 8 to 12 in. apart. Water with diluted fertilizer.

HOW TO PROVIDE CARE AND MAINTENANCE

To promote rapid, unchecked growth, for the next week or two water often enough to sustain the soil moisture. After that, water deeply during droughts. If you have planted seeds, weed around the seedlings until they have grown large enough to shade weeds out. Harvest thyme sparingly in summer's high heat.

ADDITIONAL ADVICE

Shear older plants back mercilessly in early spring and fertilize with a handful of a slow-release 10-10-10. In late summer, pot thyme in a clay container and bring it indoors to a cool, sunny spot. Water often enough to keep the soil from drying out. Thyme is evergreen here, and a mature plant will have enough foliage to allow sparing harvests during mild winters.

OTHER CULTIVARS AND SPECIES

Other good culinary species are *T.* × *citriodorus*, which has a hint of of lemon or orange, and caraway-flavored *T. herba-barona*. The decorative variegated cultivars, *T.* 'Argenteus' and 'Aureus', can be used in cooking. Between flagstones use creeping thymes, like 4-in.-high mother-of-thyme, *T. praecox*, and its subspecies, *T. p. arcticus*.

Ornamental Grasses

ONE TO TWELVE FEET TALL AND MORE, WINDBLOWN, UNTAMED, AND GRACEFUL, the ornamental grasses are the signature plants of today's strong trend toward naturalistic landscaping that requires little maintenance. Even so, your first exposure to ornamental grasses in the garden may leave you feeling, as it did me, that someone forgot to weed. But over the past ten years, I must confess that I have become a devoted fan. I love to see the new leaves unfurl as they push up from the crown of the plant after a late winter haircut. There is refreshment in the sound of wind whispering through grasses on hot summer days—a country sound especially welcome in a city garden. I am fascinated by the tall, willowy seedheads that develop late in the season and remain to grace the garden through fall and winter.

You'll be tempted to buy ornamental grass for its seedheads, but take into account several other elements before making choices. The first question to ask yourself is how the mature end-of-season height and width of the plant will fit into the site. Some are huge! The very tall grasses must be featured as specimens, with nearby plants chosen to complement them.

Also, consider the overall form of the plants. Some clump, some mound, and some fountain. The spectacular 10- to 12-ft. giant Chinese silver grass is very erect; 4- to 6-ft. maiden grass arches and the pennisetums arch over like a fountain. Consider, too, the texture of the leaves and their color during the growing season—fine, coarse, bold; bluish, greenish, reddish, gold.

Tall grasses are useful for screening, and do more for a bare masonry wall than a high-maintenance espalier. Clumps planted among native trees and shrubs create a handsome natural barrier between a dwelling, the road, and neighboring properties. The mid-height grasses planted with native wildflowers make a beautiful flowering meadow. They are the natural transition plant to a woodland or a water view. Low-growing grasses add movement, color, and contrasting texture to flower bed and pocket wild gardens.

Another vital statistic is whether the grass is a cool- or a warm-season plant. A cool-season grass shoots up in early winter soon after its annual haircut. It's a good choice for a position where it will be the main show year-round. Warm-season grasses begin to grow later, as the spring-flowering bulbs are going by. Choose a warm-season grass if you want a combination of grasses and flowers, and interplant it with spring-flowering bulbs that will bloom in sequence before, and while, the grass is growing up.

Ornamental grasses are handled very much the way perennial flowers are handled. But let the grasses remain uncut until late January, then cut them back to within a few inches of the crown. Like perennials, they begin to fill out the second season; but unlike perennials, they will not need to be divided for 8 to 10 years.

SOURCES

Some ornamental grasses are stocked by most garden centers, but for a wider choice, look to a mail-order specialist like Kurt Bluemel, Inc., 22740 Greene Lane, Baldwin, MD, 21013. Many appealing species are carried by André Viette Farm & Nursery, Route 1, Box 16, Fishersville, VA, 22939, and Milaeger's Gardens, 4838 Douglas Avenue, Racine, WI, 53402-2498. Seeds for some species are offered by W. Atlee Burpee & Co., Warminster, PA, 18974, and Park Seed Co., Cokesbury Road, Greenwood, SC, 29647-0001.

If you get as hooked as I am on grasses, you'll enjoy Carole Ottesen's book, *Ornamental Grasses/The Amber Wave*, published by McGraw-Hill. Carole offers excellent suggestions for using grasses in the landscape.

Blue Fescue

Blue fescue forms little rounded tufts 8 to 12 in. high of wiry, blue-green leaves that are evergreen in most Virginia winters. It is a cool-season grass that starts to grow soon after its January haircut and blooms in mid- to late spring. The flowers are loose, lacy panicles on stems that reach well above the foliage. The contrast between the relatively small, stiff clump and the thin gracefully arching and gently swaying flower stalks is charming. This grass is attractive used as edging for beds of shrubbery, walks, naturalized areas, and grass gardens. In a perennial border it adds contrasting texture and a welcome note of blue. *F. ovina* 'Sea Urchin' is an especially pretty cultivar that rarely needs dividing and is very long-lived. Blue fescue is sometimes used as ground cover, but I find the clumps too compact, and the foliage too stiff—it never seems quite comfortable in the role.

WHEN TO PLANT

Set out dormant, container-grown plants as soon as the ground can be worked in late winter. You can divide and replant this grass in fall, but not in summer—heat is not its friend.

WHERE TO PLANT

Plant blue fescue in full sun or in very bright shade. Without enough light, the blue will be less intense. Avoid damp spots. The foliage has a bluish-gray, waxy coat that protects it from evaporation, and wet feet can cause problems.

HOW TO PLANT

Dig roomy planting holes to which you have added 1/4 of coarse sand or chicken grit and an equal amount of compost, peat moss, chopped leaves, or other organic material. In clay soil, mix in a handful of gypsum and another of superphosphate for each plant. Set the plants high in the ground about 2 ft. apart. Water well. Mulch 2 in. deep around and between the plants.

How to Provide Care and Maintenance

Water a new planting every week or two the first season. The plant is fairly drought-resistant, so once it is established, local rainfall should be enough to keep it growing except during our mid- and late-August droughts. Allow the seedheads to ripen and stand through fall and winter. Towards the end of January, prune the plant back to the crown at ground level. Replenish the mulch until the plants have spread widely enough to shade out weeds.

Additional Advice

Blue fescue grows rapidly during cool weather, but in hot, dry periods it sulks. Do not try to force growth by watering or fertilizing. Wait for cool weather, and it will revive. Cut off the flower stalks when they begin to appear ragged. This grass benefits from division every few years.

Other Cultivars and Species

Festuca cinerea 'April Grun' is a beautiful green variety. *F. mairei*, Maire's fescue, is a pretty plant about 2 ft. tall with soft, grayish foliage. The flower is insignificant. *F. ovina* 'Elijah's Blue' forms a neat dome of blue-gray foliage that makes a fine edging or accent in a flower bed. 'Solling' withstands high heat without browning out.

Blue Oat Grass

OTHER PLANT NAME: Avena Grass

*B*lue oat grass is a lovely blue grass that is a little taller than the blue fescue. A cool-season grass that maintains its color through late winter, it starts growing very quickly after its early spring haircut, forming compact spiky tufts of striking silvery blue-green leaves 1½ to 2½ ft. high. In May, delicate, golden, oat-like flowers sway far above the foliage on graceful, erect or arching stems that extend 1 ft. or more beyond the foliage, swaying and bobbing in the wind. In summer, the flowerheads turn to a bright tan that contrasts beautifully with the foliage. This grass has many uses in the home landscape. Planted toward the middle of a large perennial border, it makes a colorful texture accent and it is beautiful massed and naturalized. I have seen it combined very effectively in wild gardens near the shore with silvery plants like artemisia, nepeta, and stachys.

WHEN TO PLANT

As soon as the ground can be worked in spring, set out container-grown plants or rooted divisions. You can divide and replant this grass in fall, but not in summer—heat is not its friend. Dig the crown, cut it apart, and replant the pieces.

WHERE TO PLANT

Plant blue oat grass in full sun or in bright shade. Without enough light, the blue will be less intense. Avoid damp spots; the foliage has a bluish-gray, waxy coat that protects it from evaporation, and wet feet can cause problems. In Zone 8, our southern shore region, avoid planting blue oat grass where it will be baked by high temperatures combined with strong sun and drying winds.

How to Plant

Helictotrichon prefers rich soil and succeeds in a wide pH range from acid 3.0 to neutral 7.0. Dig roomy planting holes and work into the soil from each hole 1/4 each of coarse sand and compost, peat moss, chopped leaves, or other acidic organic material, along with a small handful of slow-release 5-10-10 fertilizer. In clay soil, mix in a handful of gypsum and another of superphosphate for each plant. Set the plants high in the ground and about 2 ft. apart. Fill the hole, tamp the soil, and water well. Mulch 2 in. deep around and between the plants.

How to Provide Care and Maintenance

Water a new planting every week or two the first season. Once it is established, local rainfall should be enough to keep blue oat grass growing except during our mid- and late-August droughts. Allow the spikelets to ripen and stand through fall and winter. Towards the end of January, prune the plant back to the crown at ground level. Trim the plant back earlier if storms flatten the flower stems, or if it becomes less appealing.

Additional Advice

This plant grows rapidly during cool weather, but in hot, dry periods it may sulk. Do not try to force growth by watering or fertilizing. Wait for cool weather, and it will revive. Cut off the flower stalks when they begin to appear ragged. Replenish the mulch in late winter until the plants have spread widely enough to shade out weeds.

ORNAMENTAL GRASSES

Feather Reed Grass

'Stricta' is a medium-tall feather reed grass 4½ to 7 ft. high that creates a strong vertical effect—and is really showy. It is a cool-season grass that shoots right up after its winter haircut and remains attractive through hot summers. The seeds are sterile, so it never is invasive. This is one of the first ornamental grasses to bloom. Most of the spring the plant is a solid mass of medium- to dark-green foliage. By the time the late-blooming daffodils and the tulips have gone by, it is 4 ft. tall and starts to produce pale, feathery foot-long panicles of florets. Over the next weeks, the flowers evolve into erect, tan seedheads topping dark-green stems. With the coming of frost, the foliage fades to gold and platinum unless winter storms flatten the stems, and it remains handsome until it is cut back. I like this grass in mass plantings in a smaller landscape, as a specimen or a hedge against a masonry wall and interplanted among shrubs and evergreens. Its meadowy autumn golds are beautiful backing black-eyed Susans, sedum 'Autumn Glory', pale and dark-purple asters, boltonia, and fronting taller varieties of *Miscanthus*.

WHEN TO PLANT

Set out dormant, container-grown plants as soon as the ground can be worked in late winter. You can divide and replant this grass in fall, but not in summer—heat is not its friend.

WHERE TO PLANT

Plant 'Stricta' in full sun or in the bright shade of a tall tree or a building. Without enough light it will flop over. Though it thrives where its roots are fairly moist, once established it tolerates dry soil, rich or poor, as long as it is well drained.

HOW TO PLANT

Provide generous planting holes to which you have added ¼ coarse sand or chicken grit and an equal amount of compost, peat moss, chopped leaves, or other organic material, along with a handful of slow-release 5-10-10 fertilizer. In clay soil, mix in a handful of gypsum and another of superphosphate for each plant. A pH range of between 6.0 and 7.0 suits this grass. Set the plants high in the ground and about 2 ft. apart. Water well. Mulch 2 in. deep around and between the plants.

How to Provide Care and Maintenance

Water a new planting every week or two the first season. The plant is fairly drought-resistant, so once it is established local rainfall should be enough to keep it growing, except during our mid- and late-August droughts. Allow the seedheads to ripen and stand through fall and winter. Towards the end of January, prune the plant back to the crown at ground level. Trim the plant back earlier if storms flatten the stems, or if it becomes less appealing. Replenish the mulch.

Additional Advice

Calamagrostis grows rapidly during cool weather, but in hot, dry periods it may sulk. Do not try to force growth by watering or fertilizing. Wait for cool weather, and it will revive. The plants will not need dividing for 8 to 10 years or more. When they do, dig the crowns, and chop them apart with an ax.

Other Cultivars and Species

Calamagrostis × *acutiflora* 'Karl Foerster' is 5 to 6 ft. tall and a good choice for a small landscape. *C. a.* 'Overdam' has arching, white-striped foliage about 1 ft. high. Its flowers are 3-ft. pink plumes that age to gold. It requires some shade in hot regions.

ORNAMENTAL GRASSES

Japanese Blood Grass

'*R*ed Baron' produces a 12- to 18-in.-high stand of coarse grass that grows upright and is rather spiky. Its gift to the garden is leaf tops that are wine-red all season, then become blood-red in fall. The red is reddest when the plants are backlighted by the sun. This is a warm-season grass that starts to regrow only toward mid-spring; then it heads up very quickly, produces unremarkable flowers, and peaks during the dog days of late August. It can stand a lot of heat. The plants become established slowly and spread at a moderate rate. Like other grasses that start growing only as the weather warms, it is nice interplanted with medium to tall spring-flowering bulbs that screen the dormant stubble, and are in turn screened as they age
and the grass starts to grow. I like Japanese blood grass edging a bed of grasses, leading into a naturalized area, and as ground cover in an informal landscape. An interesting grouping is Japanese blood grass planted with low-growing textured plants such as leather-leaved bur-gundy bergenia, and fuzzy, silvery stachys. An attractive companion is the golden-leaved meadow foxtail, *Alopecurus pratensis* 'Aureus'.

When to Plant

Set out container-grown plants or root divisions in mid-spring. To multiply, divide the plants before new growth begins. Lift and gently break or cut the clump apart, giving each section at least one growing point.

Where to Plant

Japanese blood grass is most colorful when it receives direct sun at least part of the day, but it will grow well in light shade. In the hottest areas of Virginia, at the shore near the border to North Carolina, it may do better in semi-sun. Though it needs fairly con-stant moisture, Japanese blood grass also requires good drainage, so avoid planting it in soggy places.

How to Plant

Prepare the planting bed by digging in 2 to 4 in. (for very heavy soils) each of coarse sand or chicken grit and humusy compost. Add a light application of a slow-release 5-10-10 fertilizer. Japanese blood grass prefers soils in the neutral range, 6.0 to 7.5, so avoid acidic humus such as peat moss. In clay soil, mix in a handful of gypsum and another of superphosphate for each plant. Space the plants 12 to 18 in. apart and set them high in the ground. Water well. Mulch 2 in. deep around and between the plants.

How to Provide Care and Maintenance

Water a new planting every week or two the first season. To keep the grass thriving, maintain soil moisture at the roots and let the surface dry between waterings. This warm-season grass will start new growth only when winter is over, so wait until early spring to cut the plant back to ground level. Trim the plant back earlier if storms flatten the stems or it becomes less appealing. Replenish the mulch in late winter until the plants have spread widely enough to shade out weeds.

Additional Advice

Japanese blood grass requires moist soil, so even after the plants are established and spreading, water when late-summer drought stresses your flowers.

Red Plume Fountain Grass

*T*hough classed as hardy in Zone 6, red plume fountain grass may not survive winters in the cooler parts of Virginia. The maroon-red foliage and rose-tan flowers are so beautiful that I recommend you grow it as an annual if it does not live through winters in your area. The plant begins to grow after winter cold has ended. By early summer, it is a loose fountain of arching leaves that are plum-wine-rose in color and 3 to 4 ft. long. In July, flowering stems rise, topped by slender, rose-tan foxtails that nod and toss in the breeze. Exceptionally graceful and beautiful in flower, it is lovely in winter when it blanches to the color of silvery wheat. Red plume fountain grass sprawls, so it needs lots of space all around. A single plant makes an impressive show—a trio is spectacular. You can use it in gardens of large perennials for texture and color. Position it so the new growth will camouflage yellowing bulb foliage and fill spaces left empty as poppies and other spring perennials go by. In an urn it is regal, graceful, and smaller because the root growth is restricted.

WHEN TO PLANT

Set out container-grown plants in mid-spring as the ground begins to warm. Divide and replant this grass in early spring before heat comes. Heat is hard on it. Dig the crown, cut it apart, and replant.

WHERE TO PLANT

Red plume fountain grass is fullest, more colorful, and most beautiful growing in a spot that receives 6 hours direct sun daily. In less light, it will sprawl more and have less color.

HOW TO PLANT

Provide generous planting holes and good drainage. A pH range of between 6.0 and 7.0 suits it well. Work into the soil 1/4 each of coarse sand and of compost, peat moss, chopped leaves, or other organic material, along with a handful of slow-release 5-10-10 fertilizer. In clay soil mix in a handful gypsum and another of superphosphate for each plant. For ground cover, space the plants 2 to 3 ft. apart. If they are to be seen as specimens, allow 3 ft. all around. Set the plants high in the ground and water well. Mulch 2 in. deep around and between the plants.

HOW TO PROVIDE CARE AND MAINTENANCE

Water a new planting every week the first season. Once established, local rainfall should be enough to keep it growing except during droughts. But it prefers a damp soil surface, and if it goes dry for days on end, it will be less beautiful. Allow the seedheads to ripen and stand through fall and winter. This is a warm-season grass that will start new growth only when winter is over, so wait until late winter to cut the plant back to ground level. Trim the plant back earlier if storms flatten the stems, or it becomes less appealing.

ADDITIONAL ADVICE

Replenish the mulch in late winter until the plants have spread widely enough to shade out weeds.

OTHER CULTIVARS AND SPECIES

Pennisetum alopecuroides 'Hameln' and 'Weserbergland' are small, graceful cultivars 2 to 3 ft. tall that are used a ground cover where they are hardy. Like the species, these have green foliage and tan-gold foxtails.

Silver Grass

*M*iscanthus species are big grasses with broad, gracefully arching leaves. They start up slowly in spring and then grow tall rapidly. In late summer and fall, they produce tall, silky plumes. With cold weather, the foliage and the plumes turn to silver and tan. They are among the most beautiful of the grasses in winter. A cultivar I find attractive in the home garden is the fine-textured maiden grass, *Miscanthus sinensis* 'Gracillimus', which reaches 4 to 6 ft. in height. The long, narrow, curly leaves have a prominent white midvein. The flowers are at first reddish-pink, then turn silvery-white in autumn on curly branching panicles. Considered by some the most elegant of all the grasses, it is a frequent subject of Japanese brush artists. Red silver grass, *M. sinensis* 'Purpurascens', is a compact form 3 to 4 ft. tall that turns red, orange, and gold in fall and buff in winter. Including variegated *Miscanthus* in a large garden adds color and interest. Two of the best are *M. s.* 'Variegatus', whose leaves have a creamy stripe down the middle, and 'Zebrinus', whose leaves have crosswise stripes in green and gold.

WHEN TO PLANT

Set out container-grown plants in mid-spring as soon as the ground begins to warm. To multiply, divide before new growth begins. Lift and gently separate the clump, giving each section at least one growing point.

WHERE TO PLANT

Most *Miscanthus* species grow best in a minimum of 6 hours of direct sun, but some, including 'Gracillimus', though they will not be as full, make do with 2 to 3 hours of direct sun or the bright shade under tall trees. Miscanthus thrives where the roots have a constant supply of moisture, but established plantings sustain their growth in drier soil.

HOW TO PLANT

Miscanthus needs well-drained soil and thrives in soil that provides sustained moisture. Dig large planting holes and work into the soil from each hole 1/4 each of coarse sand or chicken grit and of compost, peat moss, chopped leaves, or other organic material. Add a handful of slow-release 10-6-4 fertilizer. In clay soil, mix in a handful of gypsum and another of superphosphate for each plant. Set the plants high in the ground. Plant with 3 to 4 ft. between the centers. Fill the holes, tamp the soil, and water well. Mulch 2 in. deep around and between the plants.

HOW TO PROVIDE CARE AND MAINTENANCE

Water a new planting every week or two the first season. Once established, some species can do with less moisture. Allow the seedheads to ripen and stand through fall and winter. *Miscanthus* is a warm-season grass that will start new growth only when winter is over, so wait until early spring, or until the plant becomes unsightly, to cut it back to ground level.

ADDITIONAL ADVICE

Replenish the mulch in late winter until the plants have spread widely enough to shade out weeds. Water during droughts until the plants are fully matured.

OTHER CULTIVARS AND SPECIES

Miscanthus sacchariflorus 'Strictus', porcupine grass, is an upright, yellow-banded, 5-ft. plant that is used as an accent plant. *M. sinensis* 'Yaku Jima', silver grass, is a beautiful compact dwarf 2 to 3 ft. high which has delicate, narrow leaves. 'Silverfeather' and 'Morning Light', which get to be 6 to 9 ft. tall, can handle more drought than most other species.

Virginia is a state where wonderful gardens have flourished for 400 years, and a wonderful state for gardening in general, with almost four seasons.

The
Gardener
who plans
reaps
the
Greatest
Reward

COOL
SPRINGS
PRESS

The Virginia Gardener's Guide
Photographic gallery of featured plants

Abelia
Abelia x grandiflora

Ageratum
Ageratum houstonianum

Alabama Fothergilla
Fothergilla major

American Beech
Fagus grandifolia

American Holly
Ilex opaca

American Sweet Gum
Liquidambar styraciflua

American Yellowwood
Cladrastis lutea

Armeria
Armeria maritima

Artemisia 'Silver King'
Artemisia ludoviciana

Aster
Aster x frikartii

Astilbe
Astilbe x arendsii

Autumn Crocus
Colchicum autumnale

Azalea
Rhododendron sp.

Bachelor's Buttons
Centaurea cyanus 'Alba'

Barberry
Berberis thunbergii

Basil
Ocimum basilicum

Bearberry, Kinnikinick
Arctostaphylos uva-ursi

Bergenia
Bergenia cordifolia

Black Gum
Nyssa sylvatica

Blue Atlas Cedar
Cedrus atlantica 'Glauca'

Blue Bugle
Ajuga genevensis

Blue False Indigo
Baptisia australis

Blue Fescue
Festuca ovina 'Glauca'

Blue Lobelia
Lobelia erinus

Blue Oat Grass
Helictotrichon sempervirens

Blue Salvia Splendens
Salvia farinacea

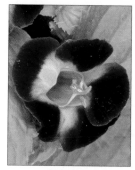

Bluewings
Torenia fournieri

Boston Ivy
Parthenocissus tricuspidata

Boxwood
Buxus sempervirens

Burning Bush
Kochia scoparia

Busy Lizzy
Impatiens sp.

Butterfly Bush
Buddleia davidii

Callery Pear
Pyrus calleryana

Carolina Hemlock
Tsuga caroliniana

Carolina Jessamine
Gelsemium sempervirens

Carolina Silverbell
Halesia tetraptera

Carpet Bugle
Ajuga reptans

Chaste Tree
Vitex agnus-castus

Chinese Balloonflower
Platycodon grandiflorus

Chives
Allium schoenoprasum

Climbing Hydrangea
Hydrangea petiolaris

Climbing Roses
Rosa sp.

Coleus
Solenostemon scuttellarioides

Columbine
Aquilegia

**Coneflower,
Black-eyed Susan**
Rudbeckia fulgida var. *sullivantii*

Coral Bells
Heuchera sp.

**Coral or Everblooming
Honeysuckle**
Lonicera x *heckrottii*

Cosmos Ladybird Mix
Cosmos sulphureus
'Ladybird MIx'

Cotoneaster
Cotoneaster dammeri

Crabapple
Malus sp.

Crape Myrtle
Lagerstroemia indica

Creeping Jenny
Lysimachia nummularia

Creeping Juniper 'Blue Rug'
Juniperus horizontalis 'Wiltonii'

Creeping Thyme
Thymus praecox
subsp. *arcticus*

Crocus
Crocus

Daffodil
Narcissus sp.

Daylily 'Stella De Oro'
Hemerocallis cv.

Dead Nettle
Lamium maculatum

Dill
Anethum graveolens

Dogwood
Cornus florida

Double Weeping Flowering Cherry
Prunus subhirtella
'Pendula Plena Rosea'

Dwarf Mondo Grass
Ophiopogon japonicus

Dwarf Winged Spindle Tree
Euonymus alatus 'Compacta'

Eastern Red Cedar
Juniperus virginiana

Elephant's-ear
Alocasia plumbea

English Ivy
Hedera helix

English Lavender
Lavandula angustifolia

Eulalia
*Miscanthus
sinensis* 'Gracillimus'

European Hornbeam
Carpinus betulus

Feather Reed Grass
Calamagrostis acutiflora

Firethorn
Pyracantha coccinea

Flowering Quince
Chaenomeles speciosa
'Cameo'

Flowering Tobacco
Nicotiana

Forsythia
Forsythia x *intermedia*

Foster Holly
Ilex x *attenuata* 'Fosteri'

Foxglove
Digitalis purpurea

Fragrant Viburnum
Viburnum x *carlcephalum*

Garden Roses
Rosa sp.

Garden Verbena
Verbena x *hybrida*

Ginkgo
Ginkgo biloba

Globe Thistle
Echinops ritro

Golden Hinoki Cypress
Chamaecyparis obtusa
'Crippsii'

Ground Cover Roses
Rosa x 'Pink Meidiland'

Heavenly Bamboo
Nandina domestica

Hedge Roses
Rosa

Holly Olive, Chinese Olive
Osmanthus heterophyllus

Hosta
Hosta

House Geranium
Pelargonium x *hortorum*

Hyacinth Bean
Lablab purpureus

Hybrid Teas
Rosa hybrid

Italian Oregano
Origanum vulgare
subsp. *hirtum*

Jackman's Clematis
Clematis x *jackmanii*

Japanese Anemone
Anemone hupehensis
var. *japonica*

Japanese Blood Grass
Imperata cylindrica
'Red Baron'

Japanese Maple
Acer palmatum

Japanese Pagoda Tree
Sophora japonica

Japanese Spirea
Spiraea japonica 'Bumalda'

Japanese Wisteria
Wisteria floribunda

Japanese Zelkova
Zelkova serrata

Koi
Cyprinus carpio

Lacebark Pine
Pinus bungeana

Lemon Grass
Cymbopogon citratus

Leyland Cypress
x *Cupressocyparis leylandii*

Lily Turf
Liriope muscari

Lotus
Nelumbo

Marigold
Tagetes

Miniatures
Rosa

Mock Orange
Philadelphus coronarius

Moonflower
Ipomoea alba

Mountain Laurel
Kalmia latifolia

Mountain Silverbell
Halesia monticola

Myrtle
Vinca minor

Northern Red Oak
Quercus rubra

Oakleaf Hydrangea
Hydrangea quercifolia

Old Garden Roses
Rosa sp.

Oriental Bittersweet
Celastrus orbiculatus

Oriental Poppy
Papaver orientale

Oriental Spruce
Picea orientalis

Ornamental Cabbage or Kale
Brassica oleracea
Acephala Group

Ornamental Peppers
Capsicum annuum

Palace Purple
Heuchera hybrid

Pansy
Viola x wittrockiana

Paperbark Maple
Acer griseum

Parsley
Petroselinum crispum

Peegee Hydrangea
Hydrangea paniculata
'Grandiflora'

Peony
Paeonia sp.

Petunia
Petunia x hybrida

Pinks
Dianthus sp.

Pink Vinca
Catharanthus roseus

Pin Oak
Quercus palustris

Plumbago
Ceratostigma plumbaginoides

Purple Coneflower
Echinacea purpurea

Pyramid Bugle
Ajuga pyramidalis

Redbud
Cercis canadensis

Red Hot Poker
Kniphofia uvaria

Red Plume Fountain Grass
Pennisetum alopecuroides

Redtip Photinia
Photinia x fraseri

Rhododendron
Rhododendron

River Birch
Betula nigra

Rock Rose
Portulaca grandiflora

Rose Mallow
Hibiscus moscheutos

Rosemary
Rosmarinus officinalis

Rose of Sharon
Hibiscus syriacus

Sage
Salvia officinalis

Sasanqua Camellia
Camellia sasanqua

Scarlet Sage
Salvia splendens

Sea Holly
Eryngium alpinum

Serviceberry
Amelanchier arborea

Serviceberry
Amelanchier canadensis

Shasta Daisy
Leucanthemum x superbum

Siberian Iris
Iris sibirica

Silver Edge Pachysandra
Pachysandra terminalis

Snapdragon
Antirrhinum majus

Sneezeweed
Helenium autumnale

Sourwood
Oxydendrum arboreum

Spearmint
Mentha spicata

Stone Crop
Sedum sp.

Strawflower
Helichrysum bracteatum

Sumac
Rhus sp.

Summer Savory
Satureja hortensis

Southern Blue Flag
Iris virginica

Swamp Maple
Acer rubrum

Sweet Alyssum
Lobularia maritima

Sweet Bay
Magnolia virginiana

Sweet Pea
Lathyrus odoratus

Sweetspire
Itea virginica

Tarragon
Artemisia dracunculus

Tickseed
Coreopsis verticillata

Trumpet Vine
Campsis radicans

Tulip Poplar
Liriodendron tulipifera

Variegated Euonymus
Euonymus fortunei 'Gracilis'

**Variegated Japanese
Silver Grass**
Miscanthus sinensis 'Variegatus'

Veronica
Veronica austriaca
ssp. *teucrium*

Viburnum
Viburnum x *burkwoodii*

Virginia Creeper
Parthenocissus quinquefolia

Virginia Witch-hazel
Hamamelis virginiana

Water Lily
Nymphaea sp.

Wax Leaf Begonia
Begonia semperflorens

White Fir
Abies concolor

White Fringe Tree
Chionanthus virginicus

White Snowflakes
Nymphoides cristata

White Water Snowflake
Hydrocleys nymphoides

Willow Oak
Quercus phellos

Winterberry
Ilex verticillata

Winter Jasmine
Jasminum nudiflorum

Yarrow
Achillea sp.

Zebra Grass
Miscanthus sinensis 'Zebrinus'

Zinnia
Zinnia elegans

Nourish the earth, and Virginia will fulfill your most cherished garden dreams.

CHAPTER EIGHT

Perennials

$\mathcal{P}$ERENNIALS ARE FLOWERING PLANTS THAT GROW FROM FIBROUS ROOTSTOCK developed from seeds, or from root or crown divisions. The crown is the upper portion of the rootstock from which stems grow. These are the flowers that come back—some for one year or two, some for three or four or five. The longest lived of all perennials is the peony. The perennials I've recommended here will survive Virginia winters.

I especially appreciate perennials borders that include aromatic herbs, the dancing, whispering grasses, and plants featuring beautiful foliage, like the foliage of the irises and heuchera. Foliage plants hold the color theme after the flowers go by. Two lovely blue foliage plants are blue oat grass and the dainty blue-green 'Jackman's Blue'. A combination that lightens and harmonizes the design is low-growing, fuzzy, white-splashed pineapple mint and silver variegated thyme backed by the grassy leaves of striped dwarf bamboo, with tall variegated silver grass behind.

In selecting perennials, keep in mind that within a species' stated period of bloom, there are varieties that will come into flower early, mid-season, or late. In cool Virginia hill country, late-blooming varieties of spring-flowering species are those likely to avoid frostbite. When it comes to perennials that bloom late in the season, early-blooming varieties are likely to avoid early frosts.

A few perennials will bloom the first year from seed sown in the garden, but most will flower only during their second year. A vigorous container-grown root division or second-year seedling planted in early spring will bloom that summer. If the perennial that you are interested in blooms in early or mid-spring—columbine, for example—you'll get better flowering if you set out a container-grown specimen in early fall than if you plant it in early spring.

Chapter Eight

Some catalogs ship perennials in spring, "bare root," with planting instructions —astilbes, for instance. In my experience, these often flower fully only in the second season.

Perennials can be grown from seed sown indoors in flats usually four to six weeks or more before transplanting time—which is after all danger of frost is past. Annuals usually germinate within 20 days, but seeds for perennials may take quite a bit longer, though a few may sprout right away. Keep seeded flats watered two, and even three months, to give all a chance to develop.

Perennials can also be started from seed sown in the garden, either in spring two weeks after the last frost date, or in summer or fall, up to two months before the first frost date. When fall sowing is recommended, it means those seeds will benefit from a chilling period, as many perennials do.

In early winter, a healthy practice is to clear the flower beds of collapsed foliage that will grow slimy after frost. Plants whose structures remain upright, like black-eyed Susans, should be left for their winter interest, and so the seedheads can feed the birds and reseed the garden. Don't pull off dead foliage, because that may damage the crown: cut it off. In spring when you clean up the perennial beds, be careful not to damage burgeoning stems while raking through perennials such as lilies.

To remain productive, most perennials must be divided and replanted every four or five years. Some need dividing more often—garden mums, for example. The rule is to divide spring-flowering perennials a month before the ground will freeze in fall, or before new growth begins in early spring. Divide autumn-flowering perennials, such as chrysanthemums, in spring before any sign of growth appears. A plant will signal when it needs dividing as the stems become crowded and leggy, and there are fewer and smaller blooms.

Artemisia 'Silver King'

*T*he artemisias are superb perennials planted for the silver
foliage that brightens early spring borders and lightens the green
and plum tones of fall and winter. They are lovely growing among
flowers in hues of pink and blue, and in collections of yellow or
orange flowers. Their small yellow or white flowers are not important.
One of the most popular is 'Silver King' artemisia, *A. ludoviciana*
variety *albula*, which will grow to 2 or 3 ft. tall, but can be pinched
back to contain the height. The leaves are finely cut and fragrant and
have a hint of red in fall and winter. The slightly shorter 'Silver Queen'
has jagged, bolder foliage. For the front of the garden and for edging,
a better plant is 12-in.-high 'Silver Mound' artemisia, *A. schmidtiana*.
The foliage is soft, feathery and silver-gray with a touch of green. This
particular artemisia suffers in summer heat. If the clump opens at the
center and flops by midsummer, cut the stems to the ground. It does
very well in dry, sandy places. *A.* 'Powis Castle' is somewhat taller, a
soft silky clump of foliage 1½ to 2 ft. tall.

WHEN TO PLANT

Plant strongly growing seedlings, or root divisions, in early spring.
Mature plants that are still near-dormant or just beginning to grow
will give the best performance. You can also set out container-grown
plants after they become dormant in fall.

WHERE TO PLANT

The artemisias do well in full sun in the cooler reaches of Virginia
(Zone 6), but elsewhere they do better in bright shade, and benefit
from protection from hot noon sun. Artemisias tolerate drought, but
cannot stand soil that is soggy in winter, so avoid damp, low-lying
areas where the soil alternately freezes and thaws.

HOW TO PLANT

Dig a hole about twice the size of the rootball. Place 2-in. layers of
coarse sand or chicken grit, and of leaf mold or sphagnum peat
moss in the hole. Add a slow-release 5-10-10 fertilizer. In clay soil,
work in a small handful of gypsum, and of superphosphate.

Unwind the roots circling the root ball. Half fill each hole with diluted fertilizer, set the plant a little higher than ground level, and press the crown down into ground. Fill the hole, watering to settle the soil. Provide a permanent 2-in. mulch starting a few inches from the main stem.

HOW TO PROVIDE CARE

Once the plant shows signs of new growth, to encourage branching, pinch out the top 3 to 4 in. of the lead stems. Water a new planting every week the first season unless you have a good soaking rain. The artemisias are drought resistant, so once established, local rainfall should be enough to keep them growing except during our mid- and late August droughts. In hot, humid areas artemisia foliage may die back in midsummer. Prune it away to promote new growth.

ADDITIONAL ADVICE FOR CARE

In late winter or early spring, fertilize by scratching a slow-release 10-10-10 fertilizer into the soil at half the rate recommended on the container, and water in well. Replenish the mulch. Remove ragged older stems. Every 3 or 4 years—or if the plant becomes less productive—divide it in very early spring or late summer.

ADDITIONAL CULTIVARS AND SPECIES

White mugwort, *A. lactiflora*, a species 4 to 5 ft. tall and handsome at the back of the border, bears creamy white, plumed flowers that last into fall. The dark green leaves are paler underneath. It usually needs staking.

Aster

hough there are spring-blooming asters, the varieties that
bloom late when the brightest of the summer flowers are gone
are the most appreciated. The plant is a 2- to 3-ft. leafy bush that
makes a good green filler, handsome at the back or front of a small
border even before it comes into bloom. The small daisy-like blossoms
are borne singly or in sprays, and they cover the plants with blue, dark
purple, lavender, pink, rosy red, or white—colors that are beautiful
with fall russet, golds and crimsons. One of the most popular asters in
Virginia is the beautiful hybrid *A. × frikartii*. Two of the best cultivars
are 'Wonder of Staffa', a handsome plant with big, clear lavender-blue
flowers, and 'Monch', with darker blue flowers. It flowers later and is
considered the finest. *A. × frikartii* and its cultivars are somewhat
mildew-resistant. Insist on mildew-resistant varieties if you live in an
area prone to mildew. Sprays of asters are superb in fresh arrangements, and they dry nicely, too.

WHEN TO PLANT

For bloom this year, plant sturdily growing seedlings.

WHERE TO PLANT

Asters flower best growing in full sun or bright shade. They tolerate
drought but cannot stand soil that is soggy in winter. Avoid damp
low-lying areas where the soil alternately freezes and thaws. Asters
do best in somewhat acidic soil—pH 5.5 to 6.5.

HOW TO PLANT

Prepare the bed by digging in 1 in. of coarse sand or chicken grit,
2 in. of humus, and a slow release 5-10-5 fertilizer. In clay soil, add
a very small handful of gypsum and of superphosphate for each
plant. Work the soil 6 to 8 in. deep. Mark planting holes 12 in. apart.
Half fill each hole with diluted fertilizer, and plant the seedlings.
Press the soil down around the stem of each seedling firmly enough
so the plant resists a tug. Water with a diluted fertilizer solution.
Provide a permanent 2-in. mulch of pine needles, or rotted leaf mold
starting a few inches from the crown.

How to Provide Care

Pinch the shoot tips back 2 to 3 in. once in spring, and again a month later to keep the plants stocky, and avoid the need to stake. Taller types may need staking to stand upright. Water a new plant every week the first season unless you have a good soaking rain. Once established, local rainfall should be enough to keep it growing except during our mid- and late August droughts. Deadhead asters after the first flush of blooming. Some will rebloom until it frosts.

Additional Advice for Care

After the ground freezes—around Christmas—provide a winter mulch of evergreen boughs. In late winter or early spring, fertilize by scratching a slow-release 5-10-10 fertilizer into the soil at half the rate recommended on the container, and water it in. Replenish the mulch. Every 2 or 3 years—or if the plant becomes less productive—in spring discard the main section and replant the outer portions.

Additional Cultivars and Species

You will find pink and other attractive colors among cultivars of the tall New England aster, *A. novae-angliae* 'Alma Potschke', which bears rose-pink flowers on 3 ft. stems, is a striking plant. 'Harrington's Pink' is an unusual salmon-pink, and comes into bloom late in the season.

Astilbe

*T*he shade-loving astilbes are beautiful feathery plants that flower
for 4 to 6 weeks in late spring and summer. The spikelike plumes
are composed of masses of small florets in shades from palest pink
and coral to bright red and creamy white. Most cultivars are 1¹/₂ to
3 or 5 ft. tall, and there are dwarfs suited to the rock gardens. The
deeply cut green or bronzed ferny foliage is attractive both before and
after flowering and is a good filler for the middle or back of the border. Massed, astilbes in a range of colors make a tapestry of color. The
cut flowers are lasting and dry well. Some of the best astilbes are cultivars of *Astilbe × arendsii*. Early, 2-ft. tall 'Fanal' is a very popular plant
with bronze leaves and red flowers. 'Deutschland', a 2-ft. creamy
white, is early, as is 3-ft. orchid-pink 'Cattleya', one of the best.
'Ostrich Plume' is a 3-ft. bright pink that flowers at mid-season.

WHEN TO PLANT

Mail-order catalogs generally ship astilbe as bare root crowns in
early spring. Follow their instructions for planting. Bare root crowns
are not always successful. I recommend instead setting out container-
grown crowns in mid-spring or late summer.

WHERE TO PLANT

Astilbe grows best in light shade in rich, moist humusy soil. In full
sun, it can succeed if the soil contains a lot of humus and is never
allowed to dry out. It tolerates drought but cannot stand soil that is
soggy in winter, so avoid damp low-lying areas where the soil alternately freezes and thaws. Astilbe tolerates a wide range of soil types
but seems to prefer a slightly acid pH.

HOW TO PLANT

For a container plant, dig a hole about twice the size of the rootball
and 4 in. deeper. Place 2-in. layers of coarse sand or chicken grit
and leaf mold or sphagnum peat moss in the hole and add a slow-
release 10-6-4 fertilizer. In clay soil, work in a small handful of
gypsum, and of superphosphate. Unwind roots circling the rootball.
Half fill each hole with diluted fertilizer, set the plant an inch higher
than ground level, and press the crown into the ground to bring it a

little above ground level. Fill the hole, watering to settle the soil. Provide a permanent 2-in. mulch of pine needles, or rotted leaf mold, starting a few inches from the crown.

How to Provide Care

Water astilbe plants every week unless you have a good soaking rain. The keys to success—particularly in the warmer reaches of Virginia—are sustained moisture and summer mulches. Fertilize lightly after the first real frost.

Additional Advice for Care

In early spring, scratch a small handful of 10-6-4 fertilizer into the soil around each plant before growth starts, or broadcast 10-6-4 at the rate of 10 to 20 pounds for each 1,000 square ft. Replenish the mulch. Every 3 to 4 years, divide the crowns any time from early spring to August.

Additional Cultivars and Species

In summer and early fall when the popular *A. × arendsii* cultivars have gone out of bloom, the little Chinese astilbes, *A. chinensis*, raise their tall mauve-pink flowerheads. Eight to 12 or 16 in. tall, these charming plants spread rapidly by underground stolons and are very attractive as an edging or ground cover.

PERENNIALS

Balloon Flower

OTHER COMMON NAME: Chinese Bellflower

*T*he balloon flower is an old-fashioned, graceful, and easy perennial. It is one of the best summer bloomers and a good choice where the somewhat similar campanula fails in our hot summers. This outstanding 1- to 2-ft. tall variety produces distinctive balloon-shaped buds along wand-like stems and they open to starry, blue, white or lilac-pink flowers up to 2 in. across. It blooms freely from early summer to early fall and has glossy foliage. The variety 'Apoyama' has violet flowers on plants 15 to 18 in. tall, and is very attractive planted with herbs. The Fuji series, a Japanese strain, is one of the best for the cutting garden. As a cut flower, it's long lasting if the stems are seared before they're put in water. In a test conducted in Zones 7 to 8 over a 5-year period, both at the shore and 600 ft. from the ocean, the balloon flower gave an excellent performance. It was grown in pure sand with Osmocote and fertilized once yearly. The plantings were deeply watered three times each month June through October, but not at all November through May.

WHEN TO PLANT

Sow seeds in early to mid-spring, mark the place, and be patient. Balloon flower is one of the last flowers to come up. As an alternative, any time after the ground can be worked in spring, set out container-grown plants or root divisions.

WHERE TO PLANT

Balloon flower succeeds in full sun in the cooler regions of Zone 6 and in semi-sun in Zones 7 and 8. It needs well-drained soil and does well in dry city conditions and by the shore.

HOW TO PLANT

Dig into the soil, or into a hole about twice the size of the rootball and 6 in. deeper, a 3-in. layer of coarse sand or chicken grit and a add a slow-release 5-10-10 fertilizer. In clay soil, work in a small handful of gypsum and of superphosphate. Sow seeds following package instructions. Or, mark planting holes for seedlings 6 to 8 in.

apart around a system of soaker hoses. Divide plants in flats with a sharp, clean knife, giving each a good root system. Half fill each hole with diluted fertilizer, plant the seedling high, and press the soil down around the stem firmly enough so the plant resists a tug. Water with a diluted fertilizer solution. Provide a permanent 2-in. mulch starting a few inches from the crown.

How to Provide Care

Water a new plant every week the first season unless you have a good soaking rain. Balloon flower is drought resistant, so once it's established, local rainfall will be enough to keep it growing. After the first flush of bloom, fertilize again. Deadhead to promote flowering.

Additional Advice for Care

In late winter or early spring, fertilize by scratching a slow-release 5-10-10 fertilizer into the soil and water it in. Replenish the mulch. Balloon flower rarely needs dividing.

Blue False Indigo

OTHER COMMON NAMES: Plains False Indigo, Wild Blue Indigo

*T*his is a vigorous 3- to 4-ft. tall plant that emerges early in spring, producing masses of attractive gray-green foliage that quickly becomes a small-size bush. It is topped in early summer by 1- to 2-ft. spikes of magnificent indigo-blue flowers which last about a month. They will remind you of lupines. The individual flowers look like the flowers on a pea vine but are much larger, showier and substantial. Black decorative seed pods 1 or 2 in. long follow the flowers and usually remain until at least the first hard frost when the plant is cut back to the crown. The seeds are fresh when they first start to rattle around in the pod. If you wish to start the plant from seed, it must be with fresh seeds. Blue false indigo creates strong vertical lines at the middle back of a large flowering border.

WHEN TO PLANT

Fresh seeds sprout easily in late summer, but setting out root divisions in early spring is far easier. It also assures the color you want. Plants that are still near-dormant or just beginning to grow will give the best performance. You can also set out plants after they become dormant in fall.

WHERE TO PLANT

Blue false indigo really needs full sun, but it can take a little filtered shade and still be very productive. In partial shade it probably will require staking. It tolerates drought but cannot stand soil that is soggy in winter, so avoid damp low-lying areas where the soil alternately freezes and thaws. Blue false indigo thrives in humusy somewhat acid soil, pH range 5.5 to 6.5.

How to Plant

Dig into a hole about twice the size of the rootball and 4 in. deeper, 2-in. layers of coarse sand or chicken grit and leaf mold or sphagnum peat moss. Add a slow-release 5-10-10 fertilizer. In clay soil, work in a small handful of gypsum and of superphosphate. Unwind roots circling the rootball. Set the plants 24 in. apart. Half fill each hole with diluted fertilizer, set the plant an inch or two higher than ground level, and press the crown down into ground to bring it an inch above ground level. Fill the hole, watering to settle the soil. Provide a permanent 2-in. mulch of pine needles or rotted leaf mold, starting a few inches from the crown.

How to Provide Care

Water every week unless you have a good soaking rain. After the first flush of bloom, fertilize again. Removing spent flowers may encourage a few more blooms, but let the end-of-season flower spikes remain for a winter show and to feed the birds. After the first hard freeze, cut the plant back to the crown.

Additional Advice for Care

In late winter or early spring, fertilize by scratching a slow-release 5-10-10 fertilizer into the soil. Water it in. Replenish the mulch. Fertilize again after the first flush of bloom. Every 4 or 5 years you will probably want to divide the plants because they become overcrowded.

PERENNIALS

Aquilegia

Columbine

*T*he columbine is one of the most beautiful of our mid- to late spring and early summer flowers, loved as much for its foliage as for its long-lasting, exquisite blossoms. These intricate nodding or upright flowers end in spurs usually in 2 shades, and they stand out against fresh blue-green scalloped foliage. The columbines do well in part shade, and are especially lovely naturalized along a sun-dappled path through woodlands. The plants are 1 to 3 ft. tall. The most extra-ordinary for flower are the hybrids. They come in a wide range of heights, and in colors and amazing bi-colors—white, yellow, blue, rusty pinks, lavenders, purples, reddish orange. Some hybrids have huge spurs—'Spring Song', for example, and the Music series. There are double-flowered strains and dwarfs, charming in a rock garden. The old-fashioned garden columbine, *A. vulgaris,* is the one to plant in a cottage garden. If the foliage begins to spoil after the flowers have bloomed, cut it way back, almost to the crown. I've found that it grows back and remains as a beautiful low filler for the rest of the season.

WHEN TO PLANT
Fresh seed gathered from plants that have gone to seed and sown in late spring or early summer produces flowers the following year. For bloom this year, in early spring set out container-grown plants or root divisions any time after the ground can be worked. You can also move young plants in cool, rainy weather regions in the fall.

WHERE TO PLANT
Aquilegias succeed in sun in mild parts of the state, and prefer some shade in warm regions. They do well in my rather shady garden in Washington, D.C. Aquilegia tolerates drought but cannot stand soil that is soggy in winter, so avoid damp low-lying areas where the soil alternately freezes and thaws. Set the plants 12 to 15 in. apart in groups of at least 3 to 5—but keep an eye out for self-sowers. They may turn up where you don't want them.

How to Plant

Dig into a hole about twice the size of the rootball and 4 in. deeper, 2-in. layers of coarse sand or chicken grit and leaf mold or sphagnum peat moss. Add a slow-release 5-10-10 fertilizer. In clay soil, work in a small handful of gypsum and of superphosphate. Unwind roots circling the rootball. Half fill each hole with diluted fertilizer, set the plant about 2 in. higher than ground level, and press the crown down into ground to bring it about an inch above ground level. Fill the hole, watering to settle the soil. Provide a permanent 2-in. mulch of pine needles, or rotted leaf mold starting a few inches from the crown.

How to Provide Care

Water every week unless you have a good soaking rain. Once established, columbine is fairly drought resistant and local rainfall should be enough to keep it growing except during our mid- and late August droughts. When blooming is over, if the foliage deteriorates, shear it back to the ground. It will regrow and stay attractive throughout the summer.

Additional Advice for Care

In late winter or early spring, fertilize by scratching a slow-release 5-10-10 fertilizer into the soil. Water it in. Replenish the mulch. Every 2 or 3 years, divide the crowns and replant.

Additional Cultivars and Species

A. flabellata 'Nana' is a lovely little columbine that does well in considerable shade. The plants are 6 to 8 in. tall and bear nodding blue and white blossoms that end in large hooked spurs. 'Nana Alba' blooms a little earlier, and is an exquisite white-on-white flower. These are easy plants that self-sow.

Coneflower

*T*he rudbeckias do very well in Virginia, and the perennial 'Goldsturm' is probably the finest of the yellow black-eyed Susan type. It blooms freely through midsummer into fall on compact, bushy plants 18 to 30 in. high. The ray florets are deep yellow and the cone-shaped centers bronze-black. It self-sows aggressively and is a good perennial for wild places. Removing spent blooms early in the flowering season encourages repeat flowering. However, in fall leave the flowerheads to ripen for the birds, for winter interest and to reseed.

WHEN TO PLANT

Sow seeds any time after the ground can be worked in spring. As an alternative, set out container-grown plants or root divisions in early spring. Plants that are still near-dormant or just beginning to grow will give the best performance.

WHERE TO PLANT

'Goldsturm' self-sows and is a good naturalizer for wild places. It withstands high heat and thrives in full sun. It blooms in dappled light, but tends to grow in the direction of full sun. It tolerates drought but cannot stand soil that is soggy in winter, so avoid damp low-lying areas where the soil alternately freezes and thaws. 'Goldsturm' prefers a pH in the range of 5.0 to 6.5.

HOW TO PLANT

Dig into a hole about twice the size of the rootball and 4 in. deeper, 2-in. layers of coarse coarse sand or chicken grit and leaf mold or sphagnum peat moss. Add a slow-release 5-10-10 fertilizer. In clay soil, work in a small handful of gypsum and of superphosphate. Sow seeds following package instructions or mark planting holes 15 to 18 in. apart. Half fill each hole with diluted fertilizer, plant the seedlings high, and press the soil down around the stem firmly enough so the plant resists a tug. Water with a diluted fertilizer solution. Provide a permanent 2-in. mulch starting a few inches from the crown.

How to Provide Care

Water a new planting every week the first season unless you have
a good soaking rain. Rudbeckia is drought resistant, so once it's
established, local rainfall should be enough to keep it growing
except during our mid- and late August droughts. After the first
flush of bloom, deadhead down to the next flower bud to promote
flowering.

Additional Advice for Care

In late winter or early spring, fertilize by scratching a slow-release
5-10-10 fertilizer into the soil and water it in. Replenish the mulch.
Every 3 or 4 years—or if the plant becomes less productive—divide
in early spring. If the transplants fail, renew the planting by sowing
fresh seed the following spring.

Additional Cultivars and Species

In the warmer reaches of Virginia, black-eyed Susan, *R. hirta*, is more
successful. A biennial or perennial grown as an annual, it blooms
August to October the second year after sowing.

Coral Bells

*I*n late spring and early summer, heuchera's eye-catching panicles of tiny bell-shaped flowers sway on 1- to 2-ft. wiry stalks that
arch high above the foliage. The leaves are semi-evergreen, scalloped,
dark green clusters that remain attractive most of the year. Hybrids
like 'Bressingham Blaze' bloom in shades of coral to deep red, pink,
and white. Heuchera does well in partial shade, but some cultivars
have the ability to withstand a lot of direct sun. Among them are:
'Firebird', deep scarlet; 'Fire Sprite', smaller; 'Mount St. Helen's',
which bears fiery red flowers all summer; 'Pluie de Feu', cherry-red;
'June Bride', superb white that flowers May through midsummer;
'Red Spangles', red; 'Scarlet Sentinel', scarlet; 'Scintillation', bright
pink tipped with red; and 'Snowflake', white. Another heuchera,
'Palace Purple', that is becoming very popular is grown for its foliage.
It produces a low mound of big, bold, burgundy-red leaves that
resemble those of the maple tree. The clumps look especially handsome in fall surrounded by the buffs and reds of the season. The
flowers are off-white.

WHEN TO PLANT
Set out container plants or root divisions any time after the ground
can be worked in spring. Plants that are still near-dormant or just
beginning to grow will give the best performance.

WHERE TO PLANT
Heuchera can stand more direct sun in the cool reaches of Zone 6,
but it needs partial shade elsewhere. It tolerates drought but cannot
stand soil that is soggy in winter, so avoid damp low-lying areas
where the soil alternately freezes and thaws. It prefers slightly acid
soil, pH 5.5 to 6.5.

HOW TO PLANT
Dig into a hole about twice the size of the rootball and 6 in. deeper,
2-in. layers of coarse sand or chicken grit and leaf mold or sphagnum peat moss. Add a slow-release 10-10-10 fertilizer. In clay soil,
work in a small handful of gypsum and of superphosphate. Unwind
roots circling the rootball. Half fill each hole with diluted fertilizer,

set the plant an inch or two higher than ground level, and press the crown down into ground to bring it an inch above ground level. Fill the hole, watering to settle the soil. Provide a permanent 2-in. mulch of pine needles, or rotted leaf mold starting a few inches from the crown.

How to Provide Care

Water a new plant every week the first season unless you have a good soaking rain. Heuchera is fairly drought-resistant, so water when you water the other perennials. In cold climates, mulch with branches of evergreens after the first solid frost.

Additional Advice for Care

In late winter or early spring, fertilize by scratching a slow-release 12-6-6 fertilizer into the soil at half the rate recommended on the container, and water it in. Replenish the mulch. Divide every 4 or 5 years.

Daylily

A collection of daylilies will keep your garden in color from early July until late August—and there are early and late varieties that extend the season. Daylilies need 2 or 3 years to peak, but once mature they produce dozens of large, trumpet- or cup-shaped reflex or double blooms on stalks usually 3 to 4 ft. tall. The individual blooms last just a day, but more open the following day. There are dwarfs less than a foot high, as well as 6-footers. The colors of the modern hybrids range from creamy yellows to coral pinks and fiery reds. For a long season of blooms, look for "rebloomer" daylilies. These varieties bloom early, then again in late summer or early fall, or from summer into frosts. Plants labelled "tetraploid" have richer, more intense colors, heavier petal texture, and unusual forms. For a small garden, I recommend little 'Stella De Oro', a superb performer. It is a dwarf miniature 10 to 20 in. tall that bears 2³/4-in. flowers that are gold with a green throat and somewhat fragrant. A 3-year-old plant produces literally hundreds of blooms. Avoid evergreen forms. They are best in frost-free areas.

WHEN TO PLANT

Plant, and when necessary, divide the tuberous roots in mid-spring or early fall. Container-grown daylilies can be planted any time in spring.

WHERE TO PLANT

Daylilies flourish in bright sun, or under tall trees such as pines that let in a lot of light, but not under maples or willows that filter the light. To naturalize or use as ground cover, mass 12 to 18 in. apart. Daylilies will crowd out the weeds and take care of themselves for years to come. To grow specimens in a mixed border, space them 3 to 6 ft. apart to allow for interplanting. They prefer somewhat acid soil, pH 5.5 to 6.5.

How to Plant

Prepare the bed by digging in 2 in. of coarse sand or chicken grit, of humus, and a slow release 5-10-5 fertilizer. In clay soil add a small handful of gypsum and of superphosphate for each plant. Work the soil 8 to 12 in. deep. If you are planting rhizomes, set them with the crowns 1/2 to 1 in. below the soil level and 1 ft. apart, 3 to 6 together. If you are planting container-grown daylilies, half fill each hole with diluted fertilizer, and set the plant in the hole with the crown above ground level. Fill the hole, watering to settle the soil. Provide a permanent 3-in. mulch of pine needles, or rotted leaf mold.

How to Provide Care

Ideally, daylilies should get an inch of water every week or two during the growing season. It will help to keep them blooming. After the first flush of bloom, fertilize. Deadhead to promote flowering.

Additional Advice for Care

In late winter or early spring, fertilize by scratching a slow-release 5-10-10 fertilizer into the soil and water it in. Replenish the mulch. The clumps need dividing when bloom production decreases, usually after 5 years. Dig and cut the clumps apart and replant in mid-spring or early fall.

Additional Cultivars and Species

Of the many beautiful daylilies that bloom over a long period in Zone 8, 'Prester John' is outstanding. It bears 5-in. double blooms that are bright gold-orange with a green throat and somewhat scented.

Dwarf Threadleaf Tickseed

*T*his is an easy, rewarding little perennial for late spring and summer bloom. Masses of sunny, starry flowers cover rounded mounds of dainty, dark green leaves. If flowering slows in midsummer, cut the plant back to within a few inches of the ground, and it will regrow and rebloom. One of the best cultivars is creamy yellow 'Moonbeam', a 1¹/₂- to 2-ft. dwarf. *C. rosea* is similar to 'Moonbeam', but has rosy or purple petals. It's tolerant of wet situations and hot summers. Other top cultivars of *C. verticillata* are bright yellow 'Golden Shower' which is 2 to 3 ft. tall and bright yellow 'Zagreb' which is just 12 in. high. If your area is really warm, 'Zagreb' and 'Golden Shower' are good choices. *C. grandiflora* 'Badengold', which reaches 2 ft., covers itself with large golden flowers late May to August if deadheaded, but tends to sprawl. 'Goldfink', under 9 in., is a lovely large-flowered dwarf. For the front of the border, or as edging for a wall, plant *C. auriculata* 'Nana', which bears its orange-gold flowers on 6- to 8-in. stems.

WHEN TO PLANT

In spring, sow seeds indoors or outdoors. For full bloom this season, plant root divisions in spring or late summer. You can also set out plants after they become dormant in fall.

WHERE TO PLANT

Coreopsis needs full sun, but half a day of full sun or all-day bright shade are acceptable, though flowering will be less. Coreopsis tolerates drought but can't stand soil that is soggy in winter, so avoid damp low-lying areas where the soil alternately freezes and thaws. Coreopsis prefers soil that is in the pH range between pH 6.0-7.0. Set the plants 1¹/₂ ft. apart.

HOW TO PLANT

Prepare the bed by digging in 3 in. of coarse sand or chicken grit, 2 in. of humus, and a slow-release 5-10-10 fertilizer. In clay soil, add a small handful of gypsum and of superphosphate for each plant. Work the soil 8 to 12 in. deep. Sow seeds following package instructions. Or, mark planting holes for seedlings 6 to 8 in. apart around a

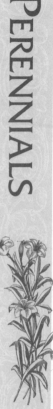

system of soaker hoses. Divide plants in flats with a sharp, clean knife, giving each a good root system. Half fill each hole with diluted fertilizer, plant the seedling high, and press the soil down around the stem firmly enough so the plant resists a tug. Water with a diluted fertilizer solution. Provide a permanent 2-in. mulch of pine needles or rotted leaf mold starting a few inches from the crown.

How to Provide Care

Water a new plant every week the first season unless you have a good soaking rain. Coreopsis is drought resistant, so once it's established, local rainfall should be enough to keep it growing except during our mid- and late August droughts. After the first flush of bloom dies down, shear the plant and fertilize again.

Additional Advice for Care

In late winter or early spring, fertilize by scratching a slow-release 5-10-10 fertilizer into the soil and water it in. Replenish the mulch. Every 2 or 3 years, reseed or divide in early spring.

Globe Thistle

*W*hen you are looking for a plant that will add texture and variety to the perennial border, investigate the globe thistle. It is a stately erect thistlelike plant, 2 to 4 ft. or taller, whose foliage has gray-green hairy undersides. In summer and early fall, it bears very handsome dryish heads of thistlelike steel-blue flowers that last for a couple of months. 'Taplow Blue' bears steel blue flowers that are about 2 in. across. It is the most popular of the cultivars. The globe thistles are handsome in groups in the wild garden, and fronting tall shrubs. They attract gold finch and nocturnal moths.

WHEN TO PLANT

Set out container-grown plants in spring. Plants that are still near-dormant or just beginning to grow will give the best performance.

WHERE TO PLANT

Plant the globe thistle in full sun. It tolerates a great deal of city living, and drought, but cannot stand soil that is soggy in winter. Avoid damp low-lying areas where the soil alternately freezes and thaws.

HOW TO PLANT

Dig into a hole about twice the size of the rootball and 6 in. deeper, 2-in. layers of coarse sand or chicken grit, and a slow-release 10-10-10 fertilizer. In clay soil, work in a small handful of gypsum and of superphosphate. Unwind roots circling the rootball. Half fill each hole with diluted fertilizer, set the plant an inch or two higher than ground level, and press the crown down into ground to bring it an inch above ground level. Fill the hole, watering to settle the soil. Provide a permanent 2-in. mulch starting a few inches from the crown.

How to Provide Care

Water a new plant every week the first season unless you have a good soaking rain. The globe thistle is drought resistant, so once it's established, local rainfall should be enough to keep it growing except during long droughts.

Additional Advice for Care

In late winter or early spring, fertilize by scratching a slow-release 10-10-10 fertilizer into the soil at half the rate recommended on the container and water it in. Replenish the mulch. Don't divide plants until they're at least 3 years old.

PERENNIALS

Heartleaf Bergenia

This is a vigorous plant 1 to 1½ ft. tall that in mid-spring produces a dozen or so graceful spires of attractive, vivid, purplish red-pink flowers. But its major gift to the garden is a clump of bold, glossy, leathery evergreen leaves that turn bronze in winter sun. The bergenias are most effective planted in groups of 5 or 10. 'Purpurea' is a tall, purple-toned variety about 20 in. tall that bears dark pink blossoms. The leaves turn a marvelous glossy burgundy when the cold comes and they remain. It is not invasive and is most effective in groups. Another first-rate, slightly taller cultivar is 'Perfecta', which has purplish leaves and rosy-red flowers that stand well above the foliage. There are white-flowered varieties—'Bressingham White', and 'Silver Light', a small plant about 12 in. tall, whose white flowers are tinged pink and have red centers.

When to Plant
Bergenia grows easily from seed, or from root divisions, planted in early spring.

Where to Plant
Bergenia tolerates full sun in cool regions, but partial shade is better farther south in the state. It colors best in full sun. It thrives in moist, well-drained soil near streams or ponds, or in flowering borders to which lots of moisture-holding humusy organic matter has been added.

How to Plant
Prepare the bed by digging in 2-in. layers of coarse sand or chicken grit, of humus, and a slow release 10-10-10 fertilizer. In clay soil add a very small handful of gypsum and of superphosphate for each plant. Work the soil 6 to 8 in. deep. Mark planting holes 8 in. apart. Half fill each hole with diluted fertilizer, and plant the seedlings or root divisions. Press the soil down around the stems firmly enough so the plant resists a tug. Water with a diluted fertilizer solution. Provide a permanent 2-in. mulch starting a few inches from the crown.

How to Provide Care

Water a new plant every week unless you have a good soaking rain. Deadhead and cut out any unattractive leaves in July and August. At the first sign of slugs, dust the area with diatomaceous earth, and repeat after every rainfall.

Additional Advice for Care

In late winter or early spring, fertilize by scratching a slow-release 10-10-10 fertilizer into the soil and water it in. Replenish the mulch. Every 3 or 4 years—or if the plant becomes crowded—divide in early spring.

Hosta

OTHER COMMON NAME: Plantain Lily

*T*he hostas are shade-loving clump-forming plants 12 to 30 in. tall that are used as foliage plants in the perennial border, and as ground cover and edging under trees. They can handle competition from trees, as well as considerable shade—dappled shade, bright shade, and even quite substantial shade. In summer and early fall, they bear lavender or white flower spikes that rise above the foliage. The flowers of varieties of the fragrant hostas, *H. plantaginea* 'Grandi-flora', have a lovely scent, especially new forms such as the pure white 'Aphrodite', which also is remarkably beautiful. Hostas' leaves are beautiful and there's almost an infinite number of varieties. They may be broad or tall, narrow or small—smooth textured, quilted, puckered, even half-twisted. The shades range from rich or muted hues of blue-green to yellow-white and there are green leaves with narrow or broad white or gold edges or splotches, and yellow-green leaves with dark-green splotching and edgings. At maturity, the clumps vary from dwarf to giant clumps 5 ft. across. It takes a hosta 3 years to mature. The older it gets, the more impressive and pleasing it will be. As a filler in the perennial border a good choice is 'Gold Edge' or 'Gold Circle', *H. sieboldiana* 'Frances Williams'. It grows into 4-ft. clumps with very large leaves as puckered as seersucker and blue-green with broad golden margins.

WHEN TO PLANT

Set out container-grown plants in early spring or in late summer or early fall. If you are planting rhizomes, do that in early to mid-spring. Catalogs ship hosta rhizomes—but hostas are slow-growing to start with, so I suggest a container plant.

WHERE TO PLANT

Hosta are not recommended for full sun, but good light does improve flowering. Some species tolerate more sun than others, especially in cool hill country. The best light for hostas is filtered. The tips of early-flowering hostas push up early and where there are late frosts they're safer under tall trees. Do not plant the larger hostas in Zone 8.

How to Plant

Dig into the planting bed, or into a hole twice the size of the root-ball, 2 in. of coarse sand or chicken grit, and 3 in. of humus, and a slow release 10-5-10 fertilizer. In clay soil, add a small handful of gypsum and of superphosphate for each plant. Set rhizomes 1 in. below soil level. If you are planting container-grown hostas, half fill each hole with diluted fertilizer, and set the plant into the hole so that the crown is a little above ground level. Fill the hole, watering to settle the soil. Provide a permanent 3-in. mulch starting 3 in. from the crown.

How to Provide Care

Even moisture is very important to hostas, especially the first 2 or 3 years, but established plants tolerate drought, wet feet, and neglect. Scratch a handful of fertilizer in around each plant toward midsummer and water it in. Remove flower stalks when they fade. To keep the plants healthy, when frost wilts the foliage, cut it off down to the crown and discard it. If you see the slightest sign of slug activity, powder the area with diatomaceous earth, and repeat after every rain.

Additional Advice for Care

In late winter or early spring, fertilize by scratching a slow-release 10-10-5 fertilizer into the soil, and water it in. Replenish the mulch. Hostas are slow to establish, but once underway, they can be halved every few years without harm to the planting. The best times to divide are early spring and early fall.

Additional Cultivars and Species

'Honeybells' is a lovely fragrant hosta. It has grass-green foliage and in July and August bears 3-ft. lavender-lilac flower spikes.

Japanese Anemone

*T*he fall-flowering anemones are late summer/early fall's most beautiful tall flowers for shaded places. The ferny foliage fills out at the base as the growing season advances, and then towards midsummer climbs to 2 or 3 ft. and for many weeks bears deep rose, pink, white or purple flowers, 2 to 3 in. in diameter. They are lovely at the edge of a woodland with ferns, hostas and epimediums. The Japanese variety blooms earlier, in midsummer to fall. It is 2 to 2¹/₂ ft. high, and similar to the beautiful hybrid described below, but it's better able to handle winter in cool regions and can take more direct sun. It also bears masses of pink flowers and tolerates sun better than the hybrid. The hybrids of the Japanese anemone, *A.* × *hybrida*, are larger and more beautiful, and have been bred to many forms and colors. The single-flowered types have 5 rounded petals around a central heart of bright yellow stamens. Historic 'Honorine Jobert' is a gleaming white single-flowered anemone 3 to 4 ft. tall. 'Margarete' is smaller and produces masses of double or semi-double bright rose-pink blooms on stems 2 to 3 ft. tall.

When to Plant

Plant a container-grown Japanese anemone after the ground has warmed in spring—April in Zone 8, mid-May in Zones 6 and 7. A plant that is still near-dormant or just beginning to grow will give the best performance.

Where to Plant

In Virginia, a Japanese anemone needs to grow in consistent bright shade. It prefers soil in the neutral range, and very well drained. To avoid soil that is soggy in winter, don't plant it in damp low-lying areas where the soil alternately freezes and thaws. These are tall plants that benefit from some protection from strong winds. Set Japanese anemones at least 24 in. apart.

How to Plant

Dig into a hole about twice the size of the rootball and 6 in. deeper, 2-in. layers of coarse sand or chicken grit and leaf mold or sphagnum peat moss. Add a slow-release 5-10-10 fertilizer. In clay soil, work in a small handful of gypsum and one of superphosphate. Unwind roots circling the rootball. Half fill each hole with diluted fertilizer, set the plant an inch or two higher than ground level, and press the crown down into the ground to bring it an in. above ground level. Fill the hole, watering to settle the soil. Provide a 2-in. mulch starting a few inches from the crown, and maintain its depth throughout summer.

How to Provide Care

Water a new plant every week unless you have a good soaking rain. Established older clumps are fairly drought resistant, but best results are obtained when plants are well watered during dry periods. Deadhead down to the ground as stems go out of bloom, and when blooming ends in fall clear away dead foliage. In Zone 6, it's a good idea to cover the Japanese hybrids with a winter mulch.

Additional Advice for Care

These plants need 2 or 3 seasons to become established and resent disturbance. Plan to divide only every 10 years. In spring, fertilize by scratching a slow-release 5-10-10 fertilizer into the soil at half the rate recommended on the container, and water in well. Replenish the mulch.

Marsh Rose-mallow

*T*he most familiar hibiscus used to be the tropical *H. rosa-sinensis*, a gorgeous funnel-shaped flower that lasts just a day, and rose-of-Sharon. And, of course, there's the shrub althaea, *H. syriacus*, a tall, woody plant or small tree described in the chapter on shrubs. But in recent years, the huge blooms of the marsh rose-mallow have captured the imagination of gardeners. It's a shrubby perennial that in midsummer bears funnel-shaped flowers 7 and 10 and 12 in. across. In late spring, new growth shoots up 3 to 6 ft. The canes eventually sprawl a little but the plant does not need staking—just lots of sprawl space. When in bloom, it's eye-catching at a distance. The rose-mallow most often planted in Virginia is a red type—for example the 'Lord Baltimore' strain that bears masses of bright red flowers and has beautifully lobed leaves. 'Satan' is a magnificent red with large fire-engine red flowers on 5-ft. plants. The 'Dixie Belle' strain is a seed-raised group of compacts a few feet high with flowers varying from red-eyed to red, rose and pink. There are, however, some beautiful cultivated varieties in other colors—for example 'Appleblossom', which bears light pink flowers that have deeper rose margins. 'Cotton Candy' is an exceptional bi-color with soft pink on white flowers.

WHEN TO PLANT
Set out container-grown or dormant roots (bare root) rose-mallow in early spring.

WHERE TO PLANT
Rose-mallow does best in full sun. In part shade, it will bloom but won't produce as many big flowers. Though it does not have to be staked, it does do well planted where there's some support—a wall, or in the angle of a fence where it gets support and air. It adapts to a wide range of soils, but does best in pH range between 5.5 and 7.0

HOW TO PLANT
Dig into a hole about twice the size of the root ball and 6 in. deeper 2-in. layers of coarse sand or chicken grit and leaf mold or sphagnum peat moss. Add a slow-release 5-10-10 fertilizer. In clay soil, work in a small handful of gypsum, and of superphosphate. Half fill

the hole with diluted fertilizer. Plant with the crown a few inches below the soil surface. Press the crown into ground to firm it in place. Fill the hole, watering to settle the soil. Provide a permanent 2-in. mulch of decayed leaves starting a few inches from the crown.

HOW TO PROVIDE CARE

Water a new plant every week the first season unless you have a good soaking rain. Rose-mallow resists some drought once it's established, so local rainfall should be enough to keep it growing except during our mid- and late August droughts. After the first flush of bloom, fertilize again. When the foliage dies down in late fall, cut the stems to the ground. New growth will appear in late spring.

ADDITIONAL ADVICE FOR CARE

In late winter or early spring, fertilize by scratching a slow-release 5-10-10 fertilizer into the soil and water it in. Replenish the mulch. Established plantings resent disturbance, so avoid dividing the crown.

PERENNIALS

Narrow Spiked Ligularia

*T*he ligularias are tall, majestic plants grown for their bold foliage and soaring spikes of ragged yellow or orange-yellow flowers. They bloom toward midsummer and are perfect for the back of a border, and are handsome naturalized at the edge of a woodland, a stream, a pond or anywhere their roots can stay moist. 'The Rocket' is suited to watery sites and moist borders. It's an exceptionally large plant—6 ft. by the time it blooms—that develops generous mounds of handsome, dark-stemmed, slightly rounded leathery leaves and long spikes of ragged lemon-yellow flowers. It's very good with Japanese iris and large-leaved hostas. 'Gregynog Gold', a cultivar of *L. × hessei* (syn. *Senecio × hessei*) is a smaller plant, 5 to 6 ft. tall, that has large, heart-shaped leathery leaves and daisy-like flowers that are orange-yellow. It's a very good cultivar.

WHEN TO PLANT

These are easy plants to grow. In early spring, set out container-grown root divisions any time after the ground can be worked. Plants that are still near-dormant or just beginning to grow will give the best performance.

WHERE TO PLANT

Ligularia does best in sun, but in hot areas it will benefit from protection from noon and late afternoon sun. It must not be allowed to dry out, and will succeed planted in a bog garden or any other wet spot. To thrive in a garden bed, the soil around the roots must be kept constantly damp.

HOW TO PLANT

Dig into a hole about twice the size of the rootball and 12 in. deeper, 2-in. layers of coarse sand or chicken grit and leaf mold or sphagnum peat moss. In clay soil, work in a small handful of gypsum, of superphosphate, and of a slow-release 5-10-10 fertilizer. Unwind roots circling the rootball. Half fill each hole with diluted fertilizer, set the plant an inch or two higher than ground level, and press the

crown down into ground to bring it an inch above ground level. Fill the hole, watering to settle the soil. Provide a permanent 2-in. mulch starting 3 in. from the crown.

How to Provide Care

Water as often as necessary to keep the soil evenly moist. Ligularia roots must not be allowed to dry out. After the first flush of bloom, fertilize again. Deadhead to promote flowering.

Additional Advice for Care

Fertilize in late winter or early spring by scratching a slow-release 5-10-10 fertilizer into the soil, and water it in. Replenish the mulch. Every 3 or 4 years—or if the plant becomes less productive—divide in early spring.

Additional Cultivars and Species

A smaller ligularia, *L. dentata* 'Desdemona', stays under 4 ft. and is a good choice for a small garden. It forms clumps of 12-in.-long leathery brownish-green leaves that are mahogany underneath. The flowering stems branch and bear large, orange flowers from mid- to late summer.

PERENNIALS

Oriental Poppy

*P*oppies come in all sizes. Silky, shiny and colorful, they're a mainstay of sunny gardens everywhere. But the stars of the poppy domain are the big, crinkled-silk Oriental poppies. The blossoms measure between 5 and 8 to 10 in. across, and they unfold in spring and early summer in vibrant reds, exquisite pinks, oranges, whites and combinations. The petals of some are splotched at the base in a contrasting color, usually black, and others have contrasting edges. The deeply cut foliage dies in late summer but reappears in fall and is evergreen or semi-evergreen in winter according to climate. Orientals are long-lived, but they hate to be disturbed and die if transplanted while flowering. Old foliage and stems must be allowed to ripen on the plant in the garden, then removed to make way for the growth of new foliage in fall. Do not plant poppies close to flowers that will require constant moisture during dormancy. The Oriental poppies are big, sprawling, and need lots of space. Since they're unsightly as the foliage is dying away, place them toward the back of the border. Front them with an attractive foliage plant that will grow up while the poppies are yellowing—baby's breath, for example, or dahlias, or liriope.

WHEN TO PLANT

The Oriental poppies transplant with difficulty. Do not divide or transplant them until late summer after the foliage has died down completely, or set out sturdy container-grown specimens in early spring.

WHERE TO PLANT

Poppies need full sun, but they can take a little filtered shade and still be productive. Poppies tolerate drought but can't stand soil that is soggy when they're dormant, or in winter.

HOW TO PLANT

Dig into a hole about twice the size of the rootball and 6 in. deeper, 2-in. layers of coarse sand or chicken grit and leaf mold or sphagnum peat moss. Add a slow-release 5-10-10 fertilizer. In clay soil, work in a small handful of gypsum and of superphosphate. Half fill each hole with diluted fertilizer, set the plant an inch or two higher than ground level, and press the crown down into ground to bring it an inch above ground level. Fill the hole, watering to settle the soil. Provide a permanent 2-in. mulch starting a few inches from the crown.

How to Provide Care

Maintain moisture during the growing period, but allow poppies to run dry during dormancy and until new growth begins. Poppy blossoms are followed by big, round, dark, decorative seedheads. It's best for the plant if you remove them.

Additional Advice for Care

Just as growth begins in fall, fertilize by scratching a slow-release 5-10-10 fertilizer into the soil. In late winter replenish the mulch. If you wish to divide the plant, do so in summer after it becomes completely dormant.

Additional Cultivars and Species

The 24-in.-high Shirley poppy is a popular strain of the field poppy, *P. rhoeas*, the little red poppy that grows wild in the fields of France. Shirleys are grown from seed planted where they will bloom. In cool regions, plant these in early spring for midsummer flowering. In warm regions, plant them in late summer or early fall for spring flowering.

Peony

here are 2 types of peonies—shrub-size herbaceous perennials, and woody tree forms. The herbaceous peonies are very long lived, showy beauties that make superb cut flowers. They bloom in April and May for 4 to 6 weeks, producing globes of crinkled silk in shades from creamy white to reds so rich they're almost purple. For small gardens and perennial borders, the doubles are the most popular, but interest is growing in the exotic single and Japanese peonies. The other type of peony is a woody tall shrub or small tree derived from the Chinese mountain peony, *P. suffruticosa*. These plants bear magnificent single or double flowers that have satiny, crinkled petals. As many as 75 flowers can bloom on one plant through mid- and late spring. The tree peony is planted as a specimen in a large garden, or as the centerpiece of a formal flower bed. Peonies must have a chilling period at below 40 degrees Fahrenheit to flower. The best bets for Zone 8 are herbaceous types that flower early and in mid-season, and the Japanese and single herbaceous peonies. Zone 7 is as far south as a tree peony can be counted on to bloom fully.

WHEN TO PLANT

Plant a container-grown herbaceous peony in early spring. Peonies are slow to adapt. Plants that are beginning to grow will give the best performance. You can also set out plants after they become dormant in fall. Plant a tree peony after the leaves fall in autumn.

WHERE TO PLANT

To bloom well, all peonies require a minimum of 6 hours of sun. Tree peonies require protection from noon sun. Peonies are successful in neutral or slightly alkaline soils, but tolerate an acid range. To avoid soil that is soggy in winter, don't plant a peony in a damp low-lying area where the soil alternately freezes and thaws.

HOW TO PLANT

Dig into a planting hole 3 times the size of the rootball 2-in. layers of coarse sand or chicken grit and sphagnum peat moss, along with a handful of dolomitic limestone. For herbaceous peonies, add 1 lb. of bonemeal—for a tree peony, 2 lbs. In clay soil, work in a small hand-

ful of gypsum. Unwind roots circling the rootball. Half fill the hole with diluted fertilizer, set the plant 2 in. higher than ground level, and press the crown into ground, bringing it an inch above ground level. Failure to bloom is one effect of planting too deeply. Fill the hole, watering to settle the soil. Provide a 3-in. mulch starting a few inches from the crown.

HOW TO PROVIDE CARE

Keep invasive ground covers and weeds away from peonies—they need all the fertilizer and water available. Remove seedheads until the plants are well established. Water a new plant every week the first season unless you have a good soaking rain. Once established, water it during droughts. When the foliage of a herbaceous peony turns from green to brown in fall, cut it to the crown and burn it. In late fall, spread a handful of fertilizer around the crown.

ADDITIONAL ADVICE FOR CARE

In late winter or early spring, spread a slow-release 5-10-10 fertilizer around the crown, and water it in. Replenish the mulch. Herbaceous peonies a century and older are not uncommon, but after transplanting they need a year or two to re-establish themselves, so divide only if and when you must. Divide in the fall after the foliage has turned from green to brown.

Pink

OTHER COMMON NAME: Miniature Carnation

*T*his group includes the big florist's carnation, but the dianthus planted in Virginia gardens is the little spicily scented pink. Pink is just one of its many colors. Others include red, salmon, white, yellow (*D. knappii*), and bi-color pinks. Some bloom in very early spring and repeat sporadically into late fall if deadheaded. They bloom in mounds of grassy foliage that is usually evergreen, fine for edging and as ground cover. The cheddar pink, *D. gratianopolitanus*, is probably the easiest plant to find—it's a rose or pink miniature 9 to 12 in. high. 'Tiny Rubies' is a very popular double-flowered deep pink variety. 'La Bourbille' is a clear pink. The cottage or grass pink, *D. plumarius*, blooms in spring and early summer and comes in a range of shades— salmon, rose, white and red. 'Mrs. Sinkins' is an old-fashioned, fully double ruffled white with a powerful fragrance. Probably the most fragrant pink is *D. superbus*, whose flowers are white, cool pink or lavender-pink and lacy. They are borne July to frosts on branching stems 12 to 16 in. high. It's usually grown as a biennial here. The Rainbow Loveliness strain bears feathered pastel flowers with a contrasting eye, and they're exceptionally clove scented.

WHEN TO PLANT

Sow seeds, plant seedlings or root divisions in early spring, or in late summer or early fall.

WHERE TO PLANT

Dianthus succeeds in full sun but in my garden in Washington, D.C., it also blooms in part sun, though less fully. It tolerates drought but can't stand soil that is soggy in winter, so avoid damp low-lying areas where the soil alternately freezes and thaws. Set the plants about 6 in. apart.

HOW TO PLANT

Prepare the bed by digging in 3 in. of coarse sand or chicken grit, 2 in. of humus, and a slow release 5-10-10 fertilizer. In clay soil, add a small handful of gypsum and of superphosphate for each plant.

Work the soil 8 to 12 in. deep. Sow seeds following package instructions. Or mark planting holes for seedlings 6 to 8 in. apart around a system of soaker hoses. Divide plants in flats with a sharp, clean knife, giving each a good root system. Half fill each hole with diluted fertilizer, plant the seedling high, and press the soil down around the stem firmly enough so the plant resists a tug. Water with a diluted fertilizer solution. Apply a 3-in. mulch starting 3 in. from the stems.

HOW TO PROVIDE CARE

Water a new plant every week the first season unless you have a good soaking rain. Dianthus is drought resistant, so once it's established, local rainfall should be enough to keep it growing except during our mid and late August droughts. After the first flush of bloom, deadhead the faded flowers, and fertilize again. If the plants show brown tips in August, cut them off, and make sure the plants don't go dry. They will freshen when fall comes, and can go on blooming until frosts.

ADDITIONAL ADVICE FOR CARE

In late winter or early spring, fertilize by scratching a slow-release 5-10-10 fertilizer into the soil at half the rate recommended on the container, and water it in. Replenish the mulch. The little pinks are easily multiplied by division in spring or early fall.

ADDITIONAL CULTIVARS AND SPECIES

D. barbutus, the sweet William, is a charming, old-fashioned dianthus species 18 in. high that for a short time in spring bears flat-topped flowerheads of small fringed carnation-type florets, often with a distinct eye in crimson. There are reds, pinks and bi-colors with flashes of white.

PERENNIALS

Purple Coneflower

*T*his big bold coneflower is one of the showiest, toughest and
longest-lived natives for meadow gardens. The coneflower grows
2 to 3 ft. tall, and it has coarse dark green foliage. The huge daisy-like
flowers consist of deep orange-bronze cones and backswept petals in
a rich, dusky rose-purple. It blooms in late spring and early summer,
and goes on intermittently into fall if you deadhead it regularly.
Butterflies love it. There are off-white varieties with orange centers,
like 'White Lustre', which is attractive growing with black-eyed
Susans. But the whites don't have anything like the eye-catching
appeal of the purple coneflowers. Purple coneflowers last well as a
cut flower, dry well and look great in winter arrangements. Cut the
stem just above the next flower bud so the stem can produce more
blooms. For the cutting garden, plant 'Bright Star', which is a rosy-
pink coneflower with a maroon center. Virtually pest and disease free
and tolerant of considerable drought, the purple coneflower is an
excellent choice for naturalizing.

WHEN TO PLANT

Sow seed in early spring where the plants are to grow, or sow fresh
seed in late summer or early fall. To have plants the first season, set
out container-grown plants or root divisions any time after the
ground can be worked in spring.

WHERE TO PLANT

Purple coneflower really needs full sun, but it can take a little filtered shade and still be very productive especially in the warmer
parts of the state. It tolerates drought but can't stand soil that is
soggy in winter, so avoid damp low-lying areas where the soil alternately freezes and thaws. It prefers soil in the somewhat acid range,
pH 5.5 to 6.0.

HOW TO PLANT

Dig into a hole about twice the size of the rootball and 6 in. deeper,
2-in. layers of coarse sand or chicken grit and leaf mold or sphagnum peat moss. Add a slow-release 5-10-10 fertilizer. In clay soil,
work in a small handful of gypsum, and of superphosphate.

Unwind roots circling the rootball. Half fill each hole with diluted fertilizer, set the plant an inch or 2 higher than ground level, and press the crown down into ground to bring it an inch above ground level. Fill the hole, watering to settle the soil. Provide a permanent 2-in. mulch of pine needles or rotted leaf mold starting a few inches from the crown.

HOW TO PROVIDE CARE

Water a new plant every week the first season unless you have a good soaking rain. Purple coneflower is drought resistant, so once it's established, local rainfall should be enough to keep it growing except during our mid and late August droughts. After the first flush of bloom, deadhead and fertilize plants growing in full sun again—but not those growing in shade. Leave the last of the flowers on the plants to feed the birds. In late winter, cut the plants back to the crowns.

ADDITIONAL ADVICE FOR CARE

In late winter or early spring, fertilize by scratching a slow-release 5-10-10 fertilizer into the soil at half the rate recommended on the container, and water it in. Replenish the mulch. Every 2 or 3 years reseed, or divide the crowns in late fall or early spring.

Red Hot Poker Plant

*N*ow that we are are looking for more drought-resistant plants, the red hot poker plant is getting a lot more attention. In late spring and summer, eye-catching flower spikes yellow on the bottom and bright red on the top and 18 to 36 in. tall stand straight as a poker, several spikes per plant. The yellow lower portion of the "pokers" are where early-blooming florets are aging: the red at the top is where new florets are just opening. The arching sword-shaped gray-green semi- or evergreen foliage is attractive when new. There are many new cultivars, and they're more compact than the old-fashioned varieties with attractive softer colors. 'Springtime' is coral with muted yellow older blooms; the colors of small (2 to 2^1/$_2$ ft.) 'Earliest of All' includes a soft coral rose.

WHEN TO PLANT

In the cool upland of Virginia, set out container-grown plants in early spring. In Zones 7 and 8, it can be set out in early fall.

WHERE TO PLANT

Red hot poker plant can stand a lot of direct sun, but can use some protection from noon sun in hot areas. It tolerates drought but can't stand soil that is soggy in winter, so avoid damp low-lying areas where the soil alternately freezes and thaws. Red hot poker plant does best when it's not constantly buffeted by strong winds.

HOW TO PLANT

Dig into a hole about twice the size of the rootball and 6 in. deeper, 2-in. layers of coarse sand or chicken grit and leaf mold or sphagnum peat moss. Add a slow-release 5-10-10 fertilizer. In clay soil, work in a small handful of gypsum and of superphosphate. Unwind roots circling the rootball. Half fill each hole with diluted fertilizer, set the plant an inch or two higher than ground level, and press the crown down into ground to bring it an inch above ground level. Fill the hole, watering to settle the soil. Provide a permanent 2-in. mulch starting a few inches from the crown.

How to Provide Care

Water a new plant every week the first month or two unless you have a good soaking rain. Red hot poker plant is drought resistant, so once it's established, local rainfall should be enough to keep it growing except during our mid and late August droughts. However, if it dries out in the budding stage the flowers will be sparse. After the first flush of bloom, fertilize again. Deadhead red hot poker plant consistently, and when the blooms fade, trim the plants back by half to get rid of some of the unsightly foliage.

Additional Advice for Care

In late winter or early spring, fertilize by scratching a slow-release 5-10-10 fertilizer into the soil and water it in. Replenish the mulch. Red hot poker plant dislikes being disturbed and rarely needs dividing. If you do divide, do so in early spring.

Sea Holly

*T*he eryngiums are cold-hardy, sea-green, thistle-like plants with colorful stems. They are among the best plants for gardens in situations that bake and dry—urban gardens and hot midtowns areas—and they are wonderfully textured. In summer this species, the most beautiful of the tribe, bears heads of small blue flowers surrounded by long, spiky, darker blue bracts and they stay in bloom almost forever. The plant is 18 to 24 in. tall, most attractive set out in groups of 3 to 5. It's an excellent flower for fresh or dried arrangements.

WHEN TO PLANT
In early spring, set out plantlets or root divisions.

WHERE TO PLANT
Sea holly grows best in full sun, but it can take a little shade at noon, especially in the warmer reaches of Virginia. It prefers dryish soil but can't stand soil that is soggy in winter, so avoid damp low-lying areas where the soil alternately freezes and thaws.

HOW TO PLANT
Dig into a hole about twice the size of the rootball and 6 in. deeper, 2-in. layers of coarse sand or chicken grit. Add a slow-release 5-10-10 fertilizer. In clay soil, work in a small handful of gypsum and of superphosphate. Half fill each hole with diluted fertilizer, set the plant an inch or two higher than ground level, and press the crown down into ground to bring it an inch above ground level. Fill the hole, watering to settle the soil. Provide a permanent 2-in. mulch of gravel around the crown.

How to Provide Care

Until the plant is established, water deeply but infrequently, to encourage plant roots to go deeper into the soil. Sea holly is drought resistant, so once it's established, local rainfall should be enough to keep it growing except during excessively long periods of drought.

Additional Advice for Care

In late winter or early spring, fertilize by scratching a slow-release 5-10-10 fertilizer into the soil at half the rate recommended on the container, and water it in. Replenish the mulch. To multiply your holdings, in early spring separate and set out the plantlets that develop at the base.

Sedum

OTHER COMMON NAME: Stonecrop

*I*ndestructible, heat and drought-resistant, sedums are valued for their succulent, evergreen, light-green foliage and for the beautiful fall color of some tall hybrids. The flowers are tiny and star-shaped and in taller forms cluster in showy flat-topped flowerheads. The little ground-hugging sedums are used in rock gardens, for filling nooks, crannies and pockets in walls and by steps. The taller types are indispensable for fall color. 'Autumn Joy' is an all-season contributor to the garden. The jade green foliage is evergreen. In spring, new stems rise, followed in early summer by fresh apple green flowerheads. These slowly change to a rich pink, then rose, salmon, bronze and finally to rosy russet. Another handsome sedum is 'Ruby Glow', a slightly smaller plant whose flower heads are irridescent ruby-red. These cultivars are superb coupled with ornamental grasses in naturalized plantings. They withstand heat and drought even when growing in sand and by the sea.

WHEN TO PLANT

Set out container-grown plants or root divisions any time after the ground can be worked in spring, or in late summer. Plants that are still near-dormant or just beginning to grow will give the best performance. In my garden, sedum self-sows here and there.

WHERE TO PLANT

Sedums flourish in full sun.

HOW TO PLANT

Dig into a hole about twice the size of the rootball and 6 in. deeper 2-in. layers of coarse sand or chicken grit. Add a slow-release 5-10-10 fertilizer. In clay soil, work in a small handful of gypsum and of superphosphate. Half fill the hole with diluted fertilizer, set the plant an inch or two higher than ground level, and press the crown down into the ground to bring it an inch above ground level.

Fill the hole, watering to settle the soil. Provide a permanent 2-in. mulch starting a few inches from the crown.

HOW TO PROVIDE CARE

Sedum prefers dry soil, but tolerates moisture. Provide weekly watering until the plant is established, then keep it on the dry side. Local rainfall should be enough to keep it growing except during protracted droughts. Let the flowerheads stand through the winter—they're very decorative, especially in snow or covered with ice—then cut them to the ground before growth begins in spring.

ADDITIONAL ADVICE FOR CARE

In late winter or early spring, fertilize by scratching a slow-release 5-10-10 fertilizer into the soil at half the rate recommended on the container, and water it in. Replenish the mulch. Cut back to the crown and divide clumps every 3 or 4 years.

Shasta Daisy

*T*think of the mums as three very different groups. There are the disposable cushion mums we buy and plant for instant fall color. There are the very similar garden mums we order from a catalog and set out in the garden as seedlings in mid-spring. Then there are the summer-flowering shasta daisies which are permanent fixtures in our perennial garden. For the home gardener, the shasta is the easiest of the mums to grow. They produce big, beautiful, single or double daisies that flower in early summer on plants 2 to 4 ft. tall. The flowers bloom on tall, strong crowns that multiply yearly, and the plants produce attractive, fresh green foliage that lasts as long as you don't let the plants dry out. The best-known of the older shastas is 'Alaska', a 2- to 4-ft. plant that bears pure white flowers 3 in. across with deep yellow centers. There are attractive smaller species. Three-ft. 'Aglaia', the lace daisy, has fringed petals and is double. 'Little Miss Moffat', a 14-in. plant, flowers in July and August and is a semi-double, very successful in Virginia.

When to Plant

Set out container-grown shasta daisies any time after the ground can be worked in spring. Plants that are still near-dormant or just beginning to grow will give the best performance. You can also set out plants after they become dormant in fall.

Where to Plant

Single shasta daisies need full sun. Doubles can do well in light shade. The shastas tolerate some drought but cannot stand soil that is soggy in winter, so avoid damp low-lying areas where the soil alternately freezes and thaws. Plant shastas 12 in. apart.

How to Plant

Dig into a hole about twice the size of the rootball and 6 in. deeper, 2-in. layers of coarse sand or chicken grit and leaf mold or sphagnum peat moss. Add a slow-release 5-10-10 fertilizer. In clay soil, work in a small handful of gypsum and of superphosphate. Unwind roots circling the rootball. Half fill each hole with diluted fertilizer,

set the plant an inch or 2 higher than ground level, and press the crown down into ground to bring it an inch above ground level. Fill the hole, watering to settle the soil. Provide a permanent 2-in. mulch starting a few inches from the crown.

HOW TO PROVIDE CARE

Water every week unless you have a good soaking rain. Deadhead to promote flowering, or shear the plant if it dries out. You may get another round of flowers. After the first flush of bloom, fertilize again.

ADDITIONAL ADVICE FOR CARE

In late winter or early spring, fertilize by scratching a slow-release 5-10-10 fertilizer into the soil at half the rate recommended on the container, and water it in. Replenish the mulch. Every 2 or 3 years— or if the plant becomes less productive—divide the crown in early spring or after the plant becomes dormant in fall.

ADDITIONAL CULTIVARS AND SPECIES

Feverfew, *Tanacetum parthenium*, is a lovely old-fashioned mum 1 to 3 ft. tall that bears masses of little 1-in. daisy-like white or yellow button flowers with yellow centers in late summer. It self-sows generously.

Siberian Iris

*T*he irises that fit best into a mixed perennial border in our area are the Siberians whose foliage is attractive all season. These irises bloom in late spring and early summer, clustering 2 or 3 flowers on stalks 24 to 40 in. tall. They are backed by slender, grasslike foliage that in winter turns an attractive rusty brown. The standards of the Siberian iris are small and don't quite meet, and the large falls are exquisite. The color range includes blue-purple, lavender, maroon, white, off-pink, and yellowish tones. It's an excellent flower for cutting and is handsome massed in a large border. The foliage remains attractive after the flowers have gone by. Among cultivars that do well in Virginia are the early 'Soft Blue', a repeat bloomer; mid-season 'Pink Haze', and the tall, late-blooming 'VI Luihn', a deep violet.

WHEN TO PLANT

The best period for planting and transplanting an iris is midsummer to early fall. An iris grows from a thick, fleshy elongated rhizome. It can remain unplanted for one to several weeks, but should go into the ground as soon as possible.

WHERE TO PLANT

Irises need full sun, but in hot regions they tolerate shade in late afternoon. Space the rhizomes 8 to 18 in. apart, depending on the size. Irises can handle some drought in summer but can't stand soil that is soggy in winter, so avoid damp low-lying areas where the soil alternately freezes and thaws. They succeed in soil whose pH is between 5.0 to 8.0, but prefer moderately acid soils.

HOW TO PLANT

Two to three weeks before planting, dig into the planting bed to a depth of 10 in., 2-in. layers of coarse sand or chicken grit and leaf mold or sphagnum peat moss. Work in bonemeal and a slow-release 5-10-10 fertilizer. In clay soil work in a small handful of gypsum for each plant. Bury the rhizomes with their tops above the surface of the soil. Set the leafy end in the direction in which you want the plants to develop. Allow 1$^{1}/_{2}$ to 2 ft. between rhizomes. Press the rhizome firmly into the soil, and water well. Provide a permanent 2-in. mulch starting 3 in. from the rhizomes.

HOW TO PROVIDE CARE

Water a new planting every week the first season unless you have a good soaking rain. Let the plants run somewhat dry after flowering. Remove spent flower stalks and trim the foliage back to a fan 12 in. high.

ADDITIONAL ADVICE FOR CARE

In late winter or early spring, fertilize by scratching a slow-release 5-10-10 fertilizer into the soil around the rhizome, and water it in. Replenish the mulch. In midsummer, July or August, every 3 or 4 years, or when the plantings become crowded, divide the rhizomes by lifting them, and slicing them apart at the angled seams.

ADDITIONAL CULTIVARS AND SPECIES

In wet places and heavy moist soils the beautiful Japanese iris, *I. ensata* (syn. *kaempferi*), does well. It thrives by streams in up to 4 inches of water. The flowers are flat and ruffled, sometimes 8 in. across, and are mottled in combinations of blue, pink, reddish-purple, mauve and white. They have slender stems and grasslike leaves.

PERENNIALS

Sneezeweed

*T*his tall, colorful flower is indispensable for late summer and fall bloom. A hardy native 4 to 5 ft. tall, it comes into flower just as most everything in the perennial garden is fading away. It blooms freely for months, producing masses of yellow, burnt orange, or purplish brown discs on well-branched plants. It can be used in groups at the back of the garden, in islands, and for naturalizing in a meadow or wild garden. The newer, cultivated varieties display a broad range of shades. For a smaller garden, 'The Bishop' is an excellent choice—24 to 30 in. high, it bears clear yellow flowers. 'Butterpat', a golden 3-ft. plant, produces masses of small flowers, and sometimes outproduces fall mums. 'Moerheim Beauty' is typical of some well-established cultivars from abroad. It's about 3 ft. tall, and the blossoms have purple-brownish-yellow petals that fade to burnt orange. 'Riverton Beauty' is a 5-ft. plant whose flowers are yellow with a glowing bronze eye.

When to Plant
Helenium grows fairly easily from seed sown in spring, but root divisions are more satisfactory. Sow seeds or plant seedlings after the soil has warmed—April in Zone 8, mid-May in Zones 6 and 7.

Where to Plant
Sneezeweed needs full sun in most of Virginia. In Zone 8, the warmer reaches of the state, it's at the bottom of its heat-hardiness zone and may do better with a bit of protection from noon sun.

How to Plant
Dig into a hole about twice the size of the rootball and 6 in. deeper, 2-in. layers of coarse sand or chicken grit, and of leaf mold, or sphagnum peat moss. Add a slow-release 5-10-10 fertilizer. In clay soil, work in a small handful of gypsum and of superphosphate. Unwind roots circling the rootball. Half fill each hole with diluted fertilizer, set the plant an inch or two higher than ground level, and

press the crown down into ground to bring it an inch above ground level. Fill the hole, watering to settle the soil. Provide a permanent 2-in. mulch starting a few inches from the crown.

HOW TO PROVIDE CARE

Pinching in late spring makes a bushier plant that may not need staking, but the flowering will come later. Stake helenium if the plant begins to topple. Water a new plant every week the first season unless you have a good soaking rain. After the first flush of bloom, fertilize again. Deadhead to promote flowering.

ADDITIONAL ADVICE FOR CARE

In late winter or early spring, fertilize by scratching a slow-release 5-10-10 fertilizer into the soil at half the rate recommended on the container, and water it in. Replenish the mulch.

*T*he veronicas are easy to grow, first-rate fillers that in mid-spring to summer bear an abundance of flowers in densely packed upright spikes. The colors of the flowers range from pale blue to lilac blue and deep blue. The foliage is attractive semi- or evergreen. 'Crater Lake Blue' is the finest of the veronicas—12 to 15 in. high with beautiful spires of gentian blue flowers. A somewhat taller species is *V. spicata*, which blooms in summer. The flowers are 1 to 3 ft. tall and their colors range from deep blue to white. There are light pinks, too. 'Blue Peter' is a well-loved cultivar. Another beautiful veronica is the smaller *V. gentianoides*, a mat-forming species approximately 6 in. tall that in spring lifts loose racemes of flowers that are pale blue, almost white, with darker veins.

WHEN TO PLANT

Any time after the ground can be worked in spring, set out root divisions. Plants that are still near-dormant or just beginning to grow will give the best performance.

WHERE TO PLANT

Veronica does best in full sun, but it stands some shade. It tolerates drought but can't stand soil that is soggy in winter, so avoid damp low-lying areas where the soil alternately freezes and thaws.

HOW TO PLANT

Dig into a hole about twice the size of the rootball and 6 in. deeper, 2-in. layers of coarse sand or chicken grit. Add a slow-release 5-10-10 fertilizer. In clay soil, work in a small handful of gypsum and of superphosphate. Unwind roots circling the rootball. Half fill each hole with diluted fertilizer, set the plant an inch or two higher than ground level, and press the crown down into ground to bring it an inch above ground level. Fill the hole, watering to settle the soil. Provide a permanent 2-in. mulch starting a few inches from the crown.

How to Provide Care

Water every week unless you have a good soaking rain. Veronica is tolerant of moisture, and must not be allowed to dry out. Deadhead to promote flowering.

Additional Advice for Care

In late winter or early spring, fertilize by scratching a slow-release 5-10-10 fertilizer into the soil at half the rate recommended on the container, and water it in. Replenish the mulch. Every 3 or 4 years— or if the plant becomes less productive—divide in early spring.

Additional Cultivars and Species

V. repens, which is called creeping speedwell, thrives in full sun in rocky places and in walls. The flowers are white-blue.

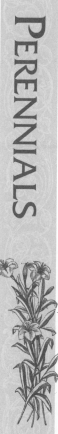

Yarrow

Y arrow is a flower for all seasons and all locations, from the formal perennial border to the herb garden. It's showy when naturalized with ornamental grasses and growing in meadow gardens. The ferny foliage of this ancient herb is strongly scented and makes a nicely textured filler for the garden. From spring through midsummer, the large flat-topped flowerheads in strong yellows, gold, off-pink, cerise, and off-white stand above woolly gray-green foliage 8 to 36 in. high. The cut flowers are long lasting in fresh bouquets. They dry easily and are a mainstay of winter arrangements. 'Coronation Gold' and 'Moonshine' are exceptionally beautiful yellow hybrids 24 to 36 in. tall, excellent with ornamental grasses. *A. millefolium* is a smaller plant that comes in a range of attractive colors—cerise-red, peach, and salmon.

WHEN TO PLANT

Any time after the ground can be worked in spring, set out container-grown plants or root divisions. Plants that are still near-dormant or just beginning to grow will give the best performance. You can also set out plants after they become dormant in fall.

WHERE TO PLANT

Yarrow really needs full sun, but it can take a little filtered shade and still be productive. It succeeds in drought, sand, and by the seashore, but can't stand soggy soil, especially in winter. Avoid damp low-lying areas where the soil alternately freezes and thaws. Yarrow is a wide-spreading plant, so allow 10 to 12 in. all around the planting hole.

HOW TO PLANT

Dig into a hole about twice the size of the rootball and 6 in. deeper, 2-in. layers of coarse sand or chicken grit and leaf mold or sphagnum peat moss. Add a slow-release 5-10-10 fertilizer. In clay soil, work in a small handful of gypsum and of superphosphate. Unwind roots circling the rootball. Half fill each hole with diluted fertilizer, set the plant an inch or two higher than ground level, and press the crown down into ground to bring it an inch above ground level. Fill the hole, watering to settle the soil. Apply a permanent 2-in. mulch starting 3 in. from the crown.

How to Provide Care

Water a new plant every week the first month or so unless you have a good soaking rain. Yarrow is drought resistant, so once it's established, local rainfall should be enough to keep it growing except during our mid- and late August droughts. Deadhead often. As fall approaches, remove spent blooms and their stems to encourage a new round of color. After the first flush of bloom, fertilize again.

Additional Advice for Care

In late winter or early spring, fertilize by scratching a slow-release 5-10-10 fertilizer into the soil at half the rate recommended on the container, and water it in. Replenish the mulch. Every 4 or 5 years—or if the plant becomes less productive—divide in early spring before growth begins.

Additional Cultivars and Species

Two species that are excellent in shore gardens are fern-leaved yarrow, *A. filipendulina*, which has silvery green, deeply cut foliage and great flat mustard-yellow flowerheads; and *A. taygetea*, a cool, sulfur-yellow flower that has beautiful, finely divided silvery leaves. It's about 18 to 24 in tall. This yarrow is not hardy north of Zone 7.

PERENNIALS

Roses

$\mathcal{R}$OSES ARE IRRESISTIBLE, IF NOT ALWAYS EASY. In 1987, a time when chemical remedies for the rose's many ills were beginning to be banned, the rose was designated by Congress as the nation's floral emblem, defeating the rugged marigold—a native flower with lots of friends and few enemies. That's the power of the rose. Its extraordinary beauty and its recently acquired spring-to-fall bloom period have made it the most popular flower in America. That wonderful ever-blooming characteristic is the gift of hybridizers who crossed fragrant, hardy, old garden roses that bloom only in spring with roses from warm regions of China that bloom all season.

But the fact remains that to grow roses, you must deal with the challenges that accompany many of these lovely shrubs. So choose a plant that will fulfill your dreams and make the effort of growing it worthwhile. And, if fragrance is part of your dream, be sure to chose a rose labeled as fragrant.

The rose problems prevalent in Virginia are Japanese beetles, black spot, and powdery mildew. I live in a neighborhood where there are few Japanese beetles. I get rid of them by knocking them off the flowers in the very early morning when they are sluggish with the cold. Then I squash them underfoot. Other solutions abound if you are willing to rise early. You can shake them onto a drop cloth and drown them in soapy water, or drop them onto large leaves and crush the bundle in the disposal.

You can also import and turn loose native species of parasitic wasps and flies, spray plants attacked by the beetles with rotenone, or apply milky disease spores to the soil to kill the larvae. Yet another solution is to fill your garden with plants that provide berries and seedheads for birds, and fertilize the roses in late winter with partially composted horse manure, which often has seeds. It does wonders for the roses, and flocks of hungry birds will swoop in to make short work of seeds, worms, and Japanese beetles.

Chapter Nine

Black spot is common, especially in hybrid teas, floribundas, and grandifloras. The solution offered is to spray plants that show signs of infection from mid-spring to mid-fall. It helps to remove every trace of infected vegetation from the plant and from the ground. If the leaves are wetted by rain or the hose, that favors black spot, so always water roses at ground level. Spraying with an 0.5 solution of baking soda may help; 1 teaspoon of baking soda to 1 quart of water. Ortho sells a combination rose control that covers black spot. It hasn't been banned as of this writing, since I can still find it in garden centers and hardware stores.

Powdery mildew, another major rose problem here, may be minimized by a spraying program of weekly applications of sulfur. My answer is a combination spray recommended by a local nursery.

But the best defense against diseases is to plant roses that are specifically designated as disease resistant. Varieties that win the All-American Rose Selections Award are generally resistant to most problems. These winners of the American Rose Society trials are identified in catalogs by the letters "BARS" and the year of the award after their names.

NOTES ON GROWING ROSES

- Set hybrid roses so the bud union is 2 in. above the soil level.

- Remove all suckers growing from below the bud union as soon as they appear.

- Leave a 5-leaf sprig on each shoot as a base for the new shoots when cutting roses for bouquets.

- Make all pruning cuts $1/2$ in. above the bud eye or sprig.

- Remember that spring-flowering roses bloom on side shoots that develop from wood maturing in late summer. Those are the growing points that will be forming flowers through winter. Do any pruning right after blooming ends, but not later.

- Roses that bloom all season, or that bloom on new wood, are pruned after real cold settles in during late fall. Remove weak canes and cut back healthy canes to 2 ft. In spring when the buds are breaking, prune them back to 12 to 18 in.

Climbing Roses

*T*he climbing roses do not actually "climb." They put forth long canes you can train to cover an arch, an arbor, a trellis, a wall, or a fence, and they generally are planted in the background. The floweriest climbers are ramblers that bear clusters of small flowers on pliant canes that rise annually from the base. Another type of climber is a tall shrub with stiff canes that bear large flowers singly or in clusters. There are climbers among other categories of roses. Miniature roses with trailing stems can be used as climbers. Some hybrid teas are trained as climbers, but most of these are not reliably winter hardy in Virginia. The climbing roses that bloom most profusely are pruned annually. Five or 6 heavy canes is all a climbing rose can handle. Remove the others and train the canes that remain in the desired direction. Trained horizontally, climbers tend to flower more abundantly. Climbing roses, along with floribunda types, are the roses used to create standard or tree forms.

WHEN TO PLANT

Plant bare root roses a few weeks before the last frost. Around Williamsburg that's April 14; Culpepper, April 17; Richmond, May 4; Washington, D.C., March 25. Container-grown roses do best set out at this time, but they succeed planted almost any time in early to mid-spring and early to mid-fall.

WHERE TO PLANT

Roses need at least 6 hours of full sun to bloom their best. They can make do with 4 to 5 hours of sun, but blooming will be sparse. Climbers flower well with some shade on the base, as long as most of the plant is in the sun. Avoid sites where the roots of your rose bushes will face competition from encroaching tree roots.

HOW TO PLANT

Dig into a hole 2 ft. wide and deep a 2-in. layer of coarse sand or chicken grit, a 4-in. layer of dried cow manure, and a trowelful of bonemeal. In clay soil, mix in a handful of gypsum and another of superphosphate. A pH range of between 6.0 and 7.0 suits roses. Spread the roots of a bare root rose over a cone of soil in the center of the planting hole at a height that places the bump of the bud union 2 in. above the soil surface. Water, fill the hole, and water again. Apply mulch to within 3 in. of the stem. Plant a container-grown rose at the level at which it was growing in the container.

HOW TO PROVIDE CARE AND MAINTENANCE

Apply a gallon of water weekly. Starting 4 to 6 weeks after planting and ending in mid-August, add to the water $1/4$ teaspoon of house-plant fertilizer. Remove spent flowers, fallen leaves, and suckers rising below the bud union. Prune back canes that have flowered: often they will grow another stem that will bloom. Cut on the diagonal, just above an outward-facing bud. Cut rose stems just above a 5-leaf stem. Every 7 to 10 days, and after rain, apply an all-purpose rose insect and disease spray. After the first frost, mound shredded leaves 1 ft. deep around the crown.

ADDITIONAL ADVICE

In mid-March, dig in around the plant a trowelful of 5-10-5 fertilizer and replenish the mulch. As buds begin swelling, remove one of the oldest canes. When pruning, leave the uppermost bud on each cane pointing outward from the center of the bush. Of the new canes that develop, save only two or three later for flowering next year. As new canes grow, arch and tie them to fencing or trellising to encourage growth of flowering laterals.

OTHER CULTIVARS AND SPECIES

To have masses of scarlet flowers (unscented) off and on all season, plant 'Blaze'. One of the most beautiful ramblers is 'Golden Showers', an All-American Rose Selections winner, that bears fragrant 5-in. daffodil-yellow flowers repeatedly until late fall.

Garden Roses

OTHER PLANT NAMES: English/Polyantha/Floribunda

*T*he David Austin English roses, the polyanthas, and the floribundas are the roses that do the most for mixed, flowering borders and make the most charming foundation plants. These are flowery, disease-resistant modern roses that produce clusters of blooms almost all season long, and many are fragrant. The very romantic-looking David Austin English roses have many-petaled, perfumed 2¹/₂- to 5-in. flowers that look like old-fashioned rose hybrids. The rich pink 'Cottage Rose' and the pristine white 'Fair Bianca' are irresistible. The shrubs are compact and easily managed. The polyanthas are smaller, 2 to 3 ft. tall, and they bear masses of clusters of charming little flowers under 2 in. across. The best known is the slightly fragrant, seashell pink 'The Fairy' which often is used as a hedge rose. The floribundas are larger shrubs 4 or 5 ft. tall whose flowers are 2 to 5 in. across and, like the polyanthas, are borne in clusters. Some have blooms in the form of hybrid tea roses. In Europe, they landscape many roadsides and parks. A favorite in local gardens and for hedges is 'Betty Prior', a vivid pink with emerald foliage.

WHEN TO PLANT

Plant bare root roses a few weeks before the last frost. Around Williamsburg that's April 14; Culpepper, April 17; Richmond, May 4; Washington, D.C., March 25. Container-grown roses do best set out at this time, but they succeed planted almost any time in early to mid-spring, and in early to mid-fall.

WHERE TO PLANT

Roses need at least 6 hours of full sun to bloom their best. They can make do with 4 to 5 hours of sun, but blooming will be sparse. Avoid sites where the roots of your rose bushes will face competition from encroaching tree roots. Floribundas 'Gruss an Aachen', a small, many-petaled pink, the deep-pink 'Playgirl', and the rosy David Austin 'Bow Bells' bloom rather well in my garden in part shade.

ROSES

How to Plant

Dig into a hole 2 ft. wide and deep a 2-in. layer of coarse sand or chicken grit, a 4-in. layer of dried cow manure, and a trowelful of bonemeal. In clay soil, mix in a handful of gypsum and another of superphosphate. A pH range of between 6.0 and 7.0 suits roses. Spread the roots of a bare root rose over a cone of soil in the center of the planting hole at a height that places the bump of the graft union 2 in. above the soil surface. Water, fill the hole, and water again. Apply mulch to within 3 in. of the stem. Plant a container-grown rose at the level at which it was growing in the container.

How to Provide Care and Maintenance

Apply a gallon of water weekly. Starting 4 to 6 weeks after planting and ending in mid-August, add to the water $1/4$ teaspoon of house-plant fertilizer. Remove spent flowers, fallen leaves, and suckers rising below the bud union. Cut rose stems just above a 5-leaf stem. Every 2 weeks or so, and after rain, apply an all-purpose rose insect and disease spray. After the first frost, mound shredded leaves 1 ft. deep around the crown.

Additional Advice

In mid-March, dig in a trowelful of 5-10-5 around each plant. Replenish the mulch. As the buds swell, cut polyanthas and flori-bundas back a third, and the English roses back by half, with the uppermost bud on each remaining cane pointing outward. Remove the oldest flowering canes and leave the plants open in the center, creating a vase-shaped framework.

Other Cultivars and Species

Other popular garden roses that are easy to maintain are the Bonicas. 'Royal Bonica' yields impressive clusters of rich pink flowers in huge clusters of up to 20 flowers. It is about 4 ft. tall. It is a new version of 'Bonica', a rose that has done well at the National Arboretum, where it is cut back in late winter to 1 to $1^1/2$ ft. high.

Ground Cover Roses or Landscape Roses

Ground cover roses spread outward rather than upward, and they are used to carpet slopes, as edgers and fillers for a garden of tall shrub roses, and as low hedges. Best known are the Meidilands, which are 3 to 4 ft. tall with a 5- to 6-ft. spread. They bloom from early summer until fall, and the only maintenance they need is pruning in late winter. The flower colors are white, cherry pink, and scarlet, and there is a pearly-white blushed with pink called 'Pearl Sevillana'. Recently introduced is a new strain of really low-growing hardy roses called "carpeting" roses that grow on their own roots. Just 2 to 2¹/₂ ft. tall, they can spread in a season to 5 ft. across. They resist pests and diseases, and given monthly feeding, will bloom all season long. The best known is 'Flower Carpet' whose flowers are lavender-pink, and slightly perfumed. 'Jeeper's Creepers' is a white version, and there's a light pink called 'Baby Blanket'. The native Virginia rose, spring-blooming rose-magenta *R. virginiana*, does very well in sandy gardens and slopes along the coast. It has brilliant autumn foliage.

WHEN TO PLANT
Ground cover roses are generally offered growing in containers. They can be planted a few weeks before the last frost. Around Williamsburg that's April 14; Culpepper, April 17; Richmond, May 4; Washington, D.C., March 25. Or set them out any time in early to mid-spring, and in early to mid-fall.

WHERE TO PLANT
Roses need at least 6 hours of full sun to bloom their best. They can make do with 4 to 5 hours of sun, but blooming will be sparse.

HOW TO PLANT
Dig into a hole 2 ft. wide and deep a 2-inch layer of coarse sand or chicken grit, a 4-in. layer of dried cow manure, and a trowelful of bonemeal. In clay soil, mix in a handful of gypsum and another of superphosphate. A pH range of between 6.0 and 7.0 suits roses. Space the plants 2 ft. apart. Set the rootball in the center of the plant-

ing hole with the crown at the level at which it was growing in the container. Water, fill the hole, and water again. Apply mulch to within 3 in. of the stem.

HOW TO PROVIDE CARE AND MAINTENANCE

Water weekly until the plants are growing vigorously. The first growing season, every month from early spring through August, give each plant a gallon of water mixed with 1/4 teaspoon of house-plant fertilizer.

ADDITIONAL ADVICE

In mid-March dig in around each plant a trowelful of 5-10-5 and replenish the mulch until the plants have spread wide enough to shade out weeds and make mulching unnecessary. As buds begin swelling, shear the plants back to 1 1/2 to 2 ft. high.

OTHER CULTIVARS AND SPECIES

Some sprawling/trailing miniature roses can serve as ground cover roses. Some leggy shrub roses, like the bourbons, are trained as ground cover by pegging the sprawling branches to the ground with a forked stick or a bent wire—interesting, but a high-maintenance endeavor!

Hedge Roses

*T*he roses used for tall hedges are the large, disease-resistant floribundas, the grandifloras, and the rugged rugosas. The floribundas, described on the preceding pages, are vigorous, cluster-producing shrubs which, in many varieties, are shaped like hybrid tea roses. They make fine repeat-blooming hedges. The grandifloras are larger and bear clusters of long-stemmed, hybrid tea-type roses. The plants make excellent high hedges and impressive specimen plantings. 'Queen Elizabeth' was the first grandiflora, a clear pink. This class is now grouped with the hybrid teas in a category called Large-flowered Shrub Roses. The big rugosa or Japanese roses, cultivars of *R. rugosa*, have tall, stiff, spiny canes that make for superb hedges. They are famous for their success by the sea; planted close together they make excellent windbreaks. Rugosas bear clove-scented single or double flowers in spring with some repeat, followed in fall by big, shiny, coral-orange rose hips and colorful foliage. One of the best is crimson 'Linda Campbell', which in a season produces 6 to 7 flushes of blooms in clusters.

WHEN TO PLANT
Plant bare root roses a few weeks before the last frost. Around Williamsburg that's April 14; Culpepper, April 17; Richmond, May 4; Washington, D.C., March 25. Container-grown roses do best set out at this time, but they succeed planted almost any time in early to mid-spring, and in early to mid-fall.

WHERE TO PLANT
Roses need at least 6 hours of full sun to bloom their best. They can make do with 4 to 5 hours of sun, but blooming will be sparse. Avoid sites where the roots of your rose bushes will face competition from encroaching tree roots.

HOW TO PLANT
Dig into a hole 2 ft. wide and deep a 2-in. layer of coarse sand or chicken grit, a 4-in. layer of dried cow manure, and a trowelful of bone meal. In clay soil, mix in a handful of gypsum and another of superphosphate. A pH range of between 6.0 and 7.0 suits roses.

Spread the roots of a bare root rose over a cone of soil in the center of the planting hole at a height that places the bump of the graft union 2 in. above the soil surface. Water, fill the hole, and water again. Apply mulch to within 3 in. of the stem. Plant a container-grown rose at the level at which it was growing in the container.

HOW TO PROVIDE CARE AND MAINTENANCE

Apply a gallon of water weekly. Starting 4 to 6 weeks after planting and ending in mid-August, add to the water $1/4$ teaspoon of house-plant fertilizer. Remove spent flowers, fallen leaves, and suckers rising below the bud union. Cut roses at a point just above a 5-leaf stem. After the first frost, mound shredded leaves 1 ft. deep around the crown.

ADDITIONAL ADVICE

As buds begin swelling, dig in around the plant a trowelful of 5-10-5 and replenish the mulch. Remove the oldest flowering canes of the grandifloras, leaving an open structure of 4 to 5 strong canes 5 or 6 in. long with the uppermost buds pointing outward. To prune floribundas, see the preceding pages. Beginning with a rugosa's fourth season, remove all canes that have already flowered.

OTHER CULTIVARS AND SPECIES

'Elizabeth Scholtz' is a strong, upright grandiflora with beautifully formed orange-red-gold flowers. Crimson 'Love' is a grandiflora with shiny foliage and perfectly formed, orange-red-gold flowers. For brilliant rose hips in fall, plant *R. rugosa* 'Alba', 'Rubra', and 'Belle de Potvin', which has almost double pink flowers.

ℋybrid ℐea ℛoses

OTHER COMMON NAME: Large-flowered Bush Roses

*T*he hybrid tea roses are gorgeous, long-stemmed cutting flowers, slender, high-centered, pointed, and semi- or double-flowered. The shrubs are upright and tidy, 3 to 6 ft. tall, and they bloom all season, but not very freely. First-rate hybrid teas, like the exquisite and enduring yellow-and-rose 'Peace', bloom in my garden in mid-spring, throw a few flowers throughout summer, and bloom well from September through October. Though the shrubs are not very ornamental, need lots of attention to do their best, and may not survive winter, these are the most popular roses. Usually, hybrid teas are grown in a bed of their own with lavender or leafy annuals disguising their legginess. The hybrid tea form has been bred into the small polyantha roses, the large-flowered floribunda roses, and into miniature roses and climbing roses. To set the florist's single-stemmed, large-flowered hybrid tea rose apart from the other hybrid tea forms, its classification has recently been changed to Large-flowered Bush Roses; but it will be a while before most nurseries and catalogs call them anything but hybrid tea roses.

WHEN TO PLANT

Plant bareroot hybrid teas a few weeks before the last frost. Around Williamsburg that's April 14; Culpepper, April 17; Richmond, May 4; Washington, D.C., March 25. Container-grown roses do best set out at this time, but they succeed planted almost any time in early to mid-spring, and in early to mid-fall.

WHERE TO PLANT

Roses need at least 6 hours of full sun to bloom their best. They can make do with 4 to 5 hours of sun, but blooming will be sparse. Avoid sites where the roots of your rose bushes will face competition from encroaching tree roots.

HOW TO PLANT

Dig into a hole 2 ft. wide and 2 ft. deep a 2-in. layer of coarse sand or chicken grit, a 4-in. layer of dried cow manure, and a trowelful of bonemeal. In clay soil, mix in a handful of gypsum and another of superphosphate. A pH range of between 5.5 to 7.0 suits hybrid teas. Spread the roots of a bareroot rose over a cone of soil in the center of the planting hole at a height that places the bump of the graft union 2 in. above the soil surface. Water, fill the hole, and water again. Apply mulch to within 3 in. of the stem. Plant a container-grown rose at the level at which it was growing in the container.

HOW TO PROVIDE CARE AND MAINTENANCE

Apply a gallon of water weekly. Starting 4 to 6 weeks after planting and ending in mid-August, add to the water 1/4 tsp. of houseplant fertilizer. Be sure to remove spent flowers, fallen petals and leaves, and suckers; do not compost them. Cut roses and spent blossoms at a point just above a 5-leaf stem. Every 7 to 10 days, and after every heavy rainfall, apply an all-purpose rose spray that controls insects and disease. After the first frost, mound leaves 1 in. deep around the central stem.

ADDITIONAL ADVICE

As buds begin swelling, dig in around the plant a trowelful of 5-10-5 and replenish the mulch. Remove the damaged canes, and the oldest flowering canes, leaving an open structure of 4 to 5 strong canes 5 or 6 in. long with the uppermost buds pointing outward.

OTHER CULTIVARS AND SPECIES

Some very fragrant favorites are 'Miss All-American Beauty', AARS 1968, a many-petaled, deep-pink rose; 'Fragrant Cloud', a vivid coral-red; 'Double Delight', AARS 1977, whose 5-in. white flowers are blushed with rich red. 'Touch of Class', AARS 1986, is a huge, slightly fragrant pink, coral, and cream rose that growers love to raise for show.

Miniature Roses

*T*he miniature roses are used as edging for rose gardens, in mixed flower borders, and those with trailing branches make graceful container and basket plants. The minis will bloom for a time indoors on a sunny windowsill. The stems of the miniatures are thin, and the close-spaced leaves are tiny. The buds and flowers are perfect little replicas of larger roses and are shaped either like hybrid teas or like many-petaled cabbage roses. They flower freely from June to frost, are hardy with some winter protection, and are easy to grow. The standard miniature is a dainty shrub 12 in. high and 6 to 18 in. across. Macro-minis reach 2 ft., and a few micro-minis, like 'Elfin Gold' and 'Tiny Flame', grow to just 6 in. high and have dime-sized flowers. Some miniature roses are fragrant, for example, the lovely little yellow 'Rise 'N Shine', a recipient of the American Rose Society Award of Excellence.

WHEN TO PLANT

Miniature roses are generally offered growing in containers. They can be planted a few weeks before the last frost. Around Williamsburg that's April 14; Culpepper, April 17; Richmond, May 4; Washington, D.C., March 25, but minis can be planted almost any time in early to mid-spring, and in early to mid-fall.

WHERE TO PLANT

Even miniature roses need at least 6 hours of full sun to bloom their best. They can make do with 4 to 5 hours of sun, but blooming will be sparse. Avoid sites where the roots of your rose bushes will face competition from encroaching shrubs and tough perennials.

HOW TO PLANT

Dig into a hole 18 in. wide and deep a 1-in. layer of coarse sand or chicken grit, a 4-in. layer of dried cow manure, and a trowelful of bonemeal. In clay soil, mix in a handful of gypsum and another of superphosphate. A pH range of between 6.5 and 7.0 is best for miniature roses. Space the plants 2 ft. apart. Set the rootball in the center of the planting hole with the crown at the level at which it was growing in the container. Water, fill the hole, and water again. Apply mulch to within 3 in. of the stem.

How to Provide Care and Maintenance

Apply a half gallon of water weekly. Starting 4 to 6 weeks after planting and ending in mid-August, add to the water 1/4 teaspoon of 20-20-20 houseplant fertilizer. Remove spent flowers and fallen leaves. Cut roses at a point just above a 5-leaf stem. Every 10 days and after every heavy rainfall, apply an all-purpose rose spray that controls insects and disease. After the first frost, mound shredded leaves 1 ft. deep around the crown.

Additional Advice

In mid-March, dig in around the plant a small handful of 5-10-5 and replenish the mulch. As buds begin swelling, remove dead, weak, and discolored canes and canes that cross. Trim all the branches back by about a third, enough to maintain a pleasing form.

Other Cultivars and Species

For hanging baskets, I recommend 'Red Cascade', a vigorous minia-ture with cascading branches almost 5 ft. across that covers itself with small crimson flowers. 'Starina', a fragrant, orange-red minia-ture, earned an Award of Excellence from the American Rose Society, and it continues to be a favorite for containers.

Old Garden Roses

OTHER COMMON NAME: Historic Roses

*T*he authentic old garden roses are full-petaled and fragrant, and have become so popular that dozens of species and varieties are being reintroduced by growers. Most flower only for 4 weeks in early or mid-spring, but what a show! A few repeat bloom. Some are tall plants to train to trellises. Though they are not billed as pest- or disease-resistant, once established in good soil in full sun, at the National Arboretum the old roses succeeded without requiring a great deal of chemical support. Among the most fragrant are the apothecary rose, *R. gallica* 'Officinalis', a spring-blooming shrub whose petals are more fragrant after drying, and the damask rose, *R. damascena*. A venerable species, the damask rose produces clusters of huge, flattish flowers with a quartered effect. Pink 'Autumn Damask' blooms recurrently. 'Madame Hardy', a fragrant white with a green-button eye, is described as one of the most beautiful white roses in the world.

WHEN TO PLANT

Plant bare root roses a few weeks before the last frost. Around Williamsburg that's April 14; Culpepper, April 17; Richmond, May 4; Washington, D.C., March 25. Container-grown roses do best set out at this time, but they succeed planted almost any time in early to mid-spring, and in early to mid-fall.

WHERE TO PLANT

Roses need at least 6 hours of full sun to bloom their best. They can make do with 4 to 5 hours of sun, but blooming will be sparse. Give these beautiful old roses plenty of space all around. Avoid sites where the roots of your rose bushes will face competition from encroaching tree roots.

HOW TO PLANT

Dig into a hole 2 ft. wide and deep a 2-in. layer of coarse sand or chicken grit, a 4-in. layer of dried cow manure, and a trowelful of bonemeal. In clay soil, mix in a handful of gypsum and another of superphosphate. A pH range of between 6.0 and 7.0 suits roses.

Spread the roots of a bare root rose over a cone of soil in the center of the planting hole at a height that places the bump of the graft union 2 in. above the soil surface. Water, fill the hole, and water again. Apply mulch to within 3 in. of the stem. Plant a container-grown rose at the level at which it was growing in the container.

How to Provide Care and Maintenance

Apply a gallon of water weekly. Starting 4 to 6 weeks after planting and ending in mid-August, add to the water 1/4 teaspoon of house-plant fertilizer. Be sure to remove spent flowers, fallen petals and leaves, and suckers at once. Do not compost. Cut roses at a point just above a 5-leaf stem. Every 7 to 10 days and after every heavy rainfall, apply an all-purpose rose spray that controls insects and disease. Prune a one-time bloomer when blooming is over. Cut on the diagonal, just above an outward-facing eye. After the first frost, mound shredded leaves 1 ft. deep around the crown.

Additional Advice

In mid-March, dig in around the plant a trowelful of 5-10-5 and replenish the mulch. As buds begin swelling, remove dead, weak, and discolored canes and canes that cross. Cut the oldest canes of recurrent bloomers back to 2 or 3 bud eyes, and remove twiggy ends. As new canes grow, arch and tie them to fencing or trellising to encourage growth of flowering laterals.

Other Cultivars and Species

R. centifolia, the cabbage rose, is the multi-petaled, very fragrant very double pink rose painted by the Dutch masters. An excellent cultivar is 'Fantin Latour'. *R. C.* 'Muscosa', the moss rose, has an attractive, often fragrant, mossy growth on the sepals and calyx. 'Gloire des Mousseuses' is an extra-fragrant pink double.

CHAPTER TEN

Shrubs

*T*HE MOST POPULAR FLOWERING SHRUB IN VIRGINIA IS CERTAINLY THE AZALEA, with a spring show that is simply breathtaking. But before they come into bloom, other shrubs are showing off their spring colors. By late March, forsythia hedges are solid gold, and the hardy camellias and quinces bloom, followed by the extraordinarily fragrant viburnums. For color in the fall, the most popular fruiting shrubs are sprawling cotoneaster and firethorn. The best fall foliage color is the gift of the barberries, and of two tall shrubs (or small trees): the dwarf winged spindle tree and sumac.

For year-round greenery, it is the tradition in Virginia to grow English boxwood. It develops slowly and can be sheared for centuries, literally, and so is ideal for hedges and edging. Other handsome evergreen shrubs include the photinias, which are covered coppery-red as new growth emerges, and dainty nandina whose winter berries turn lipstick-red just as the holly berries redden. Fragrant plants have strong appeal for me, so I recommend daphne, which blooms in summer, and holly olive, a tall, broadleaved evergreen with an insignificant little flower that perfumes the air in November.

Where a bolder and less formal plant is desired, consider a variety of yew, which I think of as the most durable evergreens. I especially like the forms with graceful, arching branches.

GROWING AND PRUNING SHRUBS

I use container-grown shrubs because they are foolproof. Young plants are often more vigorous than older plants that have been parked in containers for some time. But shrubs shipped bare root in spring by a reliable mail-order house will do well if you follow the shipper's instructions for planting. A shrub will be with you for years—decades usually—so give it a good start by providing a generous planting hole and well-drained soil.

In placing shrubs, keep in mind the size of the plant at maturity. Azaleas are shallow-rooted and move well enough, even when quite large. But any shrub that is torn out of the environment it has tied into will be checked in its development. To occupy empty space while the shrub grows up, plant a shaded area with ferns, hostas, impatiens, or caladiums; in a sunny spot plant marigolds or petunias. Don't park a shrub in a deep, airless corner. White fly, a pesky little thing that spoils the appearance of leaves, just loves hot, airless corners. (If you run into a lot of white fly, spray the area two or three times with some form of neem—it does do them in.)

Don't water shrubs overhead when they are in bloom—it harms the blossoms. Water a newly planted shrub well its first season; as it matures, it will require less extra watering than perennials. Shrubs have built-in safety processes that respond well to reasonable stress, becoming somewhat dormant in very hot, dry summers, as they do in cold winters. They can adapt to some drought if they are accustomed to it, but will suffer if they are accustomed to shallow daily watering, or if they are forced by watering and fertilizing to be lush when the weather isn't supporting that kind of growth.

The way to minimize pruning chores is to select dwarf and slow-growing varieties. If you wish to stimulate growth in young, just-developing shrubs, prune them when they are growing actively. Fresh, young shoots cut in half immediately begin to grow lateral shoots. When the plants have reached the desired height and width, prune according to the growth and flowering periods.

Prune flowering shrubs according to their bloom habit: those that bloom on the current season's wood are pruned in late winter or early spring before growth begins. Those that bloom on last season's wood should be pruned as soon after the flowering period ends as possible, because the next thing they do is initiate the buds for the following season.

Abelia

*T*his is a rounded, multi-stemmed semi-evergreen shrub about 5 ft. tall, with twiggy branches, dainty foliage, and small, slightly fragrant, funnel-shaped pink flowers. It comes into bloom in June or July and goes on blooming until it frosts. The leaves take on a purplish bronze cast in late fall and persist until early winter. In warmer areas, they're almost evergreen. Abelia makes a good bank cover and an attractive hedge.

WHEN TO PLANT

The best times for planting a balled and burlapped or container-grown abelia is in the fall before Indian summer, and in early spring while the shrub still is dormant.

WHERE TO PLANT

Abelia flowers best growing in full sun. However, like most shrubs, it succeeds with 4 to 6 hours of sun, or all-day filtered light. It thrives in well-drained soil in the acid range, but it is versatile as to pH.

HOW TO PLANT

Dig a hole 4 in. deeper than the rootball, widening toward the top. Use a spading fork to loosen the sides of the hole. In clay soil, work into the hole 1/2 cupful each of gypsum and superphosphate, and top it with 2 in. of soil. Set the shrub so the crown will be 1 in. above the ground level. If balled and burlapped, set the plant in the hole, cut the rope, slash the burlap, and push it away from the ball. For a container-grown shrub, unwind the roots circling the rootball before planting. Fill the hole, watering in to settle the soil. Apply a 3-in. mulch starting 3 in. from the stem.

SHRUBS

HOW TO PROVIDE CARE

The first year, pour a bucketful of water around the roots every week unless there's a soaking rain. Mid-fall and early winter can be a dry period in Virginia, so continue the watering program suffi- ciently to keep the soil from drying out. Abelia blooms on new wood, so in late winter prune back dead branch tips to outward facing buds. Once it has attained a size that is pleasing, you can keep it at that size by removing up to a third of the branch tips in a year.

ADDITIONAL ADVICE FOR CARE

In late winter before growth begins, broadcast an organic 5-10-10 fertilizer at half the rate recommended from the drip line out to a point at a distance equal to 1^1/$_2$ times the shrub's height. Water it in. Replenish the mulch. Fertilize again in November. Once the plant is well established, switch to a 12-6-6 fertilizer.

ADDITIONAL CULTIVARS AND SPECIES

A. × grandiflora 'Francis Mason' is a densely branched dwarf from 3 to 4 ft. tall that has richly variegated foliage blending green, red, and yellow.

Alabama Fothergilla

his is a tall, fast-growing deciduous shrub that is attractive in spring and fall. From April to early May, it bears rounded tufts of honey-scented whitish stamens. The flowers and the crinkly dark green foliage that follows are pleasant, but the fall foliage is brilliant and a major reason for planting this shrub. The leaves turn to yellow gold, orange, and scarlet, and usually with all 3 colors on the same bush. This species is a big, upright shrub, 6 to 10 ft. tall. A much smaller species, *F. gardenii*, the dwarf witch alder, is a bushy shrub 2 to 4 ft. high and as wide or wider. The forthergillas are at their best fronting evergreens against which their fall colors will stand out.

WHEN TO PLANT

Set out a container-grown or balled and burlapped plant in early spring while the shrub still is dormant.

WHERE TO PLANT

Fothergilla flowers best and produces the brightest fall colors growing in full sun, but in hot areas, it benefits from protection from noon sun in summer. To succeed, fothergilla must have soil with an acid pH, under 6.0. It is not suited to alkaline or limey soil.

HOW TO PLANT

Dig into a hole the size of a card table 3-in. layers of coarse sand or chicken grit and leaf mold or sphagnum peat moss. In clay soil, work into the hole 1 cupful each of gypsum and superphosphate. Set the shrub so the crown will be 1 in. above the ground level. If it is balled and burlapped, set the plant in the hole, cut the rope, slash the burlap, and push it away from the ball. If container grown, unwind roots circling the rootball before planting. Fill the hole, watering in to settle the soil. Make a saucer of earth to hold water. Apply a 3-in. mulch of pines needles, ground composted oak leaves, or sphagnum peat moss starting 3 in. from the stem.

SHRUBS

How to Provide Care

The first year, pour a bucketful of water around the roots every week unless there's a soaking rain. Mid-fall and early winter can be a dry period in Virginia. Continue the watering program sufficiently to keep the soil from drying out. If you wish to maintain the shape of this spring-flowering shrub, shortly after it finishes blooming, prune the branches back to outward facing buds. Flower buds form on old wood.

Additional Advice for Care

In late winter before growth begins, broadcast an organic 5-10-10 fertilizer at half the rate recommended from the drip line out to a point at a distance equal to $1^1/_2$ times the shrub's height, and water it in. Replenish the mulch. Fertilize again in November.

Azalea

*I*f we grow only one flowering shrub in Virginia, it is likely to an azalea. Azaleas belong to the *Rhododendron* tribe, but they tend to bloom earlier, and are smaller. In Washington, D.C., the earliest azaleas flower with the flowering plum trees. Evergreen azaleas are usually used as background plants, with some of the spectacular big-flowered deciduous types in front—the St. Exbury azaleas, for example, or the lovely yellow-white Ghent azaleas like 'Daviesii'. An evergreen group that does well here is the Glenn Dale type, developed by B.Y. Morrison, first director of the U.S. National Arboretum. They are lovely paired with early-blooming white 'Glacier', and with mid-season fast-growing 'Martha Hitchcock', whose blossoms are white and magenta. For later blooming, use Back Acres azaleas like 'Margaret Douglas', a low-growing plant whose flowers are strong pink with an orange border, and 'Marian Lee' whose flowers have pink-tinted white centers and red borders. Other azaleas popular here are the compact Kurume hybrids, which tolerate a lot of pruning, and the Robin Hill azaleas which can take extremes of cold and heat. 'Nancy of Robinhill', a late-blooming double, is a light purplish pink with an occasional pale red blotch.

WHEN TO PLANT

The best times for planting balled and burlapped or container-grown azaleas are in fall before Indian summer, and in early spring while the shrub still is dormant. If you want to be sure of the color, buy a plant that is beginning to bloom.

WHERE TO PLANT

An azalea tolerates full sun here as long as the soil is moist, but it will do best in the bright dappled light of tall trees. A slope that offers protection from high winds is ideal. So is the edge of a woodland, and soil that formerly supported a woodland. Azaleas require soil that is well-drained, rich in humus, and acid, between pH 4.5 and 6.0.

How to Plant

Dig into a hole the size of a card table 3 in. of sphagnum peat, ground pine bark or fibrous acid compost. Add 2 in. of coarse sand, or perlite, and a generous handful of gypsum. Mix all this in to a depth of 12 to 18 in. Set the shrub so the crown will be 2 in. above the ground level. If balled and burlapped, set the plant in the hole, cut the rope, slash the burlap, and push it away from the ball. If container-grown, cut an "X" across the bottom of the rootball before planting. Fill the hole, watering in to settle the soil. Apply a 3-in. mulch of pine needles, shredded oak leaf mulch, or sphagnum peat moss, starting 3 in. from the stem.

How to Provide Care

The first year, pour a bucketful of water around the roots every week unless there's a soaking rain. Mid-fall and early winter can be a dry period in Virginia, so continue the watering program sufficiently to keep soil from drying out. Maintain the mulch throughout the summer. If you wish to maintain the shape of an azalea, shortly after it finishes blooming, shear the the branches back to outward-facing buds. This also stimulates growth, and encourages the formation of more flowering buds for the next season.

Additional Advice for Care

In late winter before growth begins, broadcast an organic 5-10-10 fertilizer for acid-loving plants at half the rate recommended from the drip line out to a point at a distance equal to 1½ times the shrub's height. Water it in. Replenish the mulch now, and again during the summer.

Additional Cultivars and Species

Some deciduous native azaleas are fragrant, notably the sweet azalea, *R. arborescens*. Its flowers are white with a reddish eye and the foliage turns reddish in fall. The early-blooming Florida flame azalea, *R. austrinum*, has fragrant, predominantly yellow and orange to orange-red flowers.

Barberry

*T*he barberries aren't the most beautiful plants in the world, but they color brilliantly in fall, and their twiggy branches are so thorny they make almost impenetrable hedges. The deciduous varieties have pinkish or reddish new leaves in late spring that turn to green in summer, and to orange, yellow and scarlet in fall. In mid-spring, they bear small, attractive yellow flowers rather hidden by the foliage, followed by red, purplish, or bluish-black fruits in late summer. The evergreen varieties are a little less hardy than the deciduous types and adapt to considerable shade. The most colorful of these shrubs is 'Crimson Pygmy' *B. thunbergii*, a cultivar of Japanese barberry. It is a deciduous type that often is the first to leaf out in spring and makes a superb hedge. A low, dense plant 3 to 5 ft. tall and often wider than it is tall, the fall foliage is brilliant, especially when the plant is growing in full sun. 'Aurea' has bright yellow leaves that hold their color.

WHEN TO PLANT

The best times for planting balled and burlapped or container-grown barberry are in fall before Indian summer, and in early spring while the shrub is still dormant. Plant a bare root shrub while it is still dormant, any time between late fall and early spring when the buds start to break.

WHERE TO PLANT

The barberries, especially the evergreen varieties, display the brightest fall color when growing in full sun. However, like most shrubs, they succeed with 4 to 6 hours of sun, or all-day filtered light. They do well in most any soil, but prefer soil that is slightly acid.

HOW TO PLANT

Dig a hole 4 in. deeper than the rootball and wider toward the top. Use a spading fork to loosen the sides of the hole. In clay soil, work into the hole 1/2 cupful each of gypsum and superphosphate, and top it with 2 in. of soil. Set the shrub so the crown will be 1 in. above the ground level. For bare root, arrange the roots over a cone of soil in the center of the hole. For a balled and burlapped plant, set it in the hole, cut the rope, slash the burlap, and push it away from the ball. For a container-grown plant, unwind roots circling the rootball before planting. Fill the hole, watering in to settle the soil. Apply a 3-in. mulch starting 3 in. from the stem.

How to Provide Care

The first year, pour a bucketful of water around the roots every week unless there's a soaking rain. Mid-fall and early winter can be a dry period in Virginia so continue the watering program suffi- ciently to keep the soil from drying out. Shear in late winter or early spring before growth begins to maintain the shape of the shrub. You can remove up to a third of the branch tips in a year.

Additional Advice for Care

In late winter before growth begins, broadcast an organic 5-10-10 fertilizer at half the rate recommended for acid-loving plants from the drip line out to a point at a distance equal to 1^1/$_2$ times the shrub's height. Water it in. Replenish the mulch. Fertilize again in November.

Additional Cultivars and Species

Among barberry species that are semi- or evergreen here are warty barberry, *B. verruculosa*, a neat, low plant with small leaves and blue black fruit; *B. julianae*, which is similar, very winter hardy, and grows to 8 ft.; and *B.* × *mentorensis*, a fast-growing barberry 5 to 7 ft. tall. The foliage of all three turns red-plum-mahogany in fall.

Bearberry Cotoneaster

*T*he cotoneasters are handsome shrubs with interesting branching, and small white or pinkish flowers in spring and summer followed by showy fall displays of bright red or orange berries. Birds are attracted by the fruits. This species, the rapid-growing evergreen bearberry cotoneaster, is a prostrate, low-spreading species, and easy to grow. It makes a solid, glossy carpet used to hold sloping banks, as a ground cover, and as a textural element in a flowering border or a shrub border. The leaves are dark green in summer and fall, and with the cold they assume a plum-purple cast. The flowers are white and the berries are red. 'Canadian Creeper' is an excellent choice for a rock garden or a hillside. Just 6 in. high, it produces small white flowers in spring and a colorful show of red berries in fall. 'Coral Beauty' is taller, about 18 in. high and has orange-red berries.

When to Plant

Set out a container-grown or a balled and burlapped cotoneaster in early spring while the shrub still is dormant.

Where to Plant

Cotoneaster flowers well in full sun, or in a spot that provides 4 to 6 hours of sun, or all-day filtered light. It does best in soil that is in the neutral range.

How to Plant

Dig into a hole the size of a card table 2-in. layers of coarse sand or chicken grit. In clay soil, work into the hole 1 cupful each of gypsum and superphosphate. Set the shrub so the crown will be 1 in. above the ground level. For a container-grown shrub, unwind roots circling the rootball before planting. For a balled and burlapped shrub, set the plant in the hole, cut the rope, slash the burlap, and push it away from the ball. Fill the hole, watering in to settle the soil. Make a saucer of earth to hold water. Apply a 3-in. mulch starting 3 in. from the stem.

HOW TO PROVIDE CARE

The first year, pour a bucketful of water around the roots every week unless there's a soaking rain. Mid-fall and early winter can be a dry period in Virginia. Continue the watering program sufficiently to keep the soil from drying out. To maintain the shape, prune between late fall when cotoneaster goes dormant and spring when the buds break.

ADDITIONAL ADVICE FOR CARE

In late winter before growth begins, broadcast an organic 5-10-10 fertilizer at half the rate recommended from the drip line out to a point at a distance equal to the shrub's height, and water it in. Replenish the mulch. Fertilize again in November.

ADDITIONAL CULTIVARS AND SPECIES

There are taller cotoneasters. Rock cotoneaster, *C. horizontalis*, is an outstanding species with flat, layered branches 2 to 3 ft. high and a spread of 5 to 8 ft. There is a lovely little slow-growing variegated cultivar, 'Variegata', whose dainty leaves are edged with white.

Boxwood

OTHER COMMON NAME: BOX

*B*oxwood is more than just a shrub to native Virginians—it is a link to the past when clipped hedges defined the formal gardens of the great estates here and in Europe. The species is a tall shrub or small tree that grows very slowly, has very small, dainty evergreen leaves, is long lived, and can be clipped and pruned to almost any shape. It is used as a trim edging, and to create tailored formal hedges along driveways and walkways in both small city gardens and in large estates. The species most popular here is dwarf or edging box, *B. sempervirens*, 'Suffruticosa', an extremely slow-growing shrub that has been valued since Colonial times. Unpruned, it will grow to 4 or 5 ft. but plants 150 years old have been kept to 3 ft. high or less. It is used extensively in topiary work.

WHEN TO PLANT

Transplant a container-grown or balled and burlapped boxwood just before growth begins in mid-March. Before transplanting, spray the leaves with wilt-proofing. Boxwoods are easy to move because their very fibrous roots are close to the surface.

WHERE TO PLANT

Shade newly transplanted boxwoods from summer sun. Mature plants thrive in full sun or light shade. Boxwood seems to do well in both neutral soil and in somewhat acid soil, pH 6.0 to 8.0.

HOW TO PLANT

Dig into a hole twice the size of the rootball 2-in. layers of coarse sand or chicken grit and leaf mold or sphagnum peat moss. In clay soil, work into the hole 1 cupful each of gypsum and superphosphate. Set the shrub so the crown will be 1 in. above the ground level. Unwind roots circling the rootball of a container-grown plant before planting. Set a balled and burlapped plant in the hole, cut the rope, slash the burlap, and push it away from the ball. Fill the hole, watering in to settle the soil. Apply a 3-in. mulch starting 3 in. from the stem.

HOW TO PROVIDE CARE

The first year, pour a bucketful of water around the roots every week unless there's a soaking rain. When frost comes, layer 8 in. of pine needles, bark, or leafmold over the roots, 3 in. from the trunk. Replenish the mulch monthly since about an inch decomposes on the underside every month. To stimulate a flush of new growth, in early spring shear boxwood lightly all over. If the goal is to maintain the plant's size and symmetrical form, prune it back after new growth has formed in late spring.

ADDITIONAL ADVICE FOR CARE

In March, reduce the winter mulch to 3 in. and remove branches damaged by winter wind and cold. Every 2 or 3 years fertilize in late winter before growth begins, again after May 1, and again in November. Use Hollytone at a third the rate recommended on the container. Water it in.

ADDITIONAL CULTIVARS AND SPECIES

Littleleaf boxwood, *B. microphylla*, is less susceptible to extremes of heat and cold. It grows to 3 to 4 ft., with an equal spread and accepts considerable shade. 'Morris Midget' and 'Compacta' are especially dwarfish forms. 'Tide Hill' grows to 2 ft. and more than twice as wide. If your boxwood tends to brown in winter, try 'Wintergreen'.

Butterfly Bush

OTHER COMMON NAME: Summer Lilac

*B*utterflies and hummingbirds—and bees—really do love this shrub, and that is a major reason for planting butterfly bush. The species is tall, composed of wandlike stems that fountain upward and are tipped from about July on with foot-long, drooping spikes of lavender florets with an orange eye. There are cultivars in colors ranging from white to dark purple. 'White Bouquet' has white flowers. 'Black Knight' has very dark purple-violet flowers. For a small garden, dwarf butterfly bush is the better choice. *B. nanhoensis* Petite Indigo™ 'Mongo' is a pretty dwarf about 4 ft. high that bears lilac blue flowers. It is small enough to plant next to the kitchen steps where you can watch the butterflies that come to it. To get the best flowering from a buddleia, prune the shrub to the ground in late winter while the plant is still dormant. It blooms on new wood and will recover quickly.

WHEN TO PLANT

The best times for planting balled and burlapped or container-grown buddleias are in fall before Indian summer, and in early spring while the shrub still is dormant. Plant a bare root shrub in late winter or early spring before the buds start to break.

WHERE TO PLANT

Buddleia flowers are best growing in full sun. It thrives in soil in the neutral range, around pH 7.0.

HOW TO PLANT

Dig a hole 4 in. deeper than the rootball and wider toward the top. Use a spading fork to loosen the sides of the hole. In clay soil, work into the hole 1/2 cupful each of gypsum and superphosphate, and top it with 2 in. of soil. Set the shrub so the crown will be 1 in. above ground level. If the shrub is bare root, arrange the roots over a cone of soil in the center of the hole. If it is balled and burlapped, set the plant in the hole, cut the rope, slash the burlap, and push it away from the ball. If container-grown, unwind roots circling the rootball before planting. Fill the hole, watering in to settle the soil. Apply a 3-in. mulch starting 3 in. from the stem.

HOW TO PROVIDE CARE

The first year, pour a bucketful of water around the roots every week unless there's a soaking rain. Mid-fall and early winter can be a dry period in Virginia. Continue the watering program sufficiently to keep the soil from drying out. Cut the plant back to the ground in late winter while it is still dormant.

ADDITIONAL ADVICE FOR CARE

In late winter before growth begins, broadcast an organic 5-10-10 fertilizer at half the rate recommended from the drip line out to a point at a distance equal to 1^1/2 times the shrub's height and water it in. Replenish the mulch. Fertilize again in November. Once the plant is well established, switch to 5-10-5.

ADDITIONAL CULTIVARS AND SPECIES

For a large garden, or for the back of a flowering border, consider using *B. alternifolia*, which grows to 20 ft. or so. It's a graceful buddleia whose flower spikes are neat clusters of lilac-purple florets. It blooms early, in June or July.

Vitex agnus-castus

Chaste Tree

*T*his is a fast-growing multi-trunked shrub that grows into a small tree. The height is about 8 to 10 ft. and the width almost equal. It has aromatic gray-green leaves and tips its branches with extremely fragrant blue flowers from June or July through September. A number of cultivated varieties have been introduced. The cultivar 'Alba' has white flowers and 'Rosea' bears pink flowers. Chaste tree does well in a container, and makes a pretty little patio "tree." In Zone 6, our cool hill country near the West Virginia border, the chaste tree is borderline hardy. Planted in a container, it can be moved to a spot that provides protection from the north wind.

WHEN TO PLANT

Plant a container-grown chaste tree in early spring while the shrub is still dormant.

WHERE TO PLANT

Chaste tree requires full sun. It does best in neutral range soil, pH 6.0 to 7.0.

HOW TO PLANT

Dig into a hole the size of a card table 2-in. layers of coarse sand or chicken grit, and of leaf mold or sphagnum peat moss. In clay soil, work into the hole 1 cupful each of gypsum and superphosphate. Unwind roots circling the rootball before planting. Set the shrub so the crown will be 1 in. above the ground level. Fill the hole, watering in to settle the soil. Make a saucer of earth to hold water. Apply a 3-in. mulch starting 3 in. from the stem.

HOW TO PROVIDE CARE

The first year, pour a bucketful of water around the roots every week unless there's a soaking rain. Mid-fall and early winter can be a dry period in Virginia. Continue the watering program sufficiently to keep the soil from drying out. Deadhead spent flowers to encourage blooming. In spring before the buds break, prune the branches of a young plant back to within 1 ft. of the ground. An old plant can be pruned back to live wood.

ADDITIONAL ADVICE FOR CARE

In late winter before growth begins, broadcast an organic 5-10-10 fertilizer at half the rate recommended from the drip line out to a point at a distance equal to $1^1/2$ times the shrub's height, and water it in. Replenish the mulch. Fertilize again in November. Once the plant is well established, switch to 10-10-10.

ADDITIONAL CULTIVARS AND SPECIES

V. negundo 'Heterophylla' has beautiful finely divided leaves and an airy graceful texture and 8-in. panicles of fragrant lavender flowers in late summer.

Daphne

*T*he daphnes are slow-growing, low, wide, semi-evergreen to evergreen shrubs famous for fragrance. The most perfumed and easiest to grow is winter daphne, *D. odora* 'Aureo-marginata'. This is an evergreen shrub that grows slowly to 4 or 5 ft. high. In very early spring, deep crimson buds open to dense heads of fragrant white flowers. The leaves have light margins of yellow. It is winter-hardy in Zone 7 and south—not suited to our cool uplands near the West Virginia border. For Zone 6 gardens, a better choice is *D. × burkwoodii* 'Somerset'. It is a smaller, semi-evergreen plant that grows 3 or 4 ft. high and 6 ft. wide. In late spring, and often again in summer, it bears masses of star-shaped, delightfully fragrant, pale pink flowers. The cultivar 'Carol Mackie' has leaves edged with a gold band. The garland flower, *D. cneorum*, is another good choice for colder regions, but it doesn't do well in the heat of southern Virginia. It's a dense evergreen about 1 ft. high and twice as wide. Rosy, very fragrant flowers cover the plant in mid-spring and sometimes again in summer. 'Variegata' has cream-edged leaves. 'Pygmaea' has pink flowers on prostrate branches.

WHEN TO PLANT

Plant a container-grown daphne. It doesn't transplant too easily in early spring.

WHERE TO PLANT

Plant daphnes in light shade. They require soil that is in the pH range between 6.0 and 7.0.

HOW TO PLANT

Dig into a hole the size of a card table 2-in. layers of coarse sand or chicken grit and leaf mold or sphagnum peat moss. In clay soil, work into the hole 1 cupful each of gypsum and superphosphate. Unwind roots circling the rootball before planting. Set the shrub so the crown will be 1 in. above the ground level. Fill the hole, watering in to settle the soil. Apply a 3-in. mulch starting 3 in. from the stem.

HOW TO PROVIDE CARE

The first year, pour a bucketful of water around the roots every week unless there's a soaking rain. Mid-fall and early winter can be a dry period in Virginia. Continue the watering program sufficiently to keep the soil from drying out. Before cold comes, cover the plant with pine boughs, or the boughs of some other evergreen, to prevent sunburn. After the plant has become established, it should be pruned after flowering, but before mid-July.

ADDITIONAL ADVICE FOR CARE

In late winter before growth begins, broadcast an organic 5-10-10 fertilizer over the area at half the rate recommended on the container and water it in. Replenish the mulch. Fertilize again in November. Once the plant is well established, switch to a 5-10-5 fertilizer.

Dwarf-Winged Spindle Tree

Two types of euonymus are common in Virginia landscapes, deciduous forms and vining evergreens. The dwarf-winged spindle tree belongs to the deciduous group which is planted for fall color. The crimson color of 'Compacta' rivals the maple tree's most brilliant display. This is a slow-growing shrub or small tree usually 10 to 20 ft. tall, with a somewhat flat top. Around the U.S. Capitol building, it is massed with evergreens, forsythias, and other shrubs, and is unnoticed until the cold weather comes—then the color draws the eye for weeks. The corky bark "wings" edging the branches have textural interest and are sought after for flower arrangements. The euonymus called wintercreeper, *E. fortunei*, is the hardiest of the evergreen forms, fast-growing vines used as climbers and ground covers. Its most popular forms are white-veined, small-leaved selections. 'Erecta' is a catchall term for climbing types. 'Emerald Leader' and 'Emerald Beauty' are upright forms 5 or 6 ft. tall that bear exceptionally pretty fall fruits, bright pinkish-orange capsules exposing seeds that are orange-red, and attractive to birds. Be sure to buy only a scale-resistant plant.

WHEN TO PLANT

A balled and burlapped or container-grown plant of either type—deciduous or evergreen—transplants easily. The best times for planting are in early spring and in fall before Indian summer.

WHERE TO PLANT

Euonymus succeeds on dry, rocky slopes. The dwarf-winged spindle tree colors whether it is growing in full sun, part shade, or shade. Wintercreeper euonymus produces the brightest fruits growing in full sun. However, like most shrubs, it succeeds with 4 to 6 hours of sun, or all-day filtered light. Euonymus is adaptable. These 2 species thrive in soil whose pH range is between 6.0 and 8.0.

HOW TO PLANT

Dig a hole 4 in. deeper than the rootball and wider toward the top. Use a spading fork to loosen the sides of the hole. In clay soil, work into the hole 1/2 cupful each of gypsum and superphosphate, and

top it with 2 in. of soil. Set the shrub so the crown will be 1 in. above the ground level. If the shrub is balled and burlapped, set the plant in the hole, cut the rope, slash the burlap, and push it away from the ball. If it is container-grown, unwind roots circling the rootball before planting. Fill the hole, watering in to settle the soil. Apply a 3-in. mulch starting 3 in. from the stem.

HOW TO PROVIDE CARE

The first year, pour a bucketful of water around the roots every week unless there's a soaking rain. Mid-fall and early winter can be a dry period in Virginia. Continue the watering program sufficiently to keep the soil from drying out. In early spring, shear evergreen wintercreeper types of euonymus to encourage compactness. Dwarf-winged spindle tree tolerates, but does not require, pruning.

ADDITIONAL ADVICE FOR CARE

In late winter before growth begins, broadcast an organic 10-10-10 fertilizer at half the rate recommended from the drip line out to a point at a distance equal to $1^1/_2$ times the shrub's height, and water it in. Replenish the mulch. Fertilize again in November. Once the plant is well established, switch to a 12-6-6 fertilizer.

ADDITIONAL CULTIVARS AND SPECIES

Wintercreeper euonymus, *E. fortunei* 'Dart's Blanket', a Dutch culti-var with long, dark green leaves, is recommended for use as a ground cover by the ocean. The plant is less than 24 in. high, and the leaves color to bronze and plum in winter.

Firethorn

OTHER COMMON NAME: Scarlet Firethorn

*F*irethorn is a thorny, wide-branching evergreen or semi-evergreen shrub 6 to 18 ft. high that has fine foliage, and attractive
flowers in mid-spring. It is grown primarily for the clusters of brilliant
scarlet fruit that mature in fall. It is used as a free standing specimen,
and in hedges, but is most striking rising against a blank masonry or
wooden wall, or grown on a trellis where the asymmetrical branching
and bright fall fruits stand out. The species is susceptible to scale,
but in recent years several improved varieties have been introduced.
When you buy pyracantha, insist on having a scale- and fireblight-
resistant specimen. One of the most beautiful of the new introductions
is 'Mohave', an upright shrub 8 to 10 ft. tall that bears masses of
orange-red berries. It is hardy everywhere in Virginia except in Zone
6, the area near the West Virginia border. 'Fiery Cascade' is another
plant with good resistance. It is hardy to -10 degrees Fahrenheit, and
should be fine in Zone 6.

WHEN TO PLANT

Firethorn transplants with difficulty, so buy a container-grown
shrub, and plant it in early spring before growth begins. Handle
with care until established.

WHERE TO PLANT

Firethorn flowers best and produces the brightest fruits growing in
full sun. However, like most shrubs, it succeeds with 4 to 6 hours of
sun, or all-day filtered light. It thrives in soil in the pH range
between 5.5 and 7.5.

HOW TO PLANT

Dig into a hole the size of a card table 2-in. layers of coarse sand or
chicken grit and leaf mold or sphagnum peat moss. In clay soil,
work into the hole 1 cupful each of gypsum and superphosphate.
Unwind roots circling the rootball before planting. Set the shrub so

the crown will be 1 in. above the ground level. Fill the hole, watering in to settle the soil. Make a saucer of earth to hold water. Apply a 3-in. mulch starting 3 in. from the stem.

How to Provide Care

The first year, pour a bucketful of water around the roots every week unless there's a soaking rain. Mid-fall and early winter can be a dry period in Virginia. Continue the watering program sufficiently to keep the soil from drying out. Firethorn becomes very wide-spreading if left unpruned. If you wish to maintain the shape of this spring flowering shrub, shortly after it finishes blooming, prune the branches back to outward facing buds. Flower buds—and the fruit—form on old wood.

Additional Advice for Care

In late winter before growth begins, broadcast an organic 5-10-10 fertilizer at half the rate recommended from the drip line out to a point at a distance equal to 1¹/₂ times the shrub's height, and water it in. Replenish the mulch. Fertilize again in November.

Additional Cultivars and Species

'Shawnee' is a yellow-fruited plant with good resistance. A beautiful smaller variety with orange-red fruits and good resistance is 'Navajo'. For a hot, dry garden in Zone 8, down near the North Carolina border, consider using the Formosa firethorn, *P. koidzumii*. 'Victory' is resistant to scab.

SHRUBS

Flowering Quince

lowering quince in bloom is spring's most beautiful flowering
shrub. The blossoms are rather sparse, but that suits the branching very well. The shrub is broad spreading, about 10 ft. tall when
mature, with a twiggy mass of rather thorny branches. After it has dis-
played its brilliant single or double early-spring flowers, it puts out
glossy green leaves. It is a fruiting plant. The flowers are followed in
October by fragrant, waxy, yellowish 2-in. fruits that are bitter raw,
but make an excellent preserve. The branches are easy to force into
early bloom and are remarkably lovely. Flowering quince is available
in a range of colors. 'Nivalis' is white; 'Apple Blossom', white-pink;
'Phyllis Moore', pink, semidouble; 'Cardinalis', red, double; 'Rubra
Grandiflora' has large, single, deep crimson-red flowers; 'Toyo
Nishiki' blooms in lovely hues of white, apple-blossom pink, real
pink, and red.

WHEN TO PLANT

Plant a balled and burlapped or container-grown quince in fall
before Indian summer, and in early spring while the shrub still
is dormant.

WHERE TO PLANT

Quince flowers best and produces the best fruits growing in full
sun. However, like most shrubs, it succeeds with 4 to 6 hours of sun,
or all-day filtered light. Quince tolerates a broad range of soils. It
thrives in soil with a pH of 5.5, but can succeed in soil with a pH
of 7.5.

HOW TO PLANT

Dig a hole 4 in. deeper than the rootball, wider toward the top. Use
a spading fork to loosen the sides of the hole. In clay soil, work into
the hole 1/2 cupful each of gypsum and superphosphate, and top it
with 2 in. of soil. Set the shrub so the crown will be 1 in. above the
ground level. If it is balled and burlapped, set the plant in the hole,
cut the rope, slash the burlap, and push it away from the ball. If con-

tainer-grown, unwind roots circling the rootball before planting. Fill the hole, watering in to settle the soil. Apply a 3-in. mulch of pine needles, shredded oak compost or sphagnum peat moss, starting 3 in. from the stem.

How to Provide Care

The first year, pour a bucketful of water around the roots every week unless there's a soaking rain. Mid-fall and early winter can be a dry period in Virginia. Continue the watering program sufficiently to keep the soil from drying out. Quince is pruned as needed. After flowering, remove ugly older branches. If the whole plant needs renewal, after flowering cut the whole plant back to within 6 to 12 in. of the ground.

Additional Advice for Care

In late winter before growth begins, broadcast an organic 5-10-10 fertilizer for acid-loving plants at half the rate recommended from the drip line out to a point at a distance equal to $1^1/_2$ times the shrub's height, and water it in. Replenish the mulch. Fertilize again in November.

Forsythia × intermedia 'Spectabilis'

Forsythia

OTHER COMMON NAME: Border Forsythia

*F*orsythia is the herald of spring. It pops a few golden blooms in my neighbor's yard before the plum trees have even budded in my garden. The flowers bud open before the leaves, covering the wide-spreading, arching branches with small, showy yellow flowers. The small blooms last well, as long as we don't get a heat spell. When the cold comes in fall, the leaves take on an orangy-plum hue before they fall. This is a fast-growing arching shrub that roots where it touches. It develops dense thickets unless it is pruned annually, and is used as a tall ground cover for slopes. It is attractive featured as a specimen in the middle of a large lawn, or in a group with evergreen and other flowering shrubs. Tall-growing varieties get to about 8 ft. 'Arnold Giant' is one of the hardiest. 'Lynwood' has perhaps the most beautiful flowers. 'Nana' is a smaller form, 5 to 8 ft. tall, a slow-growing dwarf. Forsythia can stand a lot of shearing, so it sometimes is seen as an espalier. Branches pruned in late winter as the buds swell are easily forced into bloom indoors.

WHEN TO PLANT

Forsythia transplants easily—bare root, balled and burlapped, or container-grown. Plant a bare root shrub while dormant, any time between late fall and early spring when the buds start to break open. Plant balled and burlapped or container-grown forsythia in early spring while still dormant, or in fall after the leaves drop.

WHERE TO PLANT

Forsythia requires full sun to flower well. It does well in soil that is in the pH range between 6.0 and 8.0.

HOW TO PLANT

Dig a hole 4 in. deeper than the rootball, wider toward the top. Use a spading fork to loosen the sides of the hole. In clay soil, work into the hole 1/2 cupful each of gypsum and superphosphate, and top it with 2 in. of soil. Set the shrub so the crown will be 1 in. above the ground level. If it is bare root, arrange the roots over a cone of soil in the center of the hole. If balled and burlapped, set the plant in the hole, cut the rope, slash the burlap, and push it away from the ball. If container-grown, unwind roots circling the rootball before planting. Fill the hole, watering in to settle the soil. Apply a 3-in. mulch starting 3 in. from the stem.

How to Provide Care

The first year, pour a bucketful of water around the roots every week unless there's a soaking rain. Mid-fall and early winter can be a dry period in Virginia. Continue the watering program sufficiently to keep the soil from drying out. If you wish to maintain the shape of this spring-flowering shrub, shortly after it finishes blooming, prune the branches back to outward facing buds. Flower buds form on old wood on spring-flowering shrubs.

Additional Advice for Care

In late winter before growth begins, broadcast an organic 5-10-10 fertilizer at half the rate recommended from the drip line out to a point at a distance equal to 1^{1}/$_2$ times the shrub's height, and water it in. Replenish the mulch. Fertilize again in November.

Additional Cultivars and Species

The plant called weeping forsythia, *F. suspensa* var. *sieboldii*, has long trailing branches that can grow to 20 or 30 ft. high given support. It is attractive growing over a low wall, but does not bloom as heavily as border forsythia.

Osmanthus heterophyllus

Holly Olive

OTHER COMMON NAME: Chinese Olive

*T*he holly olive is a handsome evergreen shrub, or small tree, usually 8 to 10 ft. tall, that has very glossy, dark green, hollylike foliage and small, sweetly fragrant blooms in fall. Several are growing near Asian Valley at the National Arboretum in Washington, D.C., and on the grounds of the U.S. Capitol. They scent the air from late September or October into early November. Among excellent cultivars is 'Gulftide', which reaches 10 to 15 ft., and has very glossy foliage. 'Aureo-marginatus' has leaves margined with yellow, as does 'Aureus'. *O. heterophyllus* 'Variegatus' is offered by many nurseries. About 8 ft. tall, it is an erect shrub with dark green leaves edged with a creamy white. The holly olive is probably not winter-hardy in Zone 6, the mountain region. The most fragrant species is *O. fragrans*, the sweet or tea olive, which is hardy only in the most southern reaches of Virginia, near the North Carolina border. It is a large shrub or small tree, 20 to 30 ft. tall. The hardiest osmanthus is *O. americanus*, devilwood, which is winter-hardy at least as far north as Zone 6. Its fragrant flowers appear in late March and April. It is a lovely plant to naturalize.

WHEN TO PLANT

Plant a container-grown osmanthus in fall before Indian summer, and in early spring while the shrub still is dormant.

WHERE TO PLANT

Osmanthus flowers best growing in full sun. However, like most shrubs, it succeeds with 4 to 6 hours of sun, or all-day filtered light. It prefers well-drained, rather acid soil, but can stand some alkalinity.

HOW TO PLANT

Dig a hole 4 in. deeper than the rootball, wider toward the top. Use a spading fork to loosen the sides of the hole. In clay soil, work into the hole 1/2 cupful each of gypsum and superphosphate, and top it with 2 in. of soil. Unwind the roots circling the rootball before planting. Set the shrub so the crown will be 1 in. above the ground. Fill the hole, watering in to settle the soil. Apply a 3-in. mulch starting 3 in. from the stem.

HOW TO PROVIDE CARE

The first year, pour a bucketful of water around the roots every week unless there's a soaking rain. Mid-fall and early winter can be a dry period in Virginia. Continue the watering program sufficiently to keep the soil from drying out. If you wish to maintain the height or shape of this spring-flowering shrub, shortly after it finishes blooming, prune the branches back to outward facing buds.

ADDITIONAL ADVICE FOR CARE

In late winter before growth begins, broadcast an organic 5-10-10 fertilizer for acid-loving plants at half the rate recommended from the drip line out to a point at a distance equal to $1^1/2$ times the shrub's height. Water it in. Replenish the mulch. Fertilize again in November. Once the plant is well established, switch to a 12-6-6 fertilizer.

ADDITIONAL CULTIVARS AND SPECIES

For Virginia's Zone 8 and southward, Fortune's osmanthus, *O.* x *fortunei*, is a better choice. It gets to be 15 to 20 ft. tall but can be kept smaller by pruning. It has dark green, leathery leaves and very fragrant flowers in mid-fall.

Hydrangea

*T*he Hydrangeas are fast-growing deciduous shrubs with cane-like branches and large handsome leaves. In summer, usually late summer, they bear huge flower heads composed of dozens of florets. Hortensia, or mophead, types have rounded flower heads with open florets; lacecaps are composed of both open and unopened (sterile) florets, and may be cone-shaped or flattened. Two species are grown for their flowers. The bigleaf *Hydrangea macrophylla*, a plant 3 to 6 ft. tall and twice as wide, blooms in mid- to late summer. The flowers may be cream, rose, or dark blue. Acid soil assures blue; pH 5.0 to 5.5 results in a soft blue; 6.0 to 6.5, or slightly higher, maintains pink. There are crimson varieties and miniatures. *H. arborescens* 'Grandiflora', known as hills of snow, is a tall shrub with rounded leaves and big clusters of creamy flowers. 'Annabelle', 4 ft. tall, produces 12-in. round flower heads from early to late summer, if deadheaded. *H. quercifolia* is a big magnificent shrub grown primarily for its foliage, big oak-like leaves that color red-purple in fall. The cone-shaped flowers bloom in June and July. 'Snowflake' and 'Snowqueen' are improved forms.

WHEN TO PLANT
Set out a container-grown plant in early spring while the shrub still is dormant.

WHERE TO PLANT
Hydrangeas bloom in sun, and in bright or dappled shade; the hotter the area, the more it benefits from some shade. Bigleaf *H. macrophylla* requires acid soil, and will color to more or less intense shades of blue or pink according to the pH. See above. Hills of Snow *H. arborescens*, and oakleaf *H. quercifolia* are adaptable as to soil pH.

HOW TO PLANT
Dig into a hole the size of a card table 2-in. layers of coarse sand or chicken grit and leaf mold or sphagnum peat moss. In clay soil, work into the hole 1 cupful each of gypsum and superphosphate. Unwind roots circling the rootball before planting. Set the shrub so

the crown will be 1 in. above the ground level. Fill the hole, watering in to settle the soil. Make a saucer of earth to hold water. Apply a 3-in. mulch starting 3 in. from the stem.

HOW TO PROVIDE CARE

The first year, pour a bucketful of water around the roots every week unless there's a soaking rain. Mid-fall and early winter can be a dry period in Virginia. Continue the watering program sufficiently to keep the soil from drying out. The bigleaf *H. macrophylla* and oakleaf *H. quercifolia* must be pruned right after flowering as these bloom on buds produced on growth from the previous season. *H. arborescens* 'Grandiflora' flowers on new wood: keep the flowering and shape by cutting out the oldest canes between late fall and early spring.

ADDITIONAL ADVICE FOR CARE

In late winter before growth begins, broadcast an organic 5-10-10 fertilizer at half the rate recommended from the drip line out to a point at a distance equal to 1½ times the shrub's height, and water it in. Replenish the mulch. Use an acid type fertilizer for bigleaf *H. macrophylla*. Fertilize again in November. Once the plant is well established switch to 5-10-5.

ADDITIONAL CULTIVARS AND SPECIES

H. paniculata 'Grandiflora', the peegee hydrangea, is a treelike shrub to 20 ft. tall with smaller leaves, and in late summer mostly sterile flowers in conical clusters, creamy at first changing to rose then bronze. *H. petiolaris* is the lovely climbing hydrangea described in the chapter on vines.

Japanese Spirea

The spiraeas are very wide, 2- to 3-ft. deciduous shrubs associated with gardens of the past. They have dainty leaves, arching branches covered in mid-spring with masses of exquisite little white or pink flowers, and often are used as flowering fillers and for massing. There are dozens of species and hundreds of cultivated varieties. *Spiraea japonica* 'Bumalda' is one of the most successful of the spiraeas, and it has been much hybridized. 'Limemound', whose foliage is lemon-yellow with a russet tinge when it emerges in spring, is a beautiful cultivar. As it matures, it tends towards lime-green. The flowers appear in early summer and they're light pink. In fall, the foliage becomes orange-red on red stems. The most popular of the old-fashioned plants is 6-ft. bridal wreath spiraea, *S. × vanhouttei*. A beautiful plant with graceful branches that arch to the ground, it literally covers itself with showy, small white flowers in mid-spring. It makes a great specimen to feature, is handsome growing along a wall, and as a formal hedge.

WHEN TO PLANT

Plant a balled and burlapped or container-grown spiraea in fall before Indian summer, or in early spring while the shrub still is dormant.

WHERE TO PLANT

Spiraea flowers best in full sun and in open airy sites. However, it can stand shade a portion of the day. It does best in soil that has a moderately acid pH range between 6.0 and 7.0. It is tolerant of every soil except very wet soil.

HOW TO PLANT

Dig a hole 4 in. deeper than the rootball, wider toward the top. Use a spading fork to loosen the sides of the hole. In clay soil, work into the hole 1/2 cupful each of gypsum and superphosphate, and top it with 2 in. of soil. Set the shrub so the crown will be 1 in. above the ground level. If it is balled and burlapped, set the plant in the hole, cut the rope, slash the burlap, and push it away from the ball. If container-grown, unwind roots circling the rootball before planting. Fill the hole, watering in to settle the soil. Apply a 3-in. mulch starting 3 in. from the stem.

HOW TO PROVIDE CARE

The first year, pour a bucketful of water around the roots every week unless there's a soaking rain. Mid-fall and early winter can be a dry period in Virginia. Continue the watering program sufficiently to keep the soil from drying out. To maintain its form, and improve flowering, prune *S. japonica* 'Bumalda' in early spring before growth begins. Do not clip *S. × vanhouttei* or you will spoil the form of the arching branches. If it gets too dense inside, cut out old or dead wood in fall after the plant has become dormant.

ADDITIONAL ADVICE FOR CARE

In late winter before growth begins, broadcast an organic 5-10-10 fertilizer at half the rate recommended from the drip line out to a point at a distance equal to $1^1/_2$ times the shrub's height. Water it in. Replenish the mulch. Fertilize again in November.

ADDITIONAL CULTIVARS AND SPECIES

S. × cinerea 'Grefsheim' is a very early blooming 3- to 4-ft. shrub with gracefully arching branches that are covered with white blooms.

Mockorange

OTHER COMMON NAME: Sweet Mockorange

*T*he species is a deciduous shrub whose beautiful white flowers and delicious fragrance are an unforgettable springtime memory to anyone who grew up with this plant in the yard. It is big—a vigorous grower that soon reaches 10 to 12 ft. in height, and with time gets to be almost twice as wide. The foliage is a rather dull, dark green, brightened in May and early June by clusters of 5 to 7 crisp, beautiful little pure white florets 1 or 2 in. across. The fragrance is sweet as orange blossoms and fills the garden. If you have no sentimental interest in old-fashioned mockorange, choose from selected varieties of a wonderfully fragrant modern hybrid, *P. × lemoinei*. 'Innocence' is one of the most fragrant of its cultivars, and grows to 8 ft. tall. 'Avalanche', another very fragrant new mockorange, stays at about 4 ft. There are many double-flowered varieties to choose from and they keep their petals longer than the single-flowered types. 'Frosty Morn', a 4- to 5-ft. shrub, is one of several very cold-hardy doubles, and has a nice fragrance.

WHEN TO PLANT

Plant a balled and burlapped or container-grown mockorange in fall before Indian summer, or in early spring while the shrub still is dormant.

WHERE TO PLANT

Mockorange flowers best growing in full sun. However, like most shrubs, it succeeds with 4 to 6 hours of sun, or bright all-day dappled light. It prefers soil that is in the pH range between 6.0 and 8.0, and stands a lot of dryness in the soil.

HOW TO PLANT

Dig a hole 4 in. deeper than the rootball and wider toward the top. Use a spading fork to loosen the sides of the hole. In clay soil, work into the hole 1/2 cupful each of gypsum and superphosphate, and top it with 2 in. of soil. Set the shrub so the crown will be 1 in. above the ground level. If it is balled and burlapped, set the plant in the

SHRUBS

hole, cut the rope, slash the burlap, and push it away from the ball. If container-grown, unwind roots circling the rootball before planting. Fill the hole, watering in to settle the soil. Apply a 3-in. mulch starting 3 in. from the stem.

HOW TO PROVIDE CARE

The first year, pour a bucketful of water around the roots every week unless there's a soaking rain. Mid-fall and early winter can be a dry period in Virginia. Continue the watering program sufficiently to keep the soil from drying out. After the plant has flowered, remove old branches to control the growth and shape the plant.

ADDITIONAL ADVICE FOR CARE

In late winter before growth begins, broadcast an organic 5-10-10 fertilizer at half the rate recommended from the drip line out to a point at a distance equal to $1^1/2$ times the shrub's height. Water it in. Replenish the mulch. Fertilize again in November.

ADDITIONAL CULTIVARS AND SPECIES

There is a variegated form of sweet mockorange, *P. coronarius* 'Variegatus', whose leaves are bordered irregularly with a creamy white.

Kalmia latifolia

Mountain Laurel

*T*he mountain laurel is an exceptionally beautiful evergreen shrub 7 to 8 ft. tall with shiny, leathery leaves. In mid- to late spring, it is covered with exquisite, rounded white, pink, or variegated flower heads composed of small cup-shaped little florets. The flowers of the species have great charm, but the new cultivars are breathtaking. 'Olympic Fire' bears big scarlet buds that open to pink, and the new growth is a rich, purplish red. 'Elf' is a slow-growing smaller laurel, 4 to 6 ft. tall eventually, whose light pink buds open to white. For naturalizing, 'Kaufman's Pink' is a good choice. The buds are a rich pink opening to pale pink, and they're long lasting. Like the rhododendron, mountain laurel is a broad-leaved evergreen that is used in groupings in shaded shrub borders. It grows wild in light woodlands from Connecticut to northern Florida, providing the soil is acid, well-drained and reasonably cool in summer. Do not bother to plant mountain laurel in poor, dry soil and full sun—it will develop leaf spot and eventually die.

WHEN TO PLANT
Plant a balled and burlapped or container-grown shrub in fall before Indian summer, or in early spring while the shrub still is dormant.

WHERE TO PLANT
The mountain laurel needs a half day of sun or bright shade all day to flower well. It does best in light woodlands. It must have soil that is in the pH range between 4.5 to 6.0.

HOW TO PLANT
Dig into a hole the size of a card table 2-in. layers of coarse sand or chicken grit, and of leaf mold or sphagnum peat moss. In clay soil, work into the hole 1 cupful each of gypsum and superphosphate. Set the shrub so the crown will be 1 in. above the ground level. If it is balled and burlapped, set the plant in the hole, cut the rope, slash the burlap, and push it away from the ball. If container-grown, unwind roots circling the root ball before planting. Fill the hole,

watering in to settle the soil. Make a saucer of earth to hold water. Apply a 3-in. mulch of pine needles, shredded composted oak leaves, or sphagnum peat moss starting 3 in. from the stem.

HOW TO PROVIDE CARE

The first year, pour a bucketful of water around the roots every week unless there's a soaking rain. Mid-fall and early winter can be a dry period in Virginia. Continue the watering program sufficiently to keep the soil from drying out. Remove the flower heads as soon as they fade. If you wish to maintain the shape of the shrub, when it has finished blooming, prune the branches back to outward-facing buds.

ADDITIONAL ADVICE FOR CARE

In late winter before growth begins, broadcast an organic 5-10-10 fertilizer for acid-loving plants at half the rate recommended from the drip line out to a point at a distance equal to 1^1/$_2$ times the shrub's height. Water it in. Replenish the mulch. Fertilize again in November.

ADDITIONAL CULTIVARS AND SPECIES

The plant called 'Otto Luykens' laurel is a cherry laurel, and is described in the entry on *Flowering Cherry*.

Nandina

OTHER COMMON NAME: Heavenly Bamboo

*N*andina is a tall, airy, graceful evergreen with dainty foliage splashed with red in winter. It produces loose clusters of small whitish florets in spring that are followed in fall by lipstick-red berries in large drooping clusters. They stay on my bush until mid-spring. Nandinas are excellent in a shrub border, as a hedge, and grow well in containers. The most popular nandinas are disease-resistant cultivars that grow to about 3 ft. and have superior winter color. 'Harbor Dwarf' is a graceful form that stays to about 2 ft. tall. The foliage is touched with pink or bronze in spring, and turns orange-bronze in fall. 'Nana Purpurea' is similar, but the foliage is reddish purple in winter.

WHEN TO PLANT

Plant a container-grown nandina in fall before Indian summer, or in early spring while the shrub is still dormant.

WHERE TO PLANT

Nandina produces the most fruits growing in full sun. However, like most shrubs, it succeeds with 4 to 6 hours of sun, or all-day filtered light. It is not particular about soil pH.

HOW TO PLANT

Dig into a hole the size of a card table 2-in. layers of coarse sand or chicken grit and leaf mold or sphagnum peat moss. In clay soil, work into the hole 1 cupful each of gypsum and superphosphate. Set the shrub so the crown will be 1 in. above the ground level. If it is balled and burlapped, set the plant in the hole, cut the rope, slash the burlap, and push it away from the ball. If container-grown, unwind roots circling the rootball before planting. Fill the hole, watering in to settle the soil. Apply a 3-in. mulch starting 3 in. from the stem.

HOW TO PROVIDE CARE

The first year, pour a bucketful of water around the roots every
week unless there's a soaking rain. Mid-fall and early winter can be
a dry period in Virginia. Continue the watering program sufficiently
to keep the soil from drying out. If you wish to maintain the shape
of this spring-flowering shrub, shortly after it finishes blooming,
remove old canes right down to the ground.

ADDITIONAL ADVICE FOR CARE

In late winter before growth begins, broadcast an organic 5-10-10
fertilizer at half the rate recommended from the drip line out to a
point at a distance equal to 1^1/$_2$ times the shrub's height. Water it in.
Replenish the mulch. Fertilize again in November. Once the plant is
well established, switch to a 12-6-6 fertilizer.

Oregon Holly-Grape

*T*he mahonias are handsome evergreens with spiny holly-like leaves and yellow flowers. They are excellent shrubs for partial shade. Two species are grown in Virginia. The Oregon holly-grape, *M. aquifolium*, has dark, evergreen leaves that turn a beautiful bronze-plum in winter in my Washington, D.C., garden. And it has another great asset—in late winter and early spring, it bears clusters of small, sweetly scented, fragrant yellow flowers. The blue-black fruits that follow aren't particularly noticeable in this species. It will grow to somewhere between 3 and 6 ft., but when it gets tall, it starts to bend over and its foliage becomes sparse, so I cut the older canes out and keep only those at or under 3 ft. The other species in my garden is leatherleaf mahonia, *M. bealei*. It is a taller plant, with very large, handsome, blue-green toothed leaves that hold their color all winter. In late February and early March, it bears dropping clusters of perfumed yellow flower spikes that are followed by blue-black grapelike fruits the birds adore. It is lovely underplanted with *Sarcococca ruscifolia*, a shiny low-growing evergreen that does well in deep shade.

WHEN TO PLANT

Plant a container-grown or balled and burlapped mahonia in early spring while the shrub is still dormant.

WHERE TO PLANT

The mahonias do best in partial shade. Oregon holly-grape can stand more sun, but prefers shade. Avoid dry, hot spots, and windy, unprotected locations. The mahonias thrive in slightly acid soil, 6.0 to 7.0.

HOW TO PLANT

Dig into a hole the size of a card table 2-in. layers of coarse sand or chicken grit and leaf mold or sphagnum peat moss. In clay soil, work into the hole 1 cupful each of gypsum and superphosphate. Set the shrub so the crown will be 1 in. above the ground level. If it is balled and burlapped, set the plant in the hole, cut the rope, slash

the burlap, and push it away from the ball. If container-grown, unwind roots circling the rootball before planting. Fill the hole, watering in to settle the soil. Apply a 3-in. mulch starting 3 in. from the stem.

HOW TO PROVIDE CARE

The first year, pour a bucketful of water around the roots every week unless there's a soaking rain. Mid-fall and early winter can be a dry period in Virginia. Continue the watering program sufficiently to keep the soil from drying out. Every few years, to keep the plant shapely, cut old stems back to the ground shortly after it has finished blooming.

ADDITIONAL ADVICE FOR CARE

In late winter before growth begins, broadcast an organic 5-10-10 fertilizer for acid-loving plants at half the rate recommended from the drip line out to a point at a distance equal to $1^1/_2$ times the shrub's height. Water it in. Replenish the mulch. Fertilize again in November. Once the plant is well established, switch to a 12-6-6 fertilizer.

Redtip Photinia

raser's photinia is a very erect evergreen shrub that grows fairly quickly to between 12 and 15 ft. and about half as wide. It has shiny, dark green foliage, but its main asset is new foliage that is an eye-catching, glistening coppery red on bright red stems. In spring, photinia bears small white flowers that have an odor some find objectionable—but it does not stay in flower for very long. Since photinia is sheared annually to encourage the growth of the colorful new foliage, the shrubs tend to be exceptionally dense. In Washington, D.C., photinia is used as a privacy screen between townhouses. In the suburbs, it is planted to create tall hedges. Out in the country, it is used to create evergreen wind breaks. 'Indian Princess' is a dwarf form with orange-copper new growth. This species is reputed to be winter-hardy only as far north as Zone 7.

WHEN TO PLANT

Plant a balled and burlapped or container-grown photinia in fall before Indian summer, or in early spring while the shrub still is dormant.

WHERE TO PLANT

Photinia succeeds in partial shade or in full sun. Avoid wet soils, and airless locations.

HOW TO PLANT

Dig a hole 4 in. deeper than the rootball, wider toward the top. Use a spading fork to loosen the sides of the hole. In clay soil, work into the hole 1/2 cupful each of gypsum and superphosphate, and top it with 2 in. of soil. Set the shrub so the crown will be 1 in. above the ground level. If it is balled and burlapped, set the plant in the hole, cut the rope, slash the burlap, and push it away from the ball. If container-grown, unwind roots circling the rootball before planting. Fill the hole, watering in to settle the soil. Apply a 3-in. mulch starting 3 in. from the stem.

SHRUBS

How to Provide Care

The first year, pour a bucketful of water around the roots every week unless there's a soaking rain. Mid-fall and early winter can be a dry period in Virginia. Continue the watering program sufficiently to keep the soil from drying out. Prune photinia every year in summer to maximize the opportunity for new growth. From each cut, 2 or 3 new tips should provide good spring color. But don't prune back past the area where leaves are growing. There is a tendency to over-prune photinias.

Additional Advice for Care

In late winter before growth begins, broadcast an organic 5-10-10 fertilizer at half the rate recommended from the drip line out to a point at a distance equal to 1½ times the shrub's height, and water it in. Replenish the mulch. Fertilize again in November. Once the plant is well established, switch to a 12-6-6 fertilizer.

Rhododendron

The rhododendron group, to which azaleas belong, includes over 900 species and thousands of evergreen and deciduous cultivars. In Virginia, these tall shrubs with their huge, airy globes of exquisite flowers are among the most valued of spring and early summer flowering shrubs. The pink, rose, lavender, purple, white, or yellow flowers often are flushed, splotched or spotted with another shade or color. They reach 20 ft. and more in the wild, but most mature at 6 or 8 ft. in cultivation. Some beautiful pink cultivars that do well in Virginia are: 'Mary Fleming', a small yellow-pink; 'Janet Blair', an 9-ft. light pink; 'Parker's Pink', a 5-ft. dark pink and white bi-color; 8-ft. pink 'Scintillation'; and 10 to 12 ft. 'Cadis', a light pink. There are also some beautiful fragrant pink cultivars of the lovely 12-ft. early-blooming evergreen species *R. fortunei*, Fortune's rhododendron. Recommended for flowers in the lavender-purple color range are: 6-ft. 'Roseum Elegans', a rose-lilac; 6-ft. 'Ben Moseley', which is purple with a pink blotch; and 8-ft. 'Caroline' which is orchid and pink. Among attractive red rhododendron are 5-ft. 'Nova Zembla', and 4-ft. 'Holden', which is a rosy red.

WHEN TO PLANT

Plant a balled and burlapped or container-grown shrub in fall before Indian summer, or in early spring while the shrub still is dormant. If you want to be sure of the color, buy a plant that is beginning to bloom.

WHERE TO PLANT

A rhododendron tolerates full sun here as long as the soil is moist, but it will do best in the bright dappled light of tall trees. A slope that offers protection from high winds is ideal. So is the edge of a woodland, and soil that formerly supported a woodland. Rhododendrons require soil that is well drained, rich in humus, and acid, between pH 4.5 and 6.0.

How to Plant

Dig into a hole the size of a card table 3 in. of sphagnum peat, ground pine bark or fibrous, acid compost. Add 2 in. of coarse sand, or perlite, and a generous handful of gypsum. Mix all this in to a depth of 12 to 18 in. Set the shrub so the crown will be 2 in. above the ground level. If balled and burlapped, set the plant in the hole, cut the rope, slash the burlap, and push it away from the ball. If container-grown, cut an "X" across the bottom of the rootball before planting. Fill the hole, watering in to settle the soil. Apply a 3-in. mulch of pine needles, shredded oak leaf mulch, or sphagnum peat moss, starting 3 in. from the stem.

How to Provide Care

The first year, pour a bucketful of water around the roots every week unless there's a soaking rain. Mid-fall and early winter can be a dry period in Virginia. Continue the watering program sufficiently to keep the soil from drying out. As each flower truss withers, pluck it off, taking care not to damage the tiny buds growing in back of it. Prune a rhododendron bush after it has bloomed, removing individual branches as required to achieve a pre-determined shape.

Additional Advice for Care

In late winter before growth begins, broadcast an organic 5-10-10 fertilizer for acid-loving plants at half the rate recommended from the drip line out to a point at a distance equal to $1^1/_2$ times the shrub's height. Water it in. Replenish the mulch now, and again during the summer.

Additional Cultivars and Species

Several species of rhododendrons thrive in Virginia: *R. dauricumm*, 4- to 5-ft. very early deciduous or semi-evergreen plants with purple, pink and white flowers; evergreen 5- to 6-ft. *R. makinoi*, which bears soft pink flowers often spotted with crimson; evergreen 3- to 4-ft. *R. yakusimanum*, which bears bright rose flowers that open to white; and 'Yaku Princess' (Yakusimanum hybrid), which is apple-blossom pink.

Sasangua Camellia

*T*he camellia is a southern belle grown for its large, lustrous evergreen leaves and for the spectacular roselike flowers it bears in fall and winter in warm areas, and in early early spring in cooler areas. The National Arboretum lost its collection of the prettiest camellia, the small 12-ft. *Camellia sasanqua,* in the cold of the late 1970s and early 1980s. Now in Washington, D.C., we plant camellias where they won't get winter sun or drying winds. We also protect them with a 5- to 6-in. winter mulch and burlap barriers, or wrap them in Remay, a protective fabric. A new collection of camellias is being tried at the National Arboretum. They are said to be hardy to -12 degrees Fahrenheit. Some good choices include 'Snow Flurry', 'Winter's Interlude', 'Winter's Dream', 'Winter's Rose', and 'Winter's Charm'. 'Frost Queen' and 'Cinnamon Cindy' are other possibilities. A few cultivars are fragrant. Select with the assistance of a reliable local nursery. Among northern Virginia nurseries that carry winter-hardy camellias are
Hill's in Arlington, Betty's Azalea Ranch in Fairfax, and Behnke's in Beltsville, MD.

When to Plant

Plant a container-grown camellia in fall before Indian summer, and in early spring while the shrub still is dormant.

Where to Plant

Plant a camellia in semi-sun or the dappled shade of a tall tree, or the bright shade of a building. Too much sun or too much shade reduces the flowering. The camellia prefers soil that is acid. The sasanqua camellia succeeds in the pH range between 4.5 and 6.5.

How to Plant

Dig into a hole the size of a card table 2-in. layers of coarse sand or chicken grit and leaf mold or sphagnum peat moss. In clay soil, work into the hole 1 cupful each of gypsum and superphosphate. Unwind roots circling the root ball before planting. Set the shrub so the crown will be 1 in. above the ground level. Fill the hole, watering in to settle the soil. Make a saucer of earth to hold water. Apply a 3-in. mulch starting 3 in. from the stem.

HOW TO PROVIDE CARE

The first year, water often enough to keep the soil surface damp.
Mid-fall and early winter can be a dry period in Virginia. Continue
the watering program sufficiently to keep the soil from drying out.
Prune the sasanqua camellia after it blossoms in fall or in midwinter.
Leave the side shoots—the flowers form on these. They don't flower
on upright branches.

ADDITIONAL ADVICE FOR CARE

In late winter before growth begins, broadcast an organic 5-10-10
fertilizer at half the rate recommended from the drip line out to a
point at a distance equal to 1¹/₂ times the shrub's height, and water
it in. Replenish the mulch. Fertilize again in September. Once the
plant is well established, switch to a 5-10-5 fertilizer.

ADDITIONAL CULTIVARS AND SPECIES

Though considered less attractive, especially in a small landscape,
the Japanese camellia, *C. japonica*, may do better in Virginia than the
sasanqua. The flowers are large, up to 5 in. across, and bloom in late
winter and early spring.

Shrub Althea

OTHER COMMON NAME: Rose-of-Sharon

*T*his is an old-fashioned, tall shrub, or small tree, about 8 to 12 ft. high and just a little less wide. It bears a profusion of short-lived flowers in July and goes on blooming until the end of September. The blossoms are trumpet shaped, like its relative the tropical hibicus, but usually are just 4 to 6 in. in diameter with ruffled petals crinkled on the margin. The usual colors are white, pink, crimson and purple. Look for one of the new cultivars introduced through the National Arboretum by the late Dr. Donald Egolf. They are sterile triploids that have a longer blooming season and set less fruit which can be a nuisance. 'Diana' bears beautiful pure white flowers that last more than a day. 'Helene' is white with a deep reddish-purple eye. 'Minerva' blooms are lavender pink, and 'Aphrodite' bears deep rose-pink flowers with showy deep red eyes.

WHEN TO PLANT
Choose a young container-grown shrub, and plant it in fall before Indian summer, or in early spring while the shrub is still dormant.

WHERE TO PLANT
Althea flowers best growing in full sun. However, like most shrubs, it succeeds with 4 to 6 hours of sun, or all-day filtered light. It thrives in a wide variety of soils, pH 5.5 to 7.0.

HOW TO PLANT
Dig into a hole the size of a card table 2-in. layers of coarse sand or chicken grit and leaf mold or sphagnum peat moss. In clay soil, work into the hole 1 cupful each of gypsum and superphosphate. Unwind roots circling the rootball before planting. Set the shrub so the crown will be 1 in. above the ground level. Fill the hole, watering in to settle the soil. Make a saucer of earth to hold water. Apply a 3-in. mulch starting 3 in. from the stem.

How to Provide Care

The first year, pour a bucketful of water around the roots every week unless there's a soaking rain. Mid-fall and early winter can be a dry period in Virginia, so continue the watering program sufficiently to keep the soil from drying out. In early spring before the buds break, prune the branches back heavily to outward-facing buds. If you want larger flowers, prune the branches back to 3 or 4 outward-facing buds.

Additional Advice for Care

In late winter before growth begins, broadcast an organic 5-10-10 fertilizer at half the rate recommended from the drip line out to a point at a distance equal to 1½ times the shrub's height. Water it in. Replenish the mulch. The soil's moisture must be maintained. Fertilize again in November. Once the plant is well established, switch to a 12-6-6 fertilizer.

Additional Cultivars and Species

A near relative that is more like a very large perennial than shrub, is rose mallow, *H. moscheutos*. In mid- to late summer, it bears huge hollyhock-like pink or white flowers with a dark eye. See the chapter on perennials.

Sumac

We have been so accustomed to admiring sumac's flaming fall colors in wild places—binding the soil on slopes along railroad tracks and superhighways—that it only recently has been appreciated as a garden plant. There are now excellent cultivated varieties, but the sumacs still are most effective massed in naturalized plantings on slopes. They are versatile as to soil, tolerate drought and pollution, and spread easily. Probably the most beautiful of the sumacs is little *R. copallina*, the shining or dwarf sumac. It is a tall, deciduous shrub or small tree to 20 to 30 ft. high in the wild, and is easily distinguished by its winged leaf stalks. In summer, there are greenish flowers in dense clusters followed by red fruit. The foliage turns to a rich crimson red in fall. Another very popular species is the staghorn sumac, *R. typhina*. It has deeply divided foliage that turns gold, orange and scarlet in fall. In early summer, it bears greenish pyramidal flowers which are followed by crimson fruit clusters that persist and are attractive to many birds. 'Laciniata' is an established cultivar whose texture is finer than that of the species.

WHEN TO PLANT

Plant a balled and burlapped or container-grown sumac in fall before Indian summer, or in early spring while the shrub still is dormant.

WHERE TO PLANT

Sumac colors most brightly and produces the most fruit growing in full sun, but it can stand all-day filtered light. Shining sumac prefers soil that is in the acid range, pH 5.5 to 7.0. The staghorn sumac, *R. typhina*, does better in the acid range, pH 5.5 to 6.0. The sumacs are excellent plants to naturalize on dry, rocky, neglected slopes, but they don't tolerate wet soil.

HOW TO PLANT

Dig a hole 4 in. deeper than the rootball, wider toward the top. Use a spading fork to loosen the sides of the hole. In clay soil, work into the hole 1/2 cupful each of gypsum and superphosphate, and top it with 2 in. of soil. Set the shrub so the crown will be 1 in. above the ground level. If it is balled and burlapped, set the plant in the hole, cut the rope, slash the burlap, and push it away from the ball. If container-grown, unwind roots circling the root ball before planting. Fill the hole, watering in to settle the soil. Apply a 3-in. mulch starting 3 in. from the stem.

How to Provide Care

The first few weeks after planting, pour a bucketful of water around the roots every week unless there's a soaking rain. If you wish to maintain the shape of this summer-flowering shrub, prune the branches back to outward-facing buds between late fall when it goes dormant, and spring when the buds break.

Additional Advice for Care

In late winter before growth begins, broadcast an organic 5-10-10 fertilizer at half the rate recommended from the drip line out to a point at a distance equal to $1^1/_2$ times the shrub's height, and water it in. Replenish the mulch.

Viburnum

*T*he viburnums are rather large, deciduous, semi-evergreen or evergreen shrubs or small trees. They are valued for their flowers and the color of their foliage and fruits in fall. Those I love best are delightfully fragrant. *V.* 'Mohawk' is 6 to 8 ft. tall when it matures, and in mid-spring it is covered with dark red buds that open to white flowers with red blotched-reverse. While in bloom, the plant is enveloped in a strong, sweet spicy fragrance, something like cloves but more exotic. The glossy foliage stays green well into fall, and sometimes turns a dull wine-red. This is a wonderful viburnum. *V.* 'Cayuga' blooms before 'Mohawk', producing abundant pink buds that open white with a sweet clove scent. It is more compact and has dark green foliage that turns a brilliant red in winter. The fruits are black. It is a good choice for small gardens. *V.* 'Chesapeake' is another compact viburnum with good color in fall. *V. × juddii* is a 15-ft. viburnum suited to a larger landscape and the cooler reaches of Virginia—but not a good choice below Zone 7. It bears fragrant, semi-snowball pinkish white flowers in mid-spring, followed by black fruits.

WHEN TO PLANT

Plant a balled and burlapped or container-grown viburnum in fall before Indian summer, or in early spring while the shrub is still dormant.

WHERE TO PLANT

Viburnum flowers and colors best in full sun. However, like most shrubs, it succeeds with 6 hours of sun, or all-day filtered light. Most of the viburnums prefer soils that are slightly acid, in the pH range between 6.0 and 7.0.

HOW TO PLANT

Dig into a hole the size of a card table 2-in. layers of coarse sand or chicken grit and leaf mold or sphagnum peat moss. In clay soil, work into the hole 1 cupful each of gypsum and superphosphate. Set the shrub so the crown will be 1 in. above the ground level. If it is balled and burlapped, set the plant in the hole, cut the rope, slash the burlap, and push it away from the ball. If container-grown, unwind roots circling the rootball before planting. Fill the hole, watering in to settle the soil. Apply a 3-in. mulch starting 3 in. from the stem.

HOW TO PROVIDE CARE

The first year, pour a bucketful of water around the roots every week unless there's a soaking rain. Mid-fall and early winter can be a dry period in Virginia. Continue the watering program sufficiently to keep the soil from drying out. If you wish to maintain the shape of this spring-flowering shrub, shortly after it finishes blooming, prune protruding branches back to outward-facing buds, and cut old branches to the ground.

ADDITIONAL ADVICE FOR CARE

In late winter before growth begins, broadcast an organic 5-10-10 fertilizer at half the rate recommended from the drip line out to a point at a distance equal to $1^{1}/_{2}$ times the shrub's height, and water it in. Replenish the mulch. Fertilize again in November.

ADDITIONAL CULTIVARS AND SPECIES

The 6-ft. cultivar 'Shasta' is a magnificent shrub introduced by the National Arboretum's late great Dr. Donald R. Egolf. In spring, it tops graceful horizontal branches with clusters of pure white flowers that are almost twice the size of those on a regular doublefile viburnum. In full bloom, it reminds you of a dogwood. The flowers are followed in midsummer by bright red fruits.

Itea virginica

Virginia Sweetspire

The bright green of Virginia sweetspire's summer foliage turns brilliant, even fluorescent, red in fall. In June or July, depending on where you live, it bears fragrant, showy white flowers in dense upright clusters to 6 in. long. The shrub reaches about 8 ft. at maturity, branching near the top. 'Henry's Garnet' is a 3- to 5-ft. improved shrub with larger fragrant flowers and foliage that turns an eye-popping red-purple in fall. Itea is not an important garden plant, but it is a wonderful plant for a wet spot in the yard, and an excellent choice for a wild garden.

WHEN TO PLANT
Plant a balled and burlapped or container-grown sweetspire in early spring while the shrub is still dormant.

WHERE TO PLANT
Sweetspire flowers and colors best growing in full sun, but it thrives in shade, too. It prefers soil in the pH range between 6.0 and 7.0.

HOW TO PLANT
Dig into a hole the size of a card table 2-in. layers of coarse sand or chicken grit, and of leaf mold or sphagnum peat moss. In clay soil, work into the hole 1 cupful each of gypsum and superphosphate. Set the shrub so the crown will be 1 in. above the ground level. If it is balled and burlapped, set the plant in the hole, cut the rope, slash the burlap, and push it away from the ball. If container-grown, unwind roots circling the rootball before planting. Fill the hole, watering in to settle the soil. Apply a 3-in. mulch starting 3 in. from the stem.

How to Provide Care

The first year, pour a bucketful of water around the roots every week unless there's a soaking rain. Mid-fall and early winter can be a dry period in Virginia. Continue the watering program sufficiently to keep the soil from drying out. Sweetspire needs no special pruning, but if you want to cut it back, do so while the plant is dormant in late winter.

Additional Advice for Care

In late winter before growth begins, broadcast an organic 5-10-10 fertilizer at half the rate recommended from the drip line out to a point equal at a distance equal to $1^1/2$ times the shrub's height, and water it in. Replenish the mulch. Fertilize again in November.

Additional Cultivars and Species

I. japonica 'Beppu', a National Arboretum introduction, is a dwarfish form that grows into a 2- to 3-ft. mound whose foliage colors handsomely in the fall. The flowers are similar to those of Virginia sweetspire, but smaller.

SHRUBS

Winter Jasmine

*W*inter jasmine is a fast-growing evergreen, rambling, flowering shrub that is planted to create quick, low-maintenance cover along walls where trailing branches are an asset, and to cover slopes and areas where the soil is poor. It also is used in the garden to hide the bottoms of leggy shrubs, like roses. The species forms 3- to 4-ft. tall mounds of stems that trail or grow 12 to 15 ft., rooting where they touch moist soil. The stems also can be trained to a trellis. Once established, winter jasmine can be difficult to remove. Winter jasmine's special charm is its rush into bloom at the first warmth of the season. It flowers here between February and April, according to the season, producing small yellow flowers on the previous season's growth.

WHEN TO PLANT
Plant a balled and burlapped or container-grown winter jasmine in fall before Indian summer, or in early spring while the shrub still is dormant.

WHERE TO PLANT
Winter jasmine flowers best growing in full sun, but it will do quite well with 4 to 6 hours of sun, or all-day filtered light.

HOW TO PLANT
Dig a hole 4 in. deeper than the rootball and wider toward the top. Use a spading fork to loosen the sides of the hole. In clay soil, work into the hole 1/2 cupful each of gypsum and superphosphate, and top it with 2 in. of soil. Set the shrub so the crown will be 1 in. above the ground level. If it is balled and burlapped, set the plant in the hole, cut the rope, slash the burlap, and push it away from the ball. If container-grown, unwind roots circling the rootball before planting. Fill the hole, watering in to settle the soil. Apply a 3-in. mulch starting 3 in. from the stem.

How to Provide Care

The first year, pour a bucketful of water around the roots every week unless there's a soaking rain. Mid-fall and early winter can be a dry period in Virginia. Continue the watering program sufficiently to keep the soil from drying out. Winter jasmine benefits from being cut back to 6 in. or so every 3 to 5 years before spring growth begins.

Additional Advice for Care

In late winter before growth begins, broadcast an organic 5-10-10 fertilizer at half the rate recommended from the drip line out to a point at a distance equal to 1½ times the shrub's height, and water it in. Replenish the mulch. Fertilize again in November. Once the plant is well established, switch to 12-6-6.

Additional Cultivars and Species

The white-flowered semi-evergreen poet's jasmine, *J. officinale*, is so fragrant it is worth trying, though Zone 7 is the at the top of its hardiness range. In the hills, it can be grown as a container plant if it has a place indoors to winter. 'Grandiflorum' has large, purple-tinged flowers. There is a fragrant pink hybrid, *J. × stephanense*, Stephan's jasmine.

Hamamelis virginiana

Witchhazel

*T*his species is the native witchhazel, the first flower of the year at the National Arboretum in Washington, D.C. Given any encouragement by the weather, some time between December and late February these tall shrubs or small trees cover their branches with fragrant, ribbonlike yellow flowers. On very cold days the little ribbons roll up. The leaves appear later. In fall, the foliage turns to a very desirable shade of golden yellow. The native plant is ideal for naturalizing in a larger country landscape, but for a smaller garden, some of the cultivars of *H. × intermedia* are better choices. 'Winter Beauty', which blooms early, has small, but abundant tangerine orange flowers which are very fragrant. 'Arnold Promise', one of the last to bloom, is a beautiful hybrid whose large flowers are deep yellow and fragrant. 'Diane' has coppery red or maroon flowers, and its fall color is exceptionally rich orange-red. The witchhazels do very well in city conditions.

WHEN TO PLANT

Plant a balled and burlapped or container-grown witchhazel in early spring while the shrub is still dormant or in fall before Indian summer.

WHERE TO PLANT

Witchhazel does well in full sun or partial shade. It prefers soil that is somewhat acid, in the pH range between 6.0 and 7.0.

HOW TO PLANT

Dig into a hole the size of a card table 2-in. layers of coarse sand or chicken grit and leaf mold or sphagnum peat moss. In clay soil, work into the hole 1 cupful each of gypsum and superphosphate. Set the shrub so the crown will be 1 in. above the ground level. If it is balled and burlapped, set the plant in the hole, cut the rope, slash the burlap, and push it away from the ball. If container-grown, unwind roots circling the rootball before planting. Fill the hole, watering in to settle the soil. Apply a 3-in. mulch starting 3 in. from the stem.

How to Provide Care

The first year, pour a bucketful of water around the roots every week unless there's a soaking rain. Mid-fall and early winter can be a dry period in Virginia. Continue the watering program sufficiently to keep the soil from drying out. Witchhazel prefers somewhat moist soil. Remove suckers as they arise. If you wish to maintain the shape of this spring-flowering shrub, shortly after it finishes blooming, prune the branches back to outward-facing buds.

Additional Advice for Care

In late winter before growth begins, broadcast an organic 5-10-10 fertilizer at half the rate recommended from the drip line out to a point at a distance equal to 1½ times the shrub's height, and water it in. Replenish the mulch. Fertilize again in November. Once the plant is well established, switch to a 12-6-6 fertilizer.

Additional Cultivars and Species

H. mollis, the Chinese witchhazel, is a tall plant, to 30 ft., and its red and yellow flowers are the largest of all, and very fragrant. The fall color is clear orange-yellow.

SHRUBS

Yew

*T*he yews are a vast tribe of vigorous evergreen shrubs and
stately trees that have short, stiff, narrow, needlelike leaves. They
have been used *ad infinitum* in gardens because they're slow-growing,
tolerate yearly shearing, and are trouble-free. They are among our
most useful and versatile evergreens for foundation plantings, hedges,
screening, and massing with broadleaves and deciduous flowering
shrubs. They come in almost all sizes, shapes, and colors. Among
yews that do well in small Virginia gardens are *T. cuspidata* 'Nana',
the dwarf Japanese yew which slowly reaches 6 ft., and is dense and
compact, and 'Densa' which has wide spreading branches—an old
plant may be 4 ft. by 20 ft. across. Another good choice for Virginia is
the dwarf English yew, *T. baccata* 'Nana', a dark-needled compact
pyramid about 3 ft. high. 'Pygmaea' remains at something under 2 ft.
'Repandens' is wide with arching branches, 2 to 4 ft. tall, and 12 to 15
ft. wide. 'Standishii' is a lovely golden yew for small gardens: a nar-
rowly upright form, it slowly branches 25 ft. and may be kept small by
shearing. Another smaller cultivar, 'Washingtonii', has open branches
and leaves a rich gold that fades to yellow-green.

WHEN TO PLANT
Plant a balled and burlapped or container-grown shrub in fall before
Indian summer, or in early spring while the shrub still is dormant.

WHERE TO PLANT
A yew will do well growing in full sun or part shade, but the needles will brown in winter if the plant is exposed to strong, cold
winds. Yews generally prefer somewhat alkaline soil. They aren't
good companion plants for azaleas and rhododendrons, and they
must have excellent drainage.

HOW TO PLANT
Dig a hole 4 in. deeper than the rootball, wider toward the top. Use
a spading fork to loosen the sides of the hole. In clay soil, work into
the hole 1/2 cupful each of gypsum and superphosphate, and top it

with 2 in. of soil. Set the shrub so the crown will be 1 in. above the ground level. If it is balled and burlapped, set the plant in the hole, cut the rope, slash the burlap, and push it away from the ball. If container-grown, unwind roots circling the rootball before planting. Fill the hole, watering in to settle the soil. Apply a 3-in. mulch starting 3 in. from the stem.

HOW TO PROVIDE CARE

The first year, pour a bucketful of water around the roots every week unless there's a soaking rain. Mid-fall and early winter can be a dry period in Virginia. Continue the watering program sufficiently to keep the soil from drying out. Prune away yew dead wood any time of year, but remember that to cut beyond the area where green needles are growing means a branch won't sprout new needles.

ADDITIONAL ADVICE FOR CARE

In late winter before growth begins, broadcast an organic 5-10-10 fertilizer at half the rate recommended from the drip line out to a point at a distance equal to 1$\frac{1}{2}$ times the shrub's height. Water it in. Replenish the mulch. Fertilize again in November. Once the plant is well established, switch to a 12-6-6 fertilizer.

Vines

*V*INES ARE BEAUTIFUL, AND THEY ARE WONDERFULLY USEFUL . . . especially in a smaller yard. Generally deep-rooted, they grow vigorously, and are relatively resistant to drought. Above all, they achieve enormous visual effects while taking up a modest spot in the ground. A vine can thrive for years in a large planter or tub. For the amount of foliage they produce, you need supply relatively little water.

In Virginia a great many beautiful vines flourish. Some vines we grow for their flowers: annuals like the spring-flowering annual sweet pea, and the gorgeous summer-flowering, night-blooming moonvine, and perennials like clematis, and the climbing hydrangea. Some vines we grow for their fall color: Virginia creeper and Boston ivy turn crimson when cold comes, and Oriental bittersweet produces beautiful bright berries the birds love. Many vines grow very rapidly—up or down, or sideways, according to how you train the leading stems, and the supports you provide.

The support is the first thing to consider before deciding on a vine. Also, consider how you are going to prune it when it gets to the top of its support. Some vines grow to be very heavy—trumpet creeper is one, and wisteria is another. How a vine climbs dictates what it needs as support. Vines that climb by twining stems require a narrow support such as a wooden post, a pipe, wires, or strings. Vines that climb by twining tendrils or leaf petioles—clematis for example—require a structure of wires, or wire mesh. Vines that climb by aerial rootlets that secrete an adhesive glue, like English ivy and Virginia creeper, need only a rugged surface, such as a brick or stucco wall, or a rough, unpainted fence. Vines that eventually will be very heavy—wisteria, climbing hydrangea, and bitter-sweet—require supports built of heavy timbers, or dead trees.

Vines hold a lot of moisture. Make sure the lumber you buy to create a support for a vine is pressure-treated and weatherproofed.

Chapter Eleven

Don't set a vine to growing up a wooden wall, because its moisture can cause rot. I suggest you leave at least a 3-in. air space between foliage and any type of house wall—vines need air circulation all the way around. Avoid planting vines that climb by tendrils near trees, large shrubs, windows, or shutters.

GROWING VINES

Set a vine about 6 in. away from its support so there will be air space behind the foliage when it matures. Water it well in the early stages, and maintain a 3-in. mulch, especially in summer to keep the roots cool. If the vine is sheltered from rain, hose it down now and then in summer—but don't hose it when it is coming into, or already in bloom. Keep dead, extraneous, or weak wood pruned out. Monitor the growth of large, fast-growing vines such as wisteria, and prune them severely every year.

PRUNING VINES

When your vine will need to be pruned depends on the plant itself. Flowering vines that bloom on the wood that grows in the current year are pruned in winter, late winter usually, before growth begins. It is always best to prune vines that lose their leaves while they still are dormant. A good time is any time just after the coldest part of the winter season, and the moment when growth begins. Flowering vines that bloom in spring on the wood produced during the previous growing season are pruned as soon as possible after the flowers fade to allow the plant plenty of time to produce and mature the wood that will flower the following year. The best time to prune vines that do not flower is in summer, after the major thrust of seasonal growth is over.

Generally speaking, it is best to avoid pruning in the fall. The wounds heal more slowly during that season, and even more important is the fact that pruning stimulates growth, and late growth may be damaged by the first frosts. It isn't necessary to paint, tar, or otherwise cover a pruning cut.

Carolina Yellow Jessamine

*C*arolina yellow jessamine is a fast-growing vine with reddish, wiry, twining stems 10 to 20 ft. long. As a vine it's an undistinguished evergreen, but in my Washington, D.C., garden in late winter, it's covered with the masses of fragrant, funnel-shaped golden flowers that are pretty and very welcome in that bleak season. The foliage is dainty and attractive all season. The plant climbs by twining around anything handy, including fencing, porches or trellises. You can use it as ground cover for slopes if you pin the stems to the ground to prevent them from twining around each other. Carolina jessamine grows wild in woodlands in the South, but in my Washington, D.C. garden, severe cold regularly damages the leaf tips, and it has to be pruned back yearly to prevent it from taking over the entire porch. It is not reliably winter hardy in the cool, hilly country near the West Virginia border, Zone 6. All parts of the plant are poisonous. The cultivar called 'Pride of Augusta' is a beautiful plant with double flowers.

WHEN TO PLANT

The best times for planting Carolina jessamine are in fall before Indian summer, and in early spring before the vine blooms.

WHERE TO PLANT

Carolina yellow jessamine blooms lavishly planted in full sun, but it also does well in partial shade. It tolerates slightly acid and slightly alkaline soil.

HOW TO PLANT

Dig into a hole twice the size of the rootball 2-in. layers of coarse sand or chicken grit and leaf mold or sphagnum peat moss. In clay soil, work 1 cupful each of gypsum and superphosphate into the hole. Unwind the roots circling the rootball and plant it with the crown an inch above ground level. Fill the hole, watering in to settle the soil. Make a saucer of earth to hold water. With soft twine, tie the longer branches to whatever you want the vine to grow over. Apply a 3-in. mulch starting 3 in. from the stem.

HOW TO PROVIDE CARE

After planting, pour a half bucket of water into the saucer every week unless there's a soaking rain. If the vine is to climb, it will in time become woody, like a small tree, and is attractive underplanted with a living mulch of myrtle, ajuga, or a slow-growing, small-leaved variegated ivy.

ADDITIONAL ADVICE FOR CARE

In late winter before growth begins, broadcast an organic 5-10-5 fertilizer over the area at half the rate recommended on the container and water it in. Replenish the mulch if necessary. Repeat in November. Once the plant is well established, switch to a 7-6-19 fertilizer. Cut away stems twining around each other, and any heading in unwanted directions.

Climbing Hydrangea

*T*his slow-growing, climbing vine with its lustrous, dark-green leaves is probably the most beautiful—and formal—climber we have. A mature specimen is magnificent in late spring and early summer when it opens clusters of small, fragrant florets backed by showy white bracts. The branches extend 2 to 3 ft. outward which gives the vine a full, rich silhouette. Though not evergreen, the leaves are a fine green, and they stay that color until they fall in late fall. In time, the central stem thickens and becomes woody, and the cinnamon-colored bark exfoliates in an attractive way. The climbing hydrangea reaches heights of 60 to 80 ft., clinging by means of root-like attachments. It will grow up brick, stucco, and stone walls, chimneys, arbors and trees. It becomes massive and must have strong support. Though it's slow-growing, once a climbing hydrangea matures, it can become invasive and will need to be pruned.

When to Plant

Set out a container-grown plant in early spring, disturbing the root-ball as little as possible. It will be slow to re-establish and show new growth. Take good care of it until it's growing vigorously.

Where to Plant

The climbing hydrangea flowers best in full sun. It does well in shade, but it won't flower as bountifully. It tolerates salt air.

How to Plant

Dig into a hole the size of a card table 2-in. layers of coarse sand or chicken grit and leaf mold or sphagnum peat moss. In clay soil, work 1 cupful each of gypsum and superphosphate into the hole. Unwind the roots circling the ball and plant it with the crown an inch above ground level. Fill the hole, watering in to settle the soil. With soft twine, tie the vine to the structure that will support it. Make a saucer of earth around the plant to hold water. Apply a 3-in. mulch starting 3 in. from the stem.

HOW TO PROVIDE CARE

After planting, pour a bucketful of water into the saucer every week unless there's a soaking rain.

ADDITIONAL ADVICE FOR CARE

In late winter before growth begins, broadcast an organic 5-10-5 fertilizer for acid-loving plants over the area at half the rate recommended on the container and water it in. Replenish the mulch. Repeat in November. Once the plant is well established, switch to a 7-6-19 fertilizer. Prune after flowering if needed.

Lonicera × heckrottii

Everblooming or Coral Honeysuckle 'Goldflame'

*T*he honeysuckles are fast-spreading, climbing, twining vines or tall shrubs that bear sweetly scented flowers followed by bright, berry-like fruits attractive to many types of birds. The birds disperse the seeds, which means honeysuckle species often turn up as weeds in your garden. Various wild types volunteer in gardens all over the state. Uncontrolled, they will take over the property, endowing it with a sweet scent and the look of a jungle. Everblooming, or coral honeysuckle, considered by many to be the most beautiful of the twining, climbing types, is less invasive. It grows 10 to 20 ft. high, bears fragrant, carmine flowers that open yellow and then change to pink, and blooms from late spring to fall. The fruit is red and not borne as profusely as other species, so the plant is less likely to become invasive. For a small city garden a good choice is *L. serotina* 'Florida', a compact, slow-growing cultivar of *L. periclymenum*, that blooms early and produces masses of fragrant flowers. It does best in partial shade but tolerates full sun.

WHEN TO PLANT
The best times for planting are in fall before Indian summer and in early spring while the plant is still dormant. But container-grown honeysuckle succeeds almost any time in spring or fall.

WHERE TO PLANT
Honeysuckle flowers best and is most fragrant growing in full sun. However, with 4 to 6 hours of sun, or all-day filtered light, it performs well. Honeysuckles thrive in soils in the neutral range, pH 6.0 to 8.0.

HOW TO PLANT
Dig a modest planting hole about 6 in. deeper and wider than the rootball and wider toward the top. Work a spading fork into the sides of the hole to loosen compacted soil. In clay soil, work 1 cupful each of gypsum and superphosphate into the hole and top it with 2 in. of soil. Unwind the roots circling the ball of a containerized plant

and set it with the crown an inch above ground level. Fill the hole, watering in to settle the soil. With soft twine, tie the vine to the structure that will support it. Make a saucer of earth around the plant to hold water. Apply a 3-in. mulch starting 3 in. from the stem.

HOW TO PROVIDE CARE

After the vine has flowered, prune away shoots that are becoming unruly. After planting, pour a bucketful of water into the vine saucer every week unless there's a soaking rain. If you wish to plant the area around the vine with a living mulch, use only drought-tolerant ground covers, like myrtle, ajuga, or a slow-growing, small-leaved variegated ivy. Hostas, liriope, mondo grass, and small, spring-flowering bulbs like wood hyacinths are also acceptable ground cover.

ADDITIONAL ADVICE FOR CARE

In late winter, broadcast an organic 5-10-5 fertilizer for acid-loving plants over the area at half the rate recommended on the container and water it in. Replenish the mulch. Repeat in November. Once the plant is well established, switch to a 7-6-19 fertilizer. If the plant becomes overgrown, cut it back to the ground before growth begins. It will develop new shoots.

ADDITIONAL CULTIVARS AND SPECIES

For the seashore, I would suggest the privet honeysuckle, *L. pileata*, a shrub said to tolerate some salt as well as some shade.

Lablab purpureus (syn. Dolichos lablab)

Hyacinth Bean

The prettiest, fast-growing annual vine is the purple-stemmed hyacinth bean. In the vegetable garden at Monticello, it twines its way up training wires and covers teepees 12 to 15 ft. high with broad, dark-green leaves. In July and August, it produces graceful clusters of rose to purple, pea-like flowers that fill the air with a gentle, sweet fragrance. It is even more beautiful in late summer when it develops long, handsome, purple-green bean pods. Once up and growing, the purple hyacinth bean quickly covers a fence, trellis, or a stump, and it readily grows up training wires or twine to screen a porch. The plant belongs to the pea family, and in climates warmer than ours is a twining perennial. I suggest you buy the hyacinth bean as a vigorously growing seedling since I have not had much luck with seeding it. If it's not offered at your garden center, you will likely find seeds listed in general interest garden catalogs like Thomson & Morgan's.

WHEN TO PLANT
In mid-spring, after the weather has warmed and the soil has dried, set out seedlings or sow seeds where the plants are to grow. Hyacinth bean will grow most quickly set out 2 weeks after the last frost: in the Williamsburg area that is April 14; Culpepper, April 17; Richmond, May 4; Washington, D.C., March 25.

WHERE TO PLANT
To flower and fruit fully, hyacinth bean requires full sun. However with 6 hours of sun, or bright, filtered light all day, it will grow.

HOW TO PLANT
Prepare the bed by digging in 2 in. of humus and a slow-release 10-10-5 fertilizer. In clay soil, add a small handful of gypsum and superphosphate for each plant. Work the soil 8 to 12 in. deep. Provide a support or string twine or wires 6 to 8 in. apart for the vines to climb. Mark planting holes near the supports. Half fill each hole with diluted fertilizer, plant the seedling high, and press the soil down around the stem firmly enough so the plant resists a tug. Water with a diluted fertilizer solution. Apply a 2-in. mulch.

HOW TO PROVIDE CARE

For the next 2 or 3 weeks, promote rapid unchecked growth by watering often enough to keep the soil moist. After that, water deeply every week unless you have a soaking rain. As the vines develop, check often to make sure each one is climbing its support and not invading the neighbor's. After the first flush of bloom, fertilize and repeat every 3 to 5 weeks through July.

Jackman's Clematis

*S*trongly growing clematis will cover walls, trellises, posts, fences and arbors. The plants grow by attaching leaf stalks to the support provided, or by scrambling over other vegetation. The Jackman's clematis is a fast-growing hybrid with very beautiful blossoms 4 to 7 in. across in colors from pink to purple, crimson, lilac, sky blue and more. The species flowers in July and August on new growth, and some cultivars go on until frost. The vines expand at a rate of 5 to 10 ft. in a single season and will grow to between 8 to 20 ft., depending on conditions. Among the fastest-growing cultivars in this group are 'Comtesse de Bouchard', 'Madame Baron Veillard', 'Perle d'Azure' and 'Victoria'. Pruning affects the way the many species of clematis bloom, and its timing is critical. The Jackmans flower on new growth. To stimulate new growth in order to have lots of flowers, as the leaf buds begin to swell in spring, cut the flowering stems back to buds within 4 to 6 in. of the main branches.

WHEN TO PLANT
Clematis is finicky about transplanting, so set out healthy, vigorously growing container plants in early spring after the soil has begun to dry and warm.

WHERE TO PLANT
Plant clematis where the roots are in shade and the vines can grow up into full sun. It is important that the roots be cool and that the vines receive lots of sun. As an alternative, plant clematis in the sun and keep the roots mulched 3 in. deep. Avoid hot, dry, airless areas. Soils with a pH between 6.0 and 7.5 are recommended for clematis, but they often tolerate somewhat acid soils.

HOW TO PLANT
Dig into a hole the size of a card table 2-in. layers of coarse sand or chicken grit and of compost sweetened with lime. In clay soil, work 1 cupful each of gypsum and superphosphate into the hole. Set the rootball with the crown an inch above ground level. Fill the hole, watering in to settle the soil. Provide twine or wire for support, or to

lead the vines to a fence, a tree, a wall, or other support. Make a saucer of earth around the plant to hold water. Apply and maintain a 3-in. mulch starting 3 in. from the stems.

How to Provide Care

After planting, pour a half bucketful of water into the saucer every week unless there's a soaking rain. Check the vines often and keep them growing in the desired direction.

Additional Advice for Care

In late winter before growth begins, broadcast an organic 5-10-5 fertilizer over the area at half the rate recommended on the container and water it in. Replenish the mulch. Repeat in November. Prune Jackman's clematis as the leaf buds begin to swell. Cut the flowering stems back to buds within 4 to 6 in. of the main branches.

Additional Cultivars and Species

A fast-growing clematis grown for its fall fragrance is sweet autumn clematis, *C. maximowicziana* (syn. *paniculata*). Cut back to the ground in winter, it grows rampantly in spring and in fall produces a froth of tiny, fragrant whitish flowers. Another fragrant clematis is anemone clematis, *C. montana*, which bears 2- to 2¹/₂-in. white or pink flowers in spring.

Japanese Wisteria

*T*n April to May, as the new foliage emerges, Japanese wisteria bears lightly scented 9- to 20-in. drooping clusters of pink, white, or lilac, single or double flowers. 'Longissima Alba' bears quite fragrant white flowers in clusters up to 15 in. long. This is a very full, leafy, twining vine that grows 30 to 40 ft., and more, at a rate of 10 ft. in a single season. As it matures, the weight is considerable, so provide a strong support. Wisteria is grown on pillars and arbors, as "green roofing" for porches, and is used to soften the harsh lines of stone walls. Do not plant wisteria where it can reach windows, doors, or gutters, or near a live tree. It can invade and damage attics, and it destroys trees. The cultivars tend to do better than the species—double-flowered varieties often are damaged by rain. Use low-nitrogen fertilizers like superphosphate for wisteria, or you will get masses of foliage and few flowers.

WHEN TO PLANT

Set out container-grown plants in early spring while the vine still is dormant, and pamper until it starts to grow.

WHERE TO PLANT

Plant wisteria in full sun. It is said to do better in soil with a high pH, but it seems to succeed in soil that is somewhat acid, too.

HOW TO PLANT

Dig into a hole the size of a card table 2-in. layers of coarse sand or chicken grit and compost or leaf mold to which a handful of lime has been added. In clay soil, work 1 cupful each of gypsum and superphosphate into the hole. Unwind roots circling the rootball, and plant with the crown an inch above ground level. Fill the hole, watering in to settle the soil. Make a saucer of earth to hold water. With soft twine, tie the vine to the structure that will support it. Apply a 3-in. mulch starting 3 in. from the stem.

How to Provide Care

After planting, pour a bucketful of water into the vine saucer every week unless there's a soaking rain. If you wish to plant the area around the vine with a living mulch, use drought-tolerant ground covers, like myrtle, ajuga, or a slow-growing, small-leaved variegated ivy. Hostas, liriope, mondo grass, and small, spring-flowering bulbs like wood hyacinths, are also acceptable ground cover.

Additional Advice for Care

For wisteria to bloom well, the vine must be pruned back ruthlessly every year while it's dormant. Japanese wisteria blooms on old wood and last season's growth. Cut all big, old shoots back, leaving only 3 to 4 buds on each. Fertilize in late winter and mid-November with superphosphate, and avoid nitrogen fertilizers which will promote leaf growth at the expense of flowering. Replenish the mulch.

Additional Cultivars and Species

Our native wisterias come into bloom later and are quite lovely, though the flower clusters aren't nearly as long. Kentucky wisteria, *W. macrostachya*, blooms after the foliage develops, providing a modest, but later, show of fragrant flower clusters 10 in. long in lilac-purple. Another late wisteria, *W. frutescens*, American wisteria, from June to August produces short, but dense, clumps of fragrant, bluish-violet flowers on new wood.

Moonvine

*M*oonvine, or moonflower, is a fast-growing tender perennial vine grown as an annual here. It has 8-in. leaves and bears large, luminous, very fragrant white flowers almost 6 in. across. They look like huge, silken trumpets and bloom all summer, opening toward evening and remaining open until about noon the following day. Moonvine is grown just for the beauty of its flowers, but it also is a good source of quick screening for porches, trellises, and urban chain-link fences. It climbs by means of twining stems and can reach 10 to 20 ft. in a single season.

WHEN TO PLANT

Plant moonvine seeds, or seedlings, after the weather warms. Around Williamsburg that's April 14; Culpepper, April 17; Richmond, May 4; Washington, D.C., March 25. You can start the seed indoors in late February or March. Soak the seeds overnight in warm water before planting.

WHERE TO PLANT

Plant moonvine where it is to bloom. It requires full sun or a minimum of 6 hours of sun daily.

HOW TO PLANT

Prepare the bed by digging in 1 in. of coarse sand or chicken grit, and a slow-release 5-10-5 fertilizer. In clay soil, add a small handful of gypsum and superphosphate for each plant. Work the soil 8 to 12 in. deep. Sow seeds following package instructions or mark planting holes for seedlings 6 to 8 in. apart. Half fill each hole with diluted fertilizer, plant the seedling high, and press the soil down around the stem firmly enough so the plant resists a tug. Water with a diluted fertilizer solution. Use soft twine to support the vines or to lead the vines to the structure that will support them. Apply a 3-in. mulch starting 3 in. from the stems.

HOW TO PROVIDE CARE

To promote rapid, unchecked growth, for the next 2 or 3 weeks water often enough to sustain the soil moisture. Check often until you are sure the vine is growing in the desired direction. During the summer, water deeply every week unless you have a soaking rain. After the first flush of bloom, fertilize again and repeat every 3 to 5 weeks through August.

Oriental Bittersweet

ittersweet is a fast-growing, twining, deciduous vine with large, glossy leaves, that is grown for the vivid fruits it produces in the fall. They are brilliant red-orange seeds surrounded by woody orange capsule segments, and are very attractive to birds. Bittersweet grows to 30 or 40 ft. almost anywhere. It is handsome growing on a rustic fence or climbing a drainpipe. It is also an excellent ground cover for rocky slopes and is used to control erosion in dry places. But don't let it start to climb a tree or a shrub, because it can be smothering. It tolerates city conditions and some drought. The female plant is the one that bears lots of fruit. Most need a male plant nearby to ensure a really good display. Do not accept a plant that the nursery can't guarantee is a female, and if you know of no pollinator in your area, buy a male plant to go with it. Oriental bittersweet is at the bottom of its heat range in Zone 8. It will do better in cool regions near the West Virginia border.

WHEN TO PLANT

Set out a small container plant in early fall or spring.

WHERE TO PLANT

Bittersweet produces the most fruits when growing in full sun. However, it will produce some fruit given 4 to 6 hours of sun or all-day filtered light.

HOW TO PLANT

Dig a modest planting hole about 6 in. deeper than the rootball and wider toward the top. Work a spading fork into the sides of the hole to loosen compacted soil. In clay soil, work 1 cupful each of gypsum and superphosphate into the hole and top it with 2 in. of soil. Unwind the roots circling the rootball and plant it with the crown an inch above ground level. Fill the hole, watering in to settle the soil. With soft twine, tie the vine to the structure that will support it. Make a saucer of earth to hold water. Apply a 3-in. mulch starting 3 in. from the stem.

How to Provide Care

After planting, pour a bucketful of water into the vine saucer every week unless there's a soaking rain. Check the vine often and keep it growing in the desired direction.

Additional Advice for Care

Prune old wood in early spring to improve fruiting.

Sweet Pea

$\mathcal{T}$he old-fashioned sweet pea is a fresh little cutting flower borne by a vine that grows 4 to 6 ft. in a season, and it's first cousin to the edible pea. The flowers appear in early to mid-spring, producing masses of blooms from purple to pale lavender, ruby red, pale pink and white. There are also bi-colored and even green varieties. Mixed colors make delightful bouquets. *L. latifolius* is the everlasting species, a perennial that grows well in Virginia, where it flowers mid- to late summer and easily climbs 10 ft. a year. Garden centers sell these as container plants. *L. odoratus* is the delicately scented "sweet" pea, an annual that grows 4 to 6 ft. in a season. Cultivars include non-climbing dwarves suitable for small gardens and containers. Buy heat-resistant strains. Sweet peas use climbing tendrils to grip their support, which can be training strings or wires—or brambles, rock piles, trellises, or garden teepees.

WHEN TO PLANT

To facilitate germination, before sowing the seeds soak them in warm water overnight, or lightly file the seed coats. Plant sweet pea seeds as soon as the ground can be worked after the last frost. Around Williamsburg that is April 14; Culpepper, April 17; Richmond, May 4, and Washington, D.C., March 25. Sweet peas do well during cool weather.

WHERE TO PLANT

Sweet pea vines flower most fully when growing in full sun, but some protection from noon and afternoon sun extends the flowering period. Plant the seeds where the plants are to grow and next to a support system of some kind—a dead bramble, a teepee, or a set of strings affixed to a tall fence.

HOW TO PLANT

Prepare the bed by digging in 1 in. of coarse sand or chicken grit, and a slow-release 5-10-5 fertilizer. In clay soil, add a small handful of gypsum and superphosphate for each plant. Work the soil 8 to 12 in. deep. Sow the seeds following the instructions on the packet or mark planting holes for seedlings 6 to 8 in. apart. Half fill each hole with diluted fertilizer, plant the seedling high, and press the soil down around the stem firmly enough so the plant resists a tug. Water with a diluted fertilizer solution. Use soft twine to support the vines or to lead the vines to the structure that will support them. Apply a 3-in. mulch starting 3 in. from the stems.

HOW TO PROVIDE CARE

To promote rapid, unchecked growth, keep the bed moist. Once the seedlings are growing well, water every week unless there's a soaking rain. Check the vines often to make sure they're not straying from their supports.

ADDITIONAL ADVICE FOR CARE

If you have planted a perennial sweet pea, when the vines have died down, cut them back to the ground. In late winter before growth begins, broadcast an organic 5-10-5 fertilizer over the area at half the rate recommended on the container and water it in. Replenish the mulch.

Trumpet Vine

*T*he trumpet vine is a fast-growing deciduous climbing vine that makes a dense, leafy "green roof" for arbors and pergolas. It is also used to cover fenceposts and to soften bleak corners and bare stone and masonry walls. The vines climb by means of aerial rootlets, growing at a run to 30 to 40 ft. As trumpet vine matures, it becomes woody and very heavy, so provide a strong support. July through early fall it opens showy orange or scarlet, trumpet-shaped flowers that appeal mightily to hummingbirds. 'Madame Galen', a cultivar of *C.* × *tagliabuana*, is a superior hybrid with larger flowers. It thrives in our state.

WHEN TO PLANT

Set out container-grown plants in early spring, or in early fall.

WHERE TO PLANT

Trumpet vine grows almost anywhere in almost any soil and almost any light, but it flowers best in full sun.

HOW TO PLANT

Dig a modest planting hole about 6 in. deeper than the rootball and wider toward the top. Work a spading fork into the sides of the hole to loosen compacted soil. In clay soil, work 1 cupful each of gypsum and superphosphate into the hole and top it with 2 in. of soil. Unwind the roots circling the rootball and plant it with the crown an inch above ground level. Fill the hole, watering in to settle the soil. With soft twine, tie or lead the vine to the structure that will support it. Make a saucer of earth to hold water. Apply a 3-in. mulch starting 3 in. from the stem.

HOW TO PROVIDE CARE

For the first month or two after planting, pour a bucketful of water into the saucer every week unless there's a soaking rain. If you wish, plant the area around the vine with a living mulch, using drought-tolerant ground covers, like myrtle, ajuga, or a slow-growing, small-leaved variegated ivy. Hostas, liriope, mondo grass, and small spring-flowering bulbs, like wood hyacinths, are also acceptable ground cover.

ADDITIONAL ADVICE FOR CARE
The colorful trumpets are produced on new growth, so prune the stems back to a few buds early every spring to encourage flowering sprouts. Replenish the mulch. Prune away out-of-control vines at any season.

ADDITIONAL CULTIVARS AND SPECIES
The Chinese trumpet creeper, *C. grandiflora*, gives a late-summer show of large, vivid scarlet, or orange, flushed with pink, flowers. It does well in warmer parts of the state.

Virginia Creeper

OTHER COMMON NAME: Woodbine

The Virginia creeper is a handsome, fast-growing, invasive vine with branches that stretch 30 to 50 ft. and more to cover a wall, a tree, a rock pile and everything nearby. It is also an excellent ground cover for out-of-the-way slopes where the fact that it loses its leaves in fall won't spoil the view. In fall the leaves turn a vivid scarlet. After the leaves fall, the asymmetrical tracery of the branches remains attractive, and the reddish new growth that appears in spring is quite lovely. The flowers are insignificant, greenish clusters hidden under the foliage. The dark berries that follow are enjoyed by birds. Virginia creeper's only drawbacks are that it can damage masonry, and, if you decide to remove it, the traces are hard to wipe out. It clings by means of tendrils that end in adhesive-like tips, and they're hard to get rid of. The Japanese creeper, *P. tricuspidata*, resembles the Virginia creeper, but has a more lustrous leaf. The cultivar 'Lowii' has small leaves when young and may be a better choice for covering a small area.

WHEN TO PLANT
The best times for planting are in fall, before Indian summer, and in early spring, while the vine is still dormant. But container-grown Virginia creeper succeeds when planted almost any time in spring or fall. It grows wild in our woodlands.

WHERE TO PLANT
Virginia creeper colors best growing in full sun, but it thrives in light shade—and grows even in deep shade. It tolerates pollution, city life, and almost any soil.

HOW TO PLANT
Dig a modest planting hole about 6 in. deeper and wider than the rootball and wider toward the top. Work a spading fork into the sides of the hole to loosen compacted soil. In clay soil, work 1 cupful each of gypsum and superphosphate into the hole and top it with 2 in. of soil. Unwind roots that may be circling the rootball and set it in the hole with the crown an inch above ground level. Fill the hole,

watering in as you do to settle the soil. With soft twine, tie the vine to the structure that will support it. Make a saucer of earth around the plant to hold water. Apply a 3-in. mulch starting 3 in. from the stem.

HOW TO PROVIDE CARE

After planting, pour a half bucketful of water into the saucer every week unless there's a soaking rain. Pinch out branch tips to keep the plant growing in whatever directions you want it to go.

ADDITIONAL ADVICE FOR CARE

In late winter before growth begins, broadcast an organic 5-10-5 fertilizer for acid-loving plants over the area at half the rate recommended on the container and water it in. Replenish the mulch. Once the plant is well established, switch to a 7-6-19 fertilizer. Before growth begins, prune at will.

ADDITIONAL CULTIVARS AND SPECIES

P. henryana, the silvervein creeper, has a bluish cast and the fall red has hints of purple. It is very handsome, but it's not hardy in the cool mountain areas, Zone 6.

CHAPTER TWELVE

Water Gardens

A WATER GARDEN ADDS THE SOUND AND SPARKLE OF MOVING WATER TO THE LANDSCAPE, and is entertaining all season long. From the moment when the first warmth brings goldfish lazing to the surface after a long winter spent at the bottom of the pond, until the last of the water lilies shuts down for winter, there's always something happening.

You can install a successful water garden yourself with a little help. The pond can be as small as a tub, or as large as you wish . . . but it's best if housed in an excavation waterproofed by a liner. All naturally wet places are now controlled by the environmental protection agencies. To plant non-natives and loose goldfish in a natural body of water on your property may be forbidden; the law protects wetlands, and that law is enforced.

The first step is to decide the water garden's location and size. Don't choose the obvious: a wet place in a dip or hollow. Without good drainage, big rainstorms and winter thaws will heave the pond. A level, sunny spot is best, but a gentle slope can be terraced and leveled. Avoid sites that are favorite haunts of hungry raccoons and birds that eat fish.

The larger the pond, the more costly the equipment that keeps the water healthy. There are two types of liners: preformed fiberglass liners, and flexible rubber sheets. Ponds up to 14 ft. long are most often outfitted with preformed fiberglass liners, and flexible rubber sheets are used for larger sizes. The water garden plants are planted in shallow pans, pails, and tubs sold by water garden suppliers and garden centers. The containers rest on a shelf in the pond, or on blocks on the bottom.

The splash and shimmer of a water garden is provided by an electric pump that recirculates the water and aerates it, which is good for the fish and the plants. It usually also runs the water through a cleansing filtering system that may be inside the pond (or outside of it), returned along a stream bed or as a fall running over rock ledges. The higher the water has to be pushed by the pump, the more powerful the pump needs to be. And, the more powerful the pump, the more it costs to buy and to operate. The size of the filter and the power of the pump are dictated by the number of gallons of water in the pond, and this is determined by its size. This all sounds rather complicated, but the dealer will help you to make the right choices. There are mechanical filters and biological filters; I recommend the latter; although more costly, they require much less maintenance.

To bring power to the recirculating pump, you will need a simple, weatherproofed, standard three-prong electrical outlet with a ground fault circuit interrupter for safety. Have a licensed electrician install the power source for the pump and have it placed at least six feet away from the edge of the pond.

If you are in hill country where the pond will freeze in winter, remove the pump and filter when the weather cools, and clean and store them indoors. During the cold months, the warmest water is in the bottom of the pond and the fish live on down there. If you keep recirculating the water, it will chill the bottom and the fish will suffer. Snails sleep the winter away

Though water is a decidedly different growing medium, you will find much that is familiar in the way aquatic plants are handled. They grow in containers, respond to fertilizing, have active and dormant seasons, and are hardy or tender. There are a few hundred aquatics, so getting to know them isn't a big undertaking. The categories of plants and animals that sustain and ornament a water garden are discussed on the following pages.

Submerged Plants

*T*he submerged plants—sometimes called "oxygenating plants"—are the first plants placed in the water of a newly filled, or refilled, pond. Small, leafy perennials with stems 2 to 3 ft. long, they live below or on the surface of the water. Their role is to contribute oxygen and to use up nutrients that would encourage the algae that make a pond murky. Fish spawn among the fronds. Five types of submerged plants are recommended for Virginia. Washington grass, *Cabomba caroliniana*, is one of the prettiest. It is a lacy, fan-shaped plant that bears minuscule white or purple flowers. Anacharis, *Elodea canadensis* variety *gigantea* has fern-like fronds and is a first-rate filter that grows right up to the top of the water and bears tiny white flowers. Several species of *Myriophyllum* serve as submerged plants, all of them excellent filters. Dwarf sagittaria, *Sagittaria subulata*, is a small plant with fronds 3 to 6 in. long that make an attractive edger for a stream. *Vallisneria americana*, wild celery, is a beautiful plant with ribbon-like, leaves and it develops into an attractive green carpet. To make the pond more interesting, use all five, rather than a single type.

WHEN TO PLANT

Place the submerged plants in the pond as soon as it has been filled. To multiply your holdings, during the growing season take 5- or 6-in. cuttings of submerged plants 8 in. or longer, press the ends into containers filled with wet sand, and place them in the pond.

WHERE TO PLANT

Distribute the containers of submerged plants evenly over the bottom of the pond with 1 or 2 ft. of water overhead. Choose locations where the containers will receive at least 6 hours of sun and avoid places that will be shaded later by floating leaved plants. If the strands start to grow long and skinny, they need more sun.

HOW TO PLANT

For the submerged plants, provide pans 4 in. deep and plant only one variety in each container. Containers for aquatics have no drainage holes. Fill the pans with clean sand to within 1 in. of the rim. Rinse the submerged plants. Cut the rubber bands of those that

come bundled together and press each bunch or stem 2 in. into the sand. Cover the sand with rinsed 3/4-in. gravel and fill the containers with water.

How to Provide Care and Maintenance

This is the "magic formula" for keeping a pond in balance: it was developed by Charles Thomas, President of Lilypons Water Gardens, Buckeystown, Maryland.

For every one to two square feet of pond surface:
- 1 bunch (6 stems) submerged plants
- 1 black Japanese snail
- 2 in. of fish for fish up to 6 in. long
- 1/10 of a small, or medium-size, water lily
    (that is, 1 lily per 10 to 20 sq. ft.)
- 1/3 of a marginal or a small, floating-leaved plant
    (that is, 1 marginal plant or 1 small-leaved floater for every 3 to 6 sq. ft.)

Additional Advice

Do not add fertilizer.

Other Cultivars and Species

There are other submerged plants, but think twice before introducing them into your pond. They tend to be invasive. Two of the most beautiful are illegal in some states—water hyacinth and water lettuce. Federal statutes forbid the shipment of water hyacinth in interstate commerce.

Fish/Livestock

*F*ish, snails, and frogs are added to the water garden for their charm, and for their usefulness. The beauty of the fish and the pleasure they provide is only a part of their gift to the water garden. Their appetite for insects and larvae, especially mosquitoes, keeps the water garden free of pests. Fish wastes help to fertilize the plants. The small black or brown-black snails are the pond's most outstanding housekeepers. They creep around devouring algae and clearing up undesirable leftovers and algae. The black Japanese snail, *Viviparis malleatus*, is the best. This species does not eat the plants or come out of the water, and it reproduces only 2 or 3 times during the season. Other aquatic snails often overpopulate. Tadpoles, the young of the bullfrog, *Rana catesbiana*, help to keep the pond clear of algae and uneaten fish food. Watching its transformation to the adult stage is always fascinating. When frost comes, frogs bury themselves in mud and have a long nap. Large pet shops and aquatic nurseries sell fish, tadpoles, and snails.

WHEN TO PLACE

After the plants are in the pond, allow 2 weeks for the water to age before placing fish and livestock in the pond. Float their plastic traveling bags in the pond for 15 minutes to allow the creatures time to adjust to the temperature before slipping them into the water.

WHERE TO PLACE

Loose livestock and the fish in "aged" pond water after allowing them time to get used to the temperature of the water. Fish and tadpoles will swim off and hide. The snails will just drop down into the water and not be seen for days. Any that are dead will eventually float and should be removed at once.

HOW TO PLACE

Before placing the creature in the pond, add a broad-spectrum fish disease remedy. After the fish and livestock have adjusted to the water temperature, slide them from their containers into the water. Fish need not be fed, but if you don't they remain wild, hiding when you come. For the first 10 days, feed the fish lightly with an antibiotic medicated food. Regular fish food comes in flake, stick, pellet, and granular forms. Flakes serve all. Floating sticks and pellets are for goldfish and koi 2 in. long or more. Granular food is for fish over 1 in. long, and it sinks.

HOW TO PROVIDE CARE AND MAINTENANCE

Here is the "magic formula" for keeping a pond in balance. It was developed by Charles Thomas, President of Lilypons Water Gardens, Buckeystown, Maryland:

For every 1 to 2 sq. ft. of pond surface:

1 bunch (6 stems) submerged plants

1 black Japanese snail

2 in. of fish for fish up to 6 in. long

$1/10$ of a small, or medium-size, water lily
(that is, 1 lily per 10 to 20 sq. ft.)

$1/3$ of a marginal or a small, floating-leaved plant
(that is, 1 marginal plant or 1 small-leaved floater for every 3 to 6 sq. ft.)

ADDITIONAL ADVICE

Avoid chemical remedies unless the fish seem listless, or you see red spots on them, or a white growth which could indicate fungus. Pet shops and aquatic nurseries provide well-established remedies for such ills, but in a well-stocked pond they are uncommon.

OTHER CULTIVARS AND SPECIES

Koi are the most intelligent, the most trainable, and the most beautiful fish, but they tend to eat the water lilies.

WATER GARDENS

Nymphaea

Water Lilies

*T*he blossoms of the water lilies are the pond's stars, its most colorful flowers. They come in almost every color including blue. The large, round pads of the water lilies provide the fish with privacy and relief from hot summer sun. There are two types, and both are used in Virginia water gardens. The hardy water lilies are perennial here, though they need two to three years to bloom profusely. The tropicals are sure to bloom the first year but must winter indoors. Hardy lilies open only during the day, while the tropical lilies include both day- and exotic night-flowering plants. The hardy water lilies and the day-blooming tropical lilies open shortly after breakfast and close toward late afternoon. The heavily scented, night-blooming tropicals open as the stars come out and stay open until late morning. Two easy lilies for beginners are the hardy 'Pink Beauty', a shell pink that blooms freely its first year, and 'Dauben', a day-blooming, soft blue-violet tropical. All together, the lilies and the other ornamental aquatics should cover only 1/3 to 1/2 of a 20- by 40-ft. pond; 60 to 70% of one 10 by 10 ft. A small lily covers 90% of a tub 2 ft. square.

WHEN TO PLANT

Place the lilies in the pond as soon as it is filled. The chlorine in tap water is safe for plants. Most lilies are shipped bare root in moist materials at the right moment for planting—the best is spring, or when the water is at least 55 degrees Fahrenheit for hardy lilies, 69 degrees for tropicals.

WHERE TO PLANT

Give the lilies the sunniest positions. Arrange the containers on the pond shelf and on platforms that raise the plants to where they will be covered by the depth of water recommended by the growers. Build the platforms of stones, clean bricks, or weathered cement blocks.

HOW TO PLANT

Plant lilies in the pans, pails, and tubs sold for aquatics. They have no drainage holes. Fill the containers with heavy garden soil free of peat, manure, vermiculite, or commercial potting mixes. Aquatics

tolerate soils ranging between pH 6.0 and 8.0, but optimum is soil and pond water between pH 6.5 and 7.5. Set the plants so the growing tips are just free of the soil. Push a 10-14-8 fertilizer tablet for aquatics into the soil of each container. Cover the soil with 1/2 in. of 3/4-in. rinsed gravel. Soak the containers and place them in the pond several inches apart.

HOW TO PROVIDE CARE AND MAINTENANCE

Here is the "magic formula" for keeping a pond in balance. It was developed by Charles Thomas, President of Lilypons Water Gardens, Buckeystown, Maryland:

For every 1 to 2 sq. ft. of pond surface:

1 bunch (6 stems) of submerged plants

1 black Japanese snail

2 in. of fish for fish up to 6 in. long

1/10 of a small, or medium-size, water lily
(that is, 1 lily per 10 to 20 sq. ft.)

1/3 of a marginal or a small, floating-leaved plant
(that is, 1 marginal plant or 1 small-leaved floater for every
3 to 6 sq. ft.)

ADDITIONAL ADVICE

Remove spent blooms and yellowing foliage. Fertilize the lilies monthly during the spring and the summer. When the water temperature is over 75 degrees Fahrenheit, increase that to twice monthly. For winter, move the containers of the tropical lilies indoors to a cold garage and keep the soil moist.

OTHER CULTIVARS AND SPECIES

Among popular tropicals are night-blooming 'Wood's White Knight' which bears many large, white flowers with soft, yellow-tipped stamens and day-blooming pink 'General Pershing', 'Pink Pearl', and 'Madame Ganna Walska'.

Lotus

The lotus is a 2- to 6-ft.-tall relative of the water lily. Big, exotic leaves and exotic growth habits make one lotus a must in the water garden, even where there is not enough sun to bring it into bloom. The lotus starts the season by floating leaves that look like 12-in. lily pads. When these are complete, it puts up magnificent, wavy-edged aerial leaves, and the floating leaves come together. Then the perfumed lotus flowers rise. They are as big as a man's head and come in shades and combinations of white, pink, red, yellow, and cream. The blossoms open mornings and close at tea time for three days. The exotic seed pods that follow look like the spout of a watering can and are sought after for dried arrangements. One lotus takes up as much space as a large water lily and is all that most home ponds can host. I recommend the miniature 'Tulip Lotus' for small home ponds, and for a large pond the magnificent 'Mrs. Perry D. Slocum'. Lotus, and the other ornamentals all together should cover no more than 1/3 to 1/2 of a 20- by 40-ft. pond; 60% to 70% of one 10 by 10 ft.

WHEN TO PLANT
A lotus is shipped bare root in a plastic bag during the few weeks in spring when the rootstock is in tuber form. Plant it at once. Once the rootstock puts out runners, the tuber atrophies and planting is impossible. In late summer, the runners form tubers that can be divided the following spring and planted.

WHERE TO PLANT
Position a lotus where it will receive 6 to 8 hours of direct sun, preferably on the far side of the pond, on the pond shelf, or on a platform raised to where there will be 2 to 3 in. of water over the growing tip. Build the platforms of stones, clean bricks, or weathered cement blocks.

HOW TO PLANT
For a tuber 6 to 18 in. long, provide a pan 16 to 24 in. in diameter and 9 to 10 in. deep. A miniature requires a pan about half this size. Fill the pan with heavy garden soil free of peat, manure, vermiculite,

or commercial potting mixes. A lotus tolerates soils ranging between pH 6.0 and 8.0, but optimum is soil and pond water between pH 6.5 and 7.5. Bury the tuber 2 in. deep with the top 1/2 in. above the soil. Push a 10-14-8 water lily fertilizer tablet into the soil, and cover with 1/2 in. of 3/4-in. rinsed gravel. Soak the container and place it in the pond.

HOW TO PROVIDE CARE AND MAINTENANCE

Here is the "magic formula" for keeping a pond in balance. It was developed by Charles Thomas, President of Lilypons Water Gardens, Buckeystown, Maryland:

For every 1 to 2 sq. ft. of pond surface:
- 1 bunch (6 stems) submerged plants
- 1 black Japanese snail
- 2 in. of fish for fish up to 6 in. long
- 1/10 of a small, or medium-size, water lily or lotus (that is, 1 per 10 to 20 sq. ft.)
- 1/3 of a marginal or a small, floating-leaved plant (that is, 1 marginal plant or 1 small-leaved floater for every 3 to 6 sq. ft.)

ADDITIONAL ADVICE

Remove yellowing foliage and spent blossoms and fertilize with a water lily pellet twice a month from spring up to a month before the average first frost date for your area. For winter, move the lotus container to a depth beyond the reach of ice. If the pond freezes to the bottom, winter a lotus indoors in a garage and keep the soil moist.

OTHER CULTIVARS AND SPECIES

N. 'Momo Botan Minima' is a deep-rose dwarf with a double flower that has a golden center. The leaves spread out when the plant is growing in a pond, but in tubs and pans they stay at 12 in. It is so much in demand it can be hard to get.

Small Floating Plants

*S*everal small aquatic plants with dainty, floating leaves and flowers are used in water garden design for contrast with the big lilies and also as fillers. These plants leaf out when the water lilies begin to grow. A few bear small flowers, and some are fragrant. There are annuals, tender perennials, and hardy perennials in the group. Most grow in soil, but a few live on the water, for example parrot's-feather, *Myriophyllum aquaticum*, whose trailing stems can be trained to cascade over a tub garden or a waterfall. The annuals and tender perennials tend to grow most rapidly—some so rapidly they need severe pruning. For foliage contrast, include the tiny water clover, *Marsilea mutica*. For their flowers, choose water poppies, *Hydrocleys nymphoides*, floating-heart, *Nymphoides peltata*, and the white or yellow snowflakes, *N. cristata*, and *N. geminata*. Do not overdo the little floaters. All together the ornamentals should cover only 1/3 to 1/2 of a 20- by 40-ft. pond; 60 to 70% of one 10 by 10 ft.

WHEN TO PLANT

Place the little floaters in the pond as soon as it is filled. The chlorine in tap water is safe. Most are shipped bare root in moist materials at the right moment for planting—the best is spring, or when the water is at least 50 degrees Fahrenheit for hardy plants, 69 degrees for tender perennials.

WHERE TO PLANT

Position the containers a few feet from the lilies on the pond shelf, and on platforms raising them to where they are covered by the depths of water suggested by the grower. Build the platforms of stones, clean bricks, or weathered cement blocks. Plants that live on the surface of the water without being rooted in soil—just let loose on the pond.

HOW TO PLANT

Provide the rooted plants with pans for aquatics: they have no drainage. Fill the containers with heavy garden soil free of peat, manure, vermiculite, or commercial potting mixes. Aquatics tolerate soils ranging between pH 6.0 and 8.0, but optimum is soil and pond water between pH 6.5 and 7.5. Set the plants so the growing tips are just free of the soil. Push a 10-14-8 fertilizer tablet for aquatics into the soil of each container. Cover the soil with 1/2 in. of 3/4-in. rinsed gravel. Soak the containers and place them in the pond several feet apart.

HOW TO PROVIDE CARE AND MAINTENANCE

Here is the "magic formula" for keeping a pond in balance: it was developed by Charles Thomas, President of Lilypons Water Gardens, Buckeystown, Maryland:

For every 1 to 2 sq. ft. of pond surface:

1 bunch (6 stems) submerged plants

1 black Japanese snail

2 in. of fish for fish up to 6 in. long

1/10 of a small, or medium-size, water lily
(that is, 1 lily per 10 to 20 sq. ft.)

1/3 of a marginal or a small, floating-leaved plant
(that is, 1 marginal plant or 1 small-leaved floater for every 3 to 6 sq. ft.)

ADDITIONAL ADVICE

Remove yellowing foliage. Once a month in spring and summer press into each plant container a water lily fertilizer tablet. Keep the growth of these rapidly spreading plants pruned back. Just pinch off a stem at any point and pull out and discard the growth beyond.

OTHER CULTIVARS AND SPECIES

The water hawthorn, *Aponogeton distachyos*, bears vanilla-scented white flowers that appear before anything else in spring.

Verticals

The upright plants grown at the margins of a water garden are narrow- or broad-leaved natives of watery environments. There are annuals, tender perennials, and hardy perennials in the group, and a variety of heights and textures. Most have slender stems that move with the wind, adding the element of motion to the garden design. The most appealing combinations group narrow-leaved plants, such as irises, with broad-leaved verticals like elephant's-ear, *Colocasia*. The irises are the most colorful of the narrow-leaved verticals. They bloom early, and the sword-like foliage remains handsome. Cattails and ornamental grasses are a lovely addition to the mix. Many of the broad-leaved marginals are planted for their flowers, the bog lily, *Crinum americanum*, for example, which is a beautiful bulb flower. The water cannas are favorite broad-leaved plants, along with dainty umbrella plant, *Cyperus alternifolius,* and the arrow-shaped water arum, *Peltandra virginica*. Plant the marginals in sets of three of one type to a container: when you combine varieties, one usually over-whelms the others.

WHEN TO PLANT
Potted marginals can go in the pond as soon as it is filled. The chlorine in tap water is safe. Most are shipped in moist materials at the right moment for planting—the best is spring or when the water is at least 49 degrees Fahrenheit for hardy plants, 69 degrees for tropicals.

WHERE TO PLANT
Place the containers on the pond shelf, and on platforms that places them at the depths recommended by the growers. Build the platforms of stones, clean bricks, or weathered cement blocks. Start plants 6 in. high or less where they will have 1 in. of water over the gravel in their containers; move them to deeper water as they mature.

How to Plant

Set out individual plants in pans or pails that hold at least 3¹/₂ quarts of soil. Provide 24-in. pans for trios of plants. Pierce each container with 2 nailholes so the soil will remain wet even if the pond level drops below the rim. Partially fill the containers with heavy, slightly acid garden soil that includes a small amount of humus. Set the plants so that their growing tips are just free of the soil. Push a 10-14-8 fertilizer tablet for aquatics into the soil of each container. Cover the soil with ¹/₂ in. of ³/₄-in. rinsed gravel. Soak the containers and place them a 1 or 2 ft. apart on the pond floor or shelf.

How to Provide Care and Maintenance

Here is the "magic formula" for keeping a pond in balance. It was developed by Charles Thomas, President of Lilypons Water Gardens, Buckeystown, Maryland:

For every 1 to 2 sq. ft. of pond surface:

1 bunch (6 stems) submerged plants

1 black Japanese snail

2 in. of fish for fish up to 6 in. long

¹/₁₀ of a small, or medium-size, water lily
(that is, 1 lily per 10 to 20 sq. ft.)

¹/₃ of a marginal or a small, floating-leaved plant
(that is, 1 marginal plant or 1 small-leaved floater for every 3 to 6 sq. ft.)

Additional Advice

During the growing season, remove dead foliage and flowers. From spring until a month before the first expected frost, fertilize monthly at the strength following label directions. Before winter, discard the annuals and cut the hardy perennials back to within a few inches of their crowns.

Other Cultivars and Species

Among small attractive narrow-leaved marginals for tubs and small ponds are horsetail, *Equisetum hyemale*, red-stemmed sagittaria, *Sagittaria lancifolia* forma *ruminoides*, and the graceful cattail, *Typha laxmannii*.

APPENDIX

*T*HE GARDEN CLUB OF VIRGINIA, located in Richmond, recommends the following restored historic gardens of Virginia in a big, beautiful, coffee table book on the subject. From them, and from the many tourist service stands in Virginia, you can obtain a brochure that gives the addresses, phone numbers, and a description of these gardens.

NORTHERN VIRGINIA
Carlyle House, Alexandria
Gunston Hall, Mason Neck
Woodlawn Plantation, Mount Vernon
Oatlands, Leesburg
Burwell-Morgan Mill, Millwood
Belle Grove, Middletown
Belmont, Fredericksburg
Kenmore, Fredericksburg
Mary Washington House, Fredericksburg
Mary Washington Monument, Fredericksburg

CENTRAL AND WESTERN VIRGINIA
Montpelier, Montpelier Station
Monticello, Charlottesville
University of Virginia, Charlottesville
Point of Honor, Lynchburg
Woodrow Wilson Birthplace, Staunton
Washington and Lee University, Lexington
Fincastle Presbyterian Church, Fincastle
Smithfield Plantation, Blacksburg
Prestwould Plantation, Clarksville

Appendix

TIDEWATER VIRGINIA

Scotchtown, Beaverdam
Grace Arents Garden, Lewis Ginter Botanical Garden, Richmond
Virginia Union University, Richmond
St. John's Mews, Richmond
Kent-Valentine House, Richmond
Wilton, Richmond
Centre Hill Mansion, Petersburg
Bacon's Castle, Surry
Rolfe-Warren House, Smith's Fort Plantation, Surry
Bruton Parish Church, Williamsburg
Christ Church, Christchurch
Stratford Hall, Stratford
Historic Christ Church, Irvington
Historic Portsmouth Courthouse, Portsmouth
Adam Thoroughgood House, Virginia Beach
Kerr Place, Onancock

BIBLIOGRAPHY

$\mathcal{A}$ PARTIAL LIST OF REFERENCE WORKS consulted for generally-held information: Cornell University's *Hortus III* (Macmillan Publishing Company), and the new source for accuracy in plant nomenclature; Mark Griffiths' The Royal Horticultural Society *Index of Garden Plants* (Macmillan Publishing Company); Michael A. Dirr's *Manual of Woody Landscape Plants* (Stipes Publishing Company); *Wyman's Gardening Encyclypedia* (Macmillan Publishing Company); *American Horticultural Society Encyclopedia of Garden Plants* (Macmillan Publishing Company); *American Horticultural Society Flower Finder* (Simon & Schuster); *American Horticultural Society Encyclopedia of Gardening* (Dorling Kindersley); *Taylor's Master Guide to Gardening* (Houghton Mifflin); *National Arboretum Book of Outstanding Garden Plants* (Simon & Schuster); *Glorious Gardens* (Stewart, Tabori & Chang); *Good Housekeeping Illustrated Encyclopedia of Gardening* (Hearst); *Rodale's All-New Encyclopedia of Organic Gardening; Water Gardens* (Houghton Mifflin); *Water Gardening* (Timber Press); *Daffodils for the American Garden* (Elliott & Clark); by Elvin McDonald, *Rose Gardening,* (Meredith); Smith & Hawkin's *The Book of Outdoor Gardening* (Workman); Cathey Wilkinson Barash's *Edible Flowers* (Fulcrum); *Perennials for American Gardens* (Random House); Allan Michael Armitage's *Herbaceous Perennials Plants* (Varsity Press); Adelman Grenier Simmons' *Herb Gardening in Five Seasons* (Plume-New American Library); Carole Ottesen's book *Ornamental Grasses/The Amber Wave*, published by McGraw Hill.

INDEX

Index

Index

Index

Index

Index